BECAUSE COVID ...

PANDEMIC RESPONSES, RATIONALES AND RUSES

BECAUSE COVID ...

PANDEMIC RESPONSES, RATIONALES AND RUSES

EDITED BY SHIRLEY LEITCH AND SALLY WHEELER

Australian
National
University

ANU PRESS

AUSTRALIA AND THE WORLD

Australian
National
University

ANU PRESS

Published by ANU Press
The Australian National University
Canberra ACT 2600, Australia
Email: anupress@anu.edu.au

Available to download for free at press.anu.edu.au

ISBN (print): 9781760466916
ISBN (online): 9781760466923

WorldCat (print): 1503574290
WorldCat (online): 1506267028

DOI: 10.22459/BC.2025

Cover design and layout by ANU Press

This book is published under the aegis of the Australia and the World editorial board of ANU Press.

Contents

CONCLUSIONS

Contributors

Frank Bongiorno AM is a professor of history at The Australian National University (ANU). He is the author of *Dreamers and Schemers: A Political History of Australia* (La Trobe University Press, 2022). The second edition of *A Little History of the Australian Labor Party* (Nick Dyrenfurth and Frank Bongiorno) was published by NewSouth Books in 2024. He was president of the Australian Historical Association from 2022 to 2024 and is currently president of the Council for the Humanities, Arts and Social Sciences.

Barry Bozeman is regents' professor emeritus and Arizona Centennial Professor of Technology Policy and Public Management and founding director emeritus of the Center of Organization Research and Design at the University of Arizona. He has also previously held positions at the University of Georgia, Georgia Tech and Syracuse University. His research focuses on science and technology policy, public management and higher education policy. He is an elected fellow of both the American Association for the Advancement of Science and the National Academy of Public Administration. His most recent book is *Science Competes: Informing Policy in a Time of Distrust, Fracture, and Chaos* (MIT Press, 2025).

Chay Brown was born and raised in Mparntwe where she currently lives and works with Aboriginal women's groups to prevent violence against women. She has lived experience of domestic, family and sexual violence and speaks regularly as a victim–survivor advocate to inform policy and programmatic responses. Chay's research background focuses on perpetrator interventions, technology-facilitated abuse and what works to prevent violence against women.

Kim Cunio is head of the School of Music at Victoria University of Wellington in New Zealand. He is an activist composer interested in old and new music and the role of intercultural music in making sense of our larger world. A scholar, composer and performer, Kim embodies the skills of the artist, showing that writing and making art are part of the same paradigm of deep artistic exploration. He was previously the head of the ANU School of Music (2019–23).

Nathan Emmerich is a senior lecturer in bioethics in the School of Medicine and Psychology at ANU. He is the lead for professionalism and leadership in phase one of the MChD (doctor of medicine and surgery), convenes the honours program in the health sciences, and teaches a capstone course in bioethics to those studying for degrees in biology and the life sciences in the College of Science.

Robert L. Heath is an internationally renowned scholar on public relations, crisis communication, issues management, risk communication and business-to-business communication. Perhaps the most prolific author of academic publications in public relations, he has published numerous journal articles (100+) and many award-winning books, including *The SAGE Handbook of Public Relations* (2010), *Handbook of Risk and Crisis Communication* (2009), *Strategic Issues Management* (2nd ed., 2009), *Rhetorical and Critical Approaches to Public Relations II* (2009), and *Terrorism: Communication and Rhetorical Perspectives* (2008). He is the editor of *Encyclopedia of Public Relations* (2nd ed., 2013).

Mark Kenny is a professor and director at the Australian Studies Institute at ANU. He came to ANU after a high-profile journalistic career as chief political correspondent and national affairs editor of the *Sydney Morning Herald* and *The Age*. Host of ANU podcast 'Democracy Sausage', Mark is a widely reported commentator on politics, both in Australia and internationally. His research interests include national politics, comparative studies, democracy and the rise of populism.

Shirley Leitch is an emerita professor and professorial fellow at the Australian Studies Institute at ANU. She joined the institute after serving ANU first as dean of the College of Business and Economics and then as deputy vice-chancellor (global engagement). Her research is focused on public discourse and change, including science–society engagement in relation to controversial science and technology. Shirley is also the founding chair of a successful education technology company, Online Education Services Ltd.

Kate Ogg is a professor at the College of Law, ANU. She is a legal and socio-legal researcher with expertise in human mobility and the law, refugee law, the law of internal displacement, human rights law, litigation, feminist theory and method. Kate is the author of *Protection from Refuge: From Refugee Rights to Migration Management* (Cambridge University Press, 2022), which is the first global and comparative examination of the role courts play in refugee journeys. Along with Professor Susan Harris Rimmer, Kate is the editor of *Research Handbook on Feminist Engagement with International Law* (Edward Elgar, 2019). Kate has received funding from the Australian Research Council to undertake research on private refugee sponsorship and strategic human rights litigation. She regularly provides media commentary on developments in refugee and human rights law and has been invited to present her research at the United Nations High Commissioner for Refugees' Headquarters in Geneva and the Australian Parliament.

Rohan Pitchford is an Australian Research Council professorial fellow at the Research School of Economics, ANU. He received an honours degree in economics from ANU and a PhD from MIT. He has previously worked at the University of Sydney and the University of Queensland. He has published papers on the economics of contracts, default and sovereign debt in leading economics journals. His current research interests include liability of firms, securitisation and financial stability.

Rabee Tourky is the Trevor Swan Distinguished Professor of Economics and the director of the Research School of Economics at ANU. For many years he has worked on understanding general price equilibrium theory when there are many commodities but with missing insurance contracts. More recently he has been working on finite games dubbed imitation games and computational economics. Among other things, he is studying statistical/epistemic foundations of Bayesian games as well as novel piecewise linear techniques. Rabee has held professorial positions at the University of Melbourne, Purdue University and the University of Queensland.

Tony Ward has been a research fellow in history at the University of Melbourne since 2011. Prior to that, he had a varied career in academia, senior executive positions in the state public service and 17 years as principal of an economic consulting company. Tony has published two books: *Sport in Australian National Identity: Kicking Goals* (Routledge, 2010) and *Bridging Troubled Waters: Australia and Asylum Seekers* (Australian Scholarly Publishing, 2017). He has also published numerous articles in academic journals, ranging across the economics of inequality, sports history and

Australian migration history. In addition, he has written several well-read pieces for *The Conversation*, and contributed to several submissions to government on the economic and social impacts of public policies. He has a PhD in economic history from Monash University (1984).

Sally Wheeler OBE MRIA FAcSS FAAL is vice-chancellor of Birkbeck, University of London. Prior to taking up her role at Birkbeck, she was deputy vice-chancellor (international and corporate) and dean of law at ANU. She is a socio-legal scholar working in the areas of corporate responsibility and contractual relationships. Her work has been funded by research councils in the UK and the EU.

Acknowledgements

First, we would like to acknowledge and thank our publisher, ANU Press. As the world's first, largest and leading open-access university press, ANU Press plays a central and crucial role in sharing Australian scholarship with the world. They were the natural choice of publisher for this book and have been a delight to work with.

Thanks also to Professor Paul Pickering, who drove the establishment of the *Australia and the World* series and who has encouraged this project from start to finish.

To the two readers who peer reviewed the entire manuscript: your generous contributions are recognised and appreciated. Your many helpful insights, comments and suggestions have undeniably improved the book.

We are grateful to our excellent and very patient copyeditor, Rani Kerin, for her meticulous attention to detail and for guiding all of the authors through their revisions.

Finally, many thanks, to the staff within the Australian Studies Institute, ANU. Special thanks must go to Fiona Preston who has managed this project and its authors so expertly. Your advice, hard work and encouragement were invaluable.

Shirley Leitch and Sally Wheeler

Acronyms

ABC	Australian Broadcasting Corporation
ABS	Australian Bureau of Statistics
AI	artificial intelligence
ALP	Australian Labor Party
AMSANT	Aboriginal Medical Services Alliance Northern Territory
ANU	The Australian National University
ANZAC	Australian and New Zealand Army Corps
BBC	British Broadcasting Corporation
BMJ	*British Medical Journal*
BREXIT	United Kingdom's exit from the European Union
CDC	Centers for Disease Control and Prevention (US)
CNN	Cable News Network (US)
COVID-19	coronavirus disease identified in 2019
CSR	corporate social responsibility
DNA	deoxyriboNucleic acid
EPPM	Extended Parallel Process Model
FBI	Federal Bureau of Investigation (US)
GDP	gross domestic product
GFC	global financial crisis
GST	goods and services tax
GVC	global value chain
IAQ	indoor air quality
IDP	internally displaced people

JobKeeper	a COVID-19 support payment measure administered by the Australian Taxation Office
KWILS	Katherine Women's Information & Legal Services
LGBTQIA+	lesbian, gay, bisexual, trans and gender diverse, queer, intersex and asexual and questioning
LNP	Liberal–National Party Coalition (Australia)
mg	milligram
MIDI	music instrument digital interface
MNE	multinational enterprise
mRNA	messenger ribonucleic acid
NASA	National Aeronautics and Space Administration (US)
NSW	New South Wales (Australia)
OECD	Organisation for Economic Co-operation and Development
OzSAGE	a multidisciplinary network of Australian experts from a broad range of sectors relevant to the wellbeing of the Australian population during and after the COVID-19 pandemic
PADM	protective action decision-making
PCR	polymerase chain reaction
PhD	doctor of philosophy
PPE	personal protective equipment
PPP	Paycheck Protection Program
R&D	research and design
RATs	rapid antigen tests
RSL	Returned and Services League
SARS	severe acute respiratory syndrome
SARS-CoV-2	severe acute respiratory syndrome coronavirus 2
SBS	Special Broadcasting Service (Australia)
SLTT	state, local, territorial or tribal
SSS	social studies of science
STS	science and technology studies
UCG	Unified Coordination Group

UK	United Kingdom
UN	United Nations
UNCTAD	United Nations Conference on Trade and Development
UNESCO	United Nations Educational, Scientific and Cultural Organization
UNHCR	United Nations High Commissioner for Refugees
US	United States of America
WHO	World Health Organization

1

The Australian pandemic experience

Shirley Leitch and Sally Wheeler

A problem becomes a crisis when it challenges our ability to cope and thus threatens our identity. In the polycrisis the shocks are disparate, but they interact so that the whole is even more overwhelming than the sum of the parts. At times one feels as if one is losing one's sense of reality.

(Tooze, 2022)

From humble origins in Wuhan, China, the COVID-19 pandemic escalated rapidly and triggered a global polycrisis. With its complex web of interlocking problems, the polycrisis challenged our ability to find acceptable solutions (Morin & Kern, 1999; Tooze, 2022). In an attempt to avoid the truly horrifying epidemiological predictions of death and disease, economies were mothballed as cities locked down and nations shut their borders. In Australia, as elsewhere, the norms of everyday life were simply cast aside by citizens who largely accepted curfews, mask mandates and the shuttering of schools and workplaces in exchange for the promise of safety. Across every sphere of life, 'Because Covid' became an accepted shorthand, serving as both a response and unchallengeable rationale for actions that were previously unthinkable. Yet, it is always a mistake to take such things at face value.

In this book, we examine the strategies, policies and rhetoric adopted by Australian governments, organisations and individuals as part of – or under the guise of – their COVID-19 responses and rationales. We explore the intended as well as unintended consequences and consider what other agendas the pandemic has masked or enabled. Given that the impacts of the pandemic are so far-reaching and diverse, the book is not and could not be exhaustive in its coverage. Rather, we have drawn on a broad range of expertise, including on economic policy, bioethics, freedom of speech, freedom of movement, global supply chains, public value science, violence against women, news media practices, the arts sector, historical precedents and what we may learn about managing future risks. This diverse selection in and of itself illustrates the scale of the chaos wreaked by the pandemic. Our goal is to offer insights into the Australian experience at the very time the nation is beginning to learn how to live with COVID-19. The contemporaneous nature of this book and its object of study will speak to current policymakers, but we also intend to provide an invaluable resource for what will surely be a myriad of future researchers.

Many of our authors include comparative analyses with other nations, most often with the US under the Trump's first presidency. Australia and the US are both prosperous, Western-style democracies with market economies governed by a complicated mix of state and federal governments. Both are multicultural in a way that has moved them some distance from exclusively European heritage, and both have indigenous populations. The US features prominently in Australian political and cultural life, including through military alliances, trade agreements, scientific exchanges and the arts. Prior to and during the pandemic, the US also led the development of the mRNA vaccine technology that proved so effective against COVID-19. The US experience therefore offers an ideal point of comparison. Our authors consider the similarities and differences in the pandemic responses of governments and citizens alongside the subsequent economic and health outcomes at state and federal levels. In the process they highlight policy failures and provide guidance to improve our management of the next pandemic in both nations.

Australians faced the pandemic with a Liberal–National Party (LNP) government elected on a platform of neo-libertarian freedom, 'debt and deficit' reduction and the promised return of a budget surplus not seen since the global financial crisis (GFC). Instead, and in response to the pandemic, the government closed the nation's borders, curtailed basic freedoms and embarked on a program of spending that dwarfed the GFC stimulus policies of the predecessors they had pilloried. The LNP government was not alone. Around the world, governments of all political persuasions pumped in billions – then trillions – of dollars to prevent a global recession and the collapse of the financial system. Central banks absorbed government debt, propped up the private sector and underpinned the loans of major corporations (Lorié & Ciobica, 2021). In response, share markets and house prices took off and kept climbing. While whole sectors were mothballed others boomed; while many citizens remained locked down, elites appeared exempt from such restrictions (Baker & Lilleker, 2022); and while government stimulus policies were characterised as a swerve to the left, their impacts appear to have amplified inequality both within and between nations.

Disruption was a feature of daily life from the macro to the micro and down to the level of individuals and their families. Confined to their homes, their neighbourhoods and their states, Australians turned increasingly to the virtual world of social media. In the quotation that heads this chapter, Adam Tooze (2022) writes of the ability of polycrises to threaten not just our identity but also our very sense of reality. Such conditions create an ideal breeding ground for rumours, conspiracy theories and disinformation. A potent mix of suspicion, naivety and bad actors would lead thousands of people with free access to vaccinations to eschew them in the deluded belief that they were somehow a cause of the pandemic rather than a solution to it (Pertwee et al., 2022). Some even marched on their state parliaments or took to the road as part of a 'Convoy to Canberra' demanding an end to vaccine mandates and lockdowns. The sincerity of most who took part in these direct actions is evident, but investigations into the social media underpinnings of the 'Freedom Movement' revealed major sites to be of dubious origin (Culliford, 2022; Thomas, 2022; Wilson, 2022). Disinformation has become a profitable business for online scammers who have scant regard for the sometimes-lethal effects of their trade.

The vulnerability of people to the lies and conspiracy theories of disinformation was likely heightened by the pandemic itself. After all, during the pandemic, it felt as though everything had changed. People spoke vaguely of a 'new normal' that would emerge, with varying levels of optimism or pessimism as to the shape of that future social world. In the following chapter, Frank Bongiorno sketches the outlines of this future, posing the dual questions of how we will remember the COVID-19 years and what changes will endure beyond the pandemic. Bongiorno draws on our collective memory of prior episodes of global disruption as they were experienced in Australia, including the Spanish Influenza pandemic, the Depression and World War II. References to all of these major crises were drawn upon in attempts to make sense of the pandemic (Vivian, 2021).

For example, Prime Minister Scott Morrison drew parallels between Gallipoli and COVID-19 in a 2020 ANZAC Day announcement confirming the cancellation of the annual Dawn Service:

> This year, we will not be gathering at the local cenotaph, or attending gunfire breakfasts at the local RSL, or gathering together to bow our heads in silence and listen to the bugles at dawn. But we will still remember the sacrifice of those who gave so much for us at Gallipoli and on many fronts, as we ourselves give what we can to protect Australian lives while we face this terrible virus.
>
> (Morrison, 2020)

Reaching back into the past to make sense of the present is a well-established rhetorical tool for legitimising novel acts, especially those that appear to represent an historic rupture in tradition. Bongiorno concludes that the place of the pandemic in the sweep of global and Australian history remains uncertain. The only certainty is that it will be contested, including by politicians who will attempt to harness particular interpretations of the pandemic to serve their current political agendas.

In the years prior to the COVID-19 pandemic, one of the most politically contested areas of policy and public debate was science itself. Spearheaded by the fossil fuel industry which sought to discredit climate science, attacks on science were taken up by populist leaders as part of a more generalised attack on the very concepts of truth and expertise (Huber et al., 2022). These pre-existing tensions carried over into the pandemic and were exacerbated by it in a number of ways. In Chapter 3, Barry Bozeman argues that a central dimension of these tensions is the unsettled question of how we can justify the investment of public money in science unless there is demonstrable public value. Science policy often fails to deliver on its promise, Bozeman contends, precisely because of a 'tendency to confuse economic growth with public values'. Scientific research that, for example, produces technologies that displace workers or degrade the environment – even if it leads to economic growth – has done little to legitimise science. This is especially true when that growth is seen to disproportionately enrich some companies and individuals at the expense of broader society.

Science has figured in multiple ways in public discourse about COVID-19, including as the potential cause (with allegations the virus had originated in a Wuhan lab) and the potential saviour (through vaccinations). Bozeman compares the experience in his home country, the US, with that in Australia, to extract lessons and cautionary tales for both nations. He outlines the processes underpinning the rapid development of the COVID-19 vaccines, which stands as a case study in public value science. Yet the vaccines were still contested. While the medical profession hailed the breakthroughs in vaccine technology, the technologies of social media spread fear about their safety and efficacy. Adding to the confusion in both nations was the myriad of state and federal jurisdictions with differing views on health policy in relation to virus suppression and the dynamics of vaccine rollout. While many political leaders spoke of a 'science-led' pandemic response, their divergent views on what this meant in practice demonstrated that science did not actually provide a blueprint for action. Instead, as Rohan Pitchford and Rabee Tourky discuss in Chapter 4, government responses to the pandemic might be better characterised as a 'large-scale policy experiment'.

A major component of the Australian government's pandemic response was the JobKeeper package, which was framed as a solution to the job losses created by the pandemic and then accelerated by government-mandated lockdowns. The stated policy aim was to preserve the 'match' between employers and their staff in order to both prevent mass unemployment and enable a rapid return to business as usual. From the myriad of policy choices and delivery modalities that might have been selected (Elgin et al., 2020), the Australian government chose to pay JobKeeper payments directly to employers rather than to individual workers. As Pitchford and Tourky demonstrate, the hastily enacted policy was crude in its design. Despite the experimental nature of JobKeeper, there was little transparency as to recipients, minimal evaluation of its effectiveness, and an overreliance on unvalidated claims of economic hardship. The result was a significant overpayment to businesses of approximately $38 billion. With no clawback mechanism included, this figure represents a permanent transfer of public funds to the private sector. Even evaluated on its own terms, in relation to its stated aims, Pitchford and Tourky's analysis suggests that JobKeeper was a massive public policy failure.

A technical evaluation of pandemic policies will, however, only take us so far. Despite the oft-repeated mantra of 'science-led' decision-making, public policy is far more than a factual or technical concern. It is also, and maybe primarily so, a political and social concern that is inherently value laden. Policies are a means to an end and the desired end may in itself be contested. In his chapter, Nathan Emmerich considers whether the field of bioethics might be used to 'socially engineer the moral or normative aspects' of public policy formation in relation to medicine, healthcare and life sciences. Emmerich is sceptical of the view of some bioethicists that a 'follow the ethics' approach may serve as a replacement or an adjunct to a 'follow the science' siren call, concluding that both are equally flawed arguments. When bioethicists move from contemplative philosophical discourse to the public policy arena, he contends, they have become activists. Emmerich is especially wary of academic bioethicists being drawn into the culture wars that have raged in the US and, to a lesser extent, also in Australia. In line with Bourdieu (1989), he sets out a thoughtful case as to the value of maintaining the academic 'interest in disinterestedness', arguing that this is a primary source of strength for academic scholarship. Bioethics, like medical science, epidemiology and economics, can inform and critically evaluate public policy but it cannot tell us in any straightforward way what we ought to do.

Regardless of the calls from advocates of either science or bioethics, it is economics that has long been the dominant discourse of public policy in Australia and beyond. If the mantra of our policymakers is more akin to 'follow the economics', then a core task of academic research is to 'follow the money'. Certainly, Sally Wheeler's chapter analysing the pandemic's effects on global supply and value chains suggests that this is a fruitful track to pursue. The longstanding trend towards free trade and pan-global production that preceded the pandemic left nations vulnerable to any disruption in the movement of goods or people. Lockdowns at the national, state and local levels caused an unprecedented level of disruption to both. The global value chains of production slowed or broke down entirely. Normal patterns of consumption were upended and redirected online. Wheeler argues that the resulting costs were disproportionately borne by the poorest workers in the poorest nations. She demonstrates that this outcome was not accidental but baked into the system. At the same time, in Australia and elsewhere, nations that had lost their manufacturing base to lower cost, offshore jurisdictions with weaker labour laws and environmental regulation standards, found themselves without ready access to essential goods. Many Australians realised for the first time their reliance on, for example, India and China for basic medical supplies such as face masks and paracetamol. Concepts such as sovereign capability, manufacturing capacity and re-shoring were suddenly back in the discourse. Wheeler concludes, however, that only major changes in decades-old policy directions that have yet to be made could move Australia towards a more resilient and sustainable future.

If the burdens of COVID-19 fell most heavily on the poorest citizens of the poorest nations, so too did they fall most heavily on those who were most disadvantaged in the rich nation of Australia. Chay Brown writes of the 'shadow pandemic' that afflicted remote Aboriginal communities, which were already behind on measures of health, education and economic wealth while leading on most measures of homelessness, overcrowding, food insecurity and violence. Brown notes that the message of 'Stay home, stay safe' was especially inappropriate for women with violent partners. As experts such as Brown had predicted, rates of violence against women rose during lockdowns in Australia, with women in remote communities most affected. The pandemic had exacerbated the conditions that lead to violence while at the same time reducing available services as well as physical escape routes. Brown notes that at the start of the pandemic, hundreds of Aboriginal people living around towns such as Alice Springs were put on buses and sent to remote communities. The belief was that they would be safer away from urban centres. The reality was that remote communities were in no position to accommodate an influx of people without concomitant support. With limited local services of their own, such as healthcare, education and retail, these communities were reliant upon the distant towns from which they were now isolated by lockdowns. In the towns, people pivoted online for work, shopping, medical appointments, education and entertainment. In remote communities, the internet was poor or non-existent, and few stores would deliver to them in any case. Brown argues that there are important lessons for Australia's public policymakers to be drawn from the shadow pandemic. Foremost among these is the importance of applying a gender and domestic violence impact lens and a remote community lens over all policies to ensure that they are not just inclusive but also do not actively worsen the lives of some of our most vulnerable citizens.

One of the main – if not the main – sources of solace and joy during the pandemic years was the arts sector. The arts helped us to make sense of things at a time when normal life had been upended. In his chapter, Kim Cunio, like Brown, combines his deep expertise with personal experience to provide an insightful analysis of the arts during COVID-19. Like Wheeler and Brown, Cunio demonstrates that the pandemic disproportionately hit a sector and a group of citizens that was already disadvantaged. The Australian arts sector had been in economic decline for decades along with the real income artists derived from their creative work. At the same time, there had been major technological advances that had transformed arts production. It is clear that the economic benefits derived from these technologies have been captured elsewhere. Cunio's analysis of the sector's economic and technological context is the background against which he sets his highly moving account of a song cycle he composed during the pandemic. His work directly addresses the most tragic dimension of COVID-19 – the lives that were lost – and is a clear demonstration of how essential the arts are to our wellbeing. Cunio generously gifts us links to both the poems and music of his song cycle, *Covid Mantras* and *Covid Sonnets*.

While the tragedy of COVID-19 touched many households, including co-authors of this book, Australia was spared the high death toll experienced by many other nations. Australia's good fortune was partly due to wealth, which meant, for example, that it could introduce universal free vaccination programs. Perhaps just as important was Australia's political will to introduce hardline policies to reduce transmission of the virus until the vaccinations became available coupled with the willingness of the population to comply with these policies and to be vaccinated. However, and as briefly discussed above, not everyone was in agreement. In Chapter 10, Tony Ward turns our attention to the role that the news media played in the pandemic. More specifically, Ward examines the role of News Corporation media in promoting scepticism of the seriousness of the virus, the validity of government policies and the effectiveness of public health measures such as social distancing and face masks. Drawing on the work of US scholars, Ward summarises the research in that country on the likely effects that News Corporation media had on the spread of the virus. Boseman's earlier chapter briefly highlights the role of the Fox network in dividing US opinion by promoting opposition to pandemic measures and the eccentric views of President Trump, such as on the efficacy of horse-worming paste to combat the virus. Ward expands on this analysis, outlining the unequal impact of the virus on those who were most likely to vote Republican and follow Fox News. Most starkly, he finds that excess deaths were significantly higher among Republicans than Democrats.

Opposition to pandemic policies among Australian politicians was much more muted. The main focus of dissent was directly linked to party politics and the differing political allegiances of state governments. Differences at the level of state in terms of, for example, the length of lockdowns, the imposition of state border controls and the closure of schools, all provided fodder for political attacks. These were most marked in relation to Victoria, where Premier Daniel Andrews of the Australian Labor Party was heavily criticised in News Corporation media for his government's restrictive pandemic policies. Premier Andrews came under heavy, personal attack and was nicknamed 'Dictator Dan'. Ward provides a case study of the Victorian COVID-19 experience as background for an epidemiological analysis of the potential impact that News Corporation campaigns against pandemic health measures had on the spread of the virus. As was the case in the US, Ward's analysis suggests that News Corporation campaigns to oppose or ignore restrictions may have increased case numbers and contributed to the need for the Stage 4 lockdown they so strongly opposed.

State lockdowns and border closures are explored in more depth in Ogg's chapter, which focuses on internally displaced people (IDP). Australian citizens and permanent residents were mostly permitted to return home, but the scarcity and cost of both flights and the mandated hotel quarantine places meant that, in practice, it was difficult for many to do so. These restrictions were mirrored at the level of the state, which rendered many Australians IDP. Ogg summarises the subsequent academic literature on the validity and impacts of Australian border closures. She finds that the policies lacked nuance and, in particular, failed to consider the needs of the most vulnerable, such as children or people with disabilities, or the impact on Indigenous communities. Like Brown, Ogg argues that the pre-existing inequalities and injustices encountered by Aboriginal and Torres Strait Islander peoples were compounded by border closures and travel restrictions. Ogg notes that the issue of IDP is generally considered to be one that afflicts the so-called Global South. However, with more catastrophic events triggered or exacerbated by climate change, the issue has become more pressing even for wealthy nations like Australia. Floods and bushfires are more common and more serious, and are accompanied by the destruction of farmland, homes and entire communities. Ogg suggests that any action to better protect IDP is hindered by the absence of an Australian bill of rights or national human rights framework. These absences protected state and federal government border restrictions from legal challenge and enabled governments to ignore the intersecting vulnerabilities of Australia's most disadvantaged.

Our central challenge in considering the above issues is to learn how to do things better. Brown, Ogg and Wheeler all demonstrate the devastating consequences of policies applied without care for their impacts on vulnerable groups, such as Aboriginal and Torres Strait Islander peoples living in remote communities. Cunio's chapter takes us a step further to explore the consequences for groups – in this case, creative workers – who were intentionally excluded from policies designed to mitigate the worst effects of the pandemic. All policy decisions have winners and losers. In the case of Australia's COVID-19 policy responses, as Pitchford and Tourky argue, the big winners were major private sector organisations in no need of assistance.

They emerged with their balance sheets, if not always their reputations, intact. The losers were almost everyone else in an Australia in which income inequality continues to grow.

Our purpose in extracting lessons from recent history is, as the old adage goes, to ensure that we are not doomed to repeat our mistakes. It is appropriate then that the last words in the book are given to Robert Heath, perhaps the foremost expert in risk management and communication. Heath's conclusions directly address our central challenge: to learn how to do things better. Traversing the experiences of both the US, where he resides, and Australia, Heath concludes that 'good information must prevail against bad information, drive it out of the marketplace of ideas'. Like Ward, he is highly critical of media and leaders who 'politicised doubt' in ways that served their agendas but not the public good. Looking to the future, Heath contends that good pandemic policy couples science-based analysis with compassion. In the absence of science, all citizens will likely suffer more, but in the absence of compassion, those who have the least will almost certainly suffer the most.

References

Baker, T. A. & Lilleker, D. (2022). 'Not one rule for everyone': The impact of elite rule-breaking on public trust in the UK. In P. J. Maarek (Ed.), *Manufacturing government communication on Covid-19* (pp. 301–317). Springer Studies in Media and Political Communication. doi.org/10.1007/978-3-031-09230-5_15.

Bourdieu, P. (1989). The corporatism of the universal: The role of intellectuals in the modern world. *Telos*, 81, 99–110. doi.org/10.3817/0989081099.

Culliford, E. (2022, 8 February). Meta says it removed scammers' Canada convoy Facebook groups. *Reuters*. www.reuters.com/technology/meta-says-it-removed-scammers-canada-convoy-facebook-groups-2022-02-08/.

Elgin, C., Basbug, G. & Yalaman, A. (2020). Economic policy responses to a pandemic: Developing the COVID-19 economic stimulus index. *Covid Economics*, 1(3), 40–53.

Huber, R. A., Greussing, E. & Eberl, J.-M. (2022). From populism to climate scepticism: The role of institutional trust and attitudes towards science. *Environmental Politics*, 31(7), 1115–1138. doi.org/10.1080/09644016.2021.1978200.

Lorié, J. & Ciobica, J. (2021). COVID-19 government support reinforces zombification. *Journal of Risk Management in Financial Institutions, 14*(4), 345–354.

Morin, E. & Kern, B. (1999). *Homeland earth: A manifesto for the new millennium.* Hampton Press.

Morrison, S. (2020, 19 April). *Honour the service and sacrifice at home for ANZAC Day* [Media release]. pmtranscripts.pmc.gov.au/release/transcript-42789.

Pertwee, E., Simas, C. & Larson, H. J. (2022). An epidemic of uncertainty: Rumors, conspiracy theories and vaccine hesitancy. *Nature Medicine, 28*, 456–459. doi.org/10.1038/s41591-022-01728-z.

Thomas, E. (2022, 24 February). Fake 'Freedom Convoy' Facebook groups are being run by foreign networks for profit. *Institute for Strategic Dialogue.* www.isdglobal.org/digital_dispatches/fake-freedom-convoy-facebook-groups-are-being-run-by-foreign-networks-for-profit/.

Tooze, A. (2022, 29 October). Welcome to the world of the polycrisis. *Financial Times.* www.ft.com/content/498398e7-11b1-494b-9cd3-6d669dc3de33.

Vivian, S. (2021, 26 October). From Spanish flu to COVID in Australia, parallels in pandemics more than a century apart. *ABC News.* www.abc.net.au/news/2021-10-26/when-spanish-flu-hit-australian-shores-nt-ss-mataram-covid/100517650.

Wilson, C. (2022, 10 February). Fake, international Facebook accounts behind the convoy to Canberra protests. *Crikey.* www.crikey.com.au/2022/02/10/fake-international-facebook-accounts-convoy-canberra-protests/.

2

History, the pandemic and the future

Frank Bongiorno

The COVID-19 pandemic exposed various features of Australian society, culture and values less visible during 'ordinary times'. In particular, government's handling of the crisis indicated the utilitarian caste of the nation's politics. While collective memory of various episodes from the country's twentieth-century history – such as the Spanish Influenza pandemic, the Depression and World War II – would be mobilised during the COVID-19 pandemic, the place of this event in the sweep of global and Australian history remains uncertain.

T. S. Eliot's line from 'The Hollow Men' – 'Not with a bang but a whimper' – has been recalled to describe how pandemics end (Oster, 2020). Yet, even more than four years after the beginning of the pandemic, it was still difficult to imagine quite what post-COVID life might look like. Is there even something that might be called 'post-COVID'? When I recently completed a political history of Australia, I called the concluding chapter, covering the 2019–22 period, 'In the Age of COVID-19' (Bongiorno, 2022). A reader of the manuscript in the autumn of 2022 thought this title might be changed: that it was likely to date as we all emerged out of the pandemic. But it was a matter on which I pushed back: it seemed to me that we were likely to be living in something that might reasonably be called a COVID era for some time yet. A new and virulent wave of infections occurred in the winter. I retained the chapter title.

COVID-19 is unlikely to be a demographic turning point like the Black Death of the fourteenth century (1346–53), which some modern historical research suggests wiped out as much as 60 per cent of the European population, or 50 million people, but had transformative – and often positive – economic, technological and cultural impacts (Belich, 2022; Benedictow, 2005). Twentieth-century epidemics and pandemics have not carried off anything like such high proportions of the population – not even the Spanish Influenza, which might nonetheless also have killed 50 million. COVID-19 has, however, reduced life expectancy in many countries and there are growing concerns about its long-term health effects, such as on heart-related disease; notably, historians of the Spanish Influenza have begun searching for signs of its longer-term impacts on public health in the decades that followed 1918–19 (Chavez, 2023). COVID-19 has also disrupted supply chains and labour mobility, both of great importance to Australia given its diminished pre-COVID industrial capacity and high permanent and temporary immigration rates. The Albanese Labor government, elected in May 2022, is committed to boosting local self-sufficiency and lowering barriers to some immigration. The task of economic recovery has become all the more difficult against the background of the Russian invasion of Ukraine.

Some recent research suggests that vaccination might well have been more effective in the Spanish Influenza pandemic than historians have normally assumed, even in the absence of an understanding that the disease was viral (Roth, 2023). In the absence of effective vaccines, COVID-19 would have killed many more people in general, with the old and frail being most vulnerable – a different age profile from Spanish Influenza, which killed many younger people. Even in Australia with its high COVID-19 vaccination rate, few people have had more than two shots. The low booster uptake may well have assisted the spread of infection, although it cannot on its own account for Australia's slide down the international league tables (Toole & Crabb, 2022).

The public health system in Australia, like in other places around the world, will, to some extent, need to be geared to the management of COVID-19 for years to come. Periodic vaccination and COVID-19 wards – along with antiretroviral drugs – will form part of our lives for some time, at least among people in the developed world fortunate enough to enjoy such access. And so will measures to control infections and hospitalisations, although the apparent complacency involving high numbers of deaths in Australia during 2022 and 2023 has formed a strong contrast with the earlier years of the pandemic. I suggest a possible explanation for that paradox below.

There will be likely effects on civility – on the way we think and behave in everyday life. The great German sociologist Norbert Elias in *The Civilizing Process* (originally published in 1939) traced changes in personal and social behaviour across centuries, explaining how and why behaviour considered perfectly acceptable in one era would be transformed, via various forms of restraint, into the rudeness of another – and vice versa:

> People who ate together in the way customary in the Middle Ages, taking meat with their fingers from the same dish, wine from the same goblet, soup from the same pot or the same plate ... stood in a different relationship to one another than we do. And this involves not only the level of clear, rational consciousness; their emotional life also had a different structure and character.

The introduction of a fork, in such circumstances, could (and apparently did) become a cause of scandal. What Elias called 'the thresholds of embarrassment and shame' (Elias, 1994, pp. 55–56) shifted according to culture and context; good and bad manners are not fixed for all time.

How will COVID-19 affect our social interactions, our sense of the difference between civil and uncivil, considerate and inconsiderate, good and bad? Will we come to see turning up in certain situations without a mask in the way we came to regard body odour and having cigarette smoke blown in your face? Already, the signs are that, in Australia at least, mask wearing will not take on this significance; however, a minority does continue to criticise the failure of people to wear masks in social situations where infection could spread, as well as the complacency of governments and even some medical professionals about infection, hospitalisations and deaths. Given the continuing spread of the virus, and that during January 2023 (to take an example) the rolling seven-day national average of COVID-associated deaths exceeded 50, they surely have a point (Australian Government, n.d.).

There are many other forms of social interaction that may well still be reshaped by the experience of COVID-19. What about standing too close to someone in a queue? Will we shake hands as readily as before, or greet an old friend with a kiss on the cheek? Will we see cleanliness and dirtiness in new ways, with all the social, cultural and moral baggage that we know is connected with those distinctions? And what of the attitude of the vaccinated to the unvaccinated?

Will we see collective responsibility differently? Until 2020, many people went along to their workplaces with bad colds or flu symptoms, marching on like a trooper: 'Soldier on, with Codral, soldier on', an old TV advertisement for cough medicine urged us. This was despite the possibility that the virus one was carrying, and possibly spreading, would eventually kill somebody. It is almost impossible to imagine a marketing campaign of this kind in the wake of COVID-19. Will we ever quite look at someone with a bad cough, a croaky voice or a dripping nose in the same way? These are not trivial matters because they form the essence of social life and express wider understandings of what it means to belong fully to a community, our sense of obligation to one another.

The pandemic will also likely affect our understanding of how to manage work and leisure time, given that so many of us were forced to invite our jobs into every corner of our homes. And as well as reshaping domestic space, COVID-19 might have long-term effects on our urban spaces: will the daily ritual of commuting to a city office ever quite resume its pre-pandemic patterns? So far, the signs are that working more frequently from home will, for certain occupations, be more common. That is a potential source of freedom and flexibility for workers, but also of potential conflict with employers, and between employees.

Will we, more generally, regard the meaning of freedom differently? If you had asked Australians before the pandemic which freedoms they thought most important, they might have said freedom of speech or freedom from discrimination. Some might even have nominated religious freedom, which was a matter on which the Morrison Coalition government would try – and fail – to legislate in early 2022. But they would probably not have thought of freedom of movement: the freedom to travel across state boundaries, to leave one's home, to go overseas, or to come home to Australia. These freedoms were all taken for granted; borders between states and territories had long been treated as soft by most people even while differences between jurisdictions might be an inconvenience in fields such as education and business. But understandings of freedom are cultural and historical. If one had asked a Soviet citizen or a black South African in the 1970s whether they thought freedom of movement important, their experience might well have led them to say that it was. Indigenous Australians of the 1950s might have felt the same way, as would a Palestinian in the Occupied Territories today. Australians are never likely to look at their passports, their state boundaries – or even perhaps their own gardens, if they have one – in quite the same way again.

Or perhaps, as the years pass, the experience will not be etched in collective memory, or will be recalled in ways that would seem inaccurate to many of us now. Memory scholars in the humanities and social sciences have shown that the ways the past registers as collective memory are subject to complex cultural and historical (as well as biological) processes. Both individual and collective memory change as personal and social contexts change. Individual memories can be sensitive to shifts in wider public narratives; testimony that might not pass muster historiographically is nonetheless true in the way it expresses lived experience (Thomson, 1994). Lucy Taksa, in a study of memory of the Spanish Influenza in Australia, found that several of her informants recalled living through the 'Bubonic Plague' in 1919. In reality, Sydney had experienced this epidemic in 1900, but for those who had lived through the events of 1919, the term 'Bubonic Plague' expressed 'the collective experience of a rampant and deadly disease' (Taksa, 1994, p. 81). We can expect that the evolution of memory of COVID-19 will have its own complexities, although we can barely even begin to speculate what they might be.

The pandemic will likely affect how Australians view political authority, as we have been reminded that governments still have something like power of life and death over us. People had politics and government thrust on them: government decision-making determined whether or not one could walk to the end of the street to buy a cup of coffee and then, if you could, the circumstances in which you were allowed to drink it. The Australian pandemic response also seems rooted in the deeper patterns of the country's political culture. Scholars have called Australia a Benthamite society, arguing that rights are seen not as existing in the abstract, but as emerging out of law and politics (Collins, 1985). In 1930 the historian W. K. Hancock famously presented Australian democracy as having 'come to look upon the State as a vast public utility, whose duty it is to provide the greatest happiness for the greatest number'. The citizen, Hancock explained, claimed not 'natural rights' but rights received 'from the State and through the State'. Collective power was, in this way, mobilised in the service of individual rights, so that Australians saw 'no opposition between … individualism and … reliance upon Government' (Hancock, 1930, pp. 72–73).

These strains have been evident during the COVID-19 pandemic, reminding us of their deep cultural embeddedness. Many Australians longed for greater freedom, but most were willing to accept not just that there is individual responsibility for the collective welfare, but that government should play the predominant role in defining where the boundaries between individual rights and common good lie. Outside extreme libertarianism, a minority taste in Australia, there tends to be only mild political disagreement. Otherwise, most people get on with their lives, expecting the state to set reasonable parameters for individual behaviour while allowing people a wide scope to pursue their private interests as individuals and families.

They also look to government to protect them. We might see in this a continuation of the ethic of the government store, or the commissariat. It played a critical role in the early history of New South Wales as its central economic institution. Importantly, it was a public institution, adapted from the military, although one that was embedded in an emerging private economy. It issued rations to convicts and bought the produce of local farms operated by military officers and a few free settlers. The commissariat was also a de facto banker; its receipts were treated like currency in a colony that had no official coinage and, before 1817, no bank. It would ensure that no colonist, however lowly and however harsh the times, would starve, but it was also a source of profit for canny – and sometimes unscrupulous – entrepreneurs. Military officers were in a particularly strong position to make money from their dealings with the government store when there was no governor around, such as in the interregnum that followed Arthur Phillip's departure in 1792, and in the period following the overthrow of William Bligh in 1808. It provided them with a guaranteed market for their produce, at good prices, all compliments of the British Treasury (Hirst, 2014; McLean, 2012).

It does not take a vivid imagination to see how schemes such as JobKeeper and JobSeeker were descendants of the commissariat. They, too, provided government support for the viability of businesses, and they ensured that despite the lack of an income, people could more or less get by, however modestly. And, like the commissariat, JobKeeper proved a fruitful source of profit for some businesses. While many Australians would have preferred that companies that took JobKeeper and yet reported large profits should have returned the money received from government, most pragmatically accepted business profiteering as a price to be paid for the security offered by the hastily assembled government schemes. In any case, their government gave them no choice and clearly judged that it would not suffer politically in the process. And it is not clear that it did, despite exposure to the scale of subsidy provided to businesses recording healthy profits (Conifer, 2021).

COVID-19 disclosed other dimensions of Australia's political culture and the wider habits of mind on which the practice of politics and crafting of policy depend. A nation that has spent so much of its history worrying over the uninvited arrival of people in boats drew on this history in various ways, some predictable, and some less so. Certainly, border control quickly came to be seen as the best way to keep COVID-19 out of the country, even when it became apparent that it could not do so. But there were novelties this time around. It extended to internal state borders in a way that had not occurred since 1919 (Finnane, 2021). The restrictions on the country's external borders, moreover, were directed at 'our own people' – Australian citizens and permanent residents wanting to come home. Australian governments – and large sections of the population – reminded us that there was a distinction between 'Australia' and 'Australians', and that they recognised a reduced responsibility to those in the latter category who found themselves outside the country's borders. Australia has a long record of solid consular assistance to its citizens in difficulty overseas, so this distinction might be thought surprising. But when the Australian government criminalised entry from India in 2021, threatening those who tried to land with heavy fines and prison sentences of up to five years, some heard the echoes of a longer racial history, since those affected were very likely to be Australian citizens or permanent residents of Indian descent. It was indeed remarkable how readily Australians stranded overseas were 'othered'. Whereas the queue-jumping asylum-seeker had been part of Australian anti-refugee political discourse for decades, in 2020–21 some complained of Australians who had had ample opportunity to return home but had failed to do so. Bizarrely, such censure sometimes even extended to people who left their state for a holiday at Christmas, despite their having been urged by advertising campaigns to do so. The cultural historian John Williams published a book in the 1990s about Australian artistic anti-modernism between the two world wars called *The Quarantined Culture* (Williams, 1995). It was an evocative title that not only captured something important about Australia of that era but also a deeper psychological and cultural vein that could be mined in other historical contexts as well. It was thoroughly exploited by governments during this pandemic. As public policy, it, for a time, helped create enormous benefits, contributing to low infection and death rates.

In due course, it became a trap: vaccination seemed less urgent given that other methods had seemed to work rather well in keeping infections low by international standards.

COVID-19 was, in this way and others, an 'exposure site' for society's strengths and weaknesses. Problems identified before the pandemic came into sharper relief under the stresses that COVID-19 imposed. The inadequacies of aged care, the stinginess of unemployment benefits, the social costs of the gig economy, the indignities of homelessness, the sufferings of family violence and the vulnerabilities of Aboriginal communities: the pandemic brought them into stark relief. Despite Australia's national pretence of egalitarianism, expensive government relief packages were generous towards those who wear high-vis vests – particularly men – but government was rather less interested in service work done by women, or in fields such as the arts or higher education. Those normally in permanent work were treated as more deserving than those who worked casually. The voices of the young and the old were muted, even more than usual. Children who had been heard over climate change were mainly silenced over matters such as their own health and education. Politicians and journalists discussed pre-existing health conditions, and even simply old age, as if this made someone responsible for their own demise and excused official negligence. Some commentators were even willing to argue that the economic and social cost of locking down populations was so great that the right of the elderly to the protection of their lives should be demoted in any rational order of priorities. 'Is a person who has lived into their late 70s, 80s or 90s owed the same priority to preserve life as a person in their 20s or 30s who typically has more than 50 years still to live?', asked *Australian Financial Review* economics editor John Kehoe. 'Many seniors have had time to enjoy careers, children and grandchildren. My father is 68 and insists he's had a good run' (Kehoe, 2020).

Surveys in 2020 told us that the pandemic restored some public trust in government. The Scanlon Foundation, based at Monash University, had 36 per cent of respondents agreeing that government in Canberra could be trusted to do the right thing in 2019, before the pandemic, but a result of 54 per cent in July 2020 was indicative of COVID's impact (Markus, 2021a). Trust in government had declined to 44 per cent a year later, still above the average (2010–18) of 29 per cent. In July 2022, the figure was still well above the pre-pandemic level, at 41 per cent (O'Donnell, 2022).

The Australian Election Study also found that, on its measure of 'trust in democracy', support had increased from 59 per cent to 70 per cent between the 2019 and 2022 elections (Cameron & McAllister, 2022, p. 100).

Government failures across a whole range of responsibilities – from quarantine and the regulation of aged care facilities through to vaccinations – likely undermined trust in both the government and Prime Minister Scott Morrison. Confidence in the Morrison government's handling of the pandemic itself dropped from 85 per cent in 2020 to 52 per cent in mid-2021 (Markus, 2021b). Morrison's personal approval rating also plunged. State government performance was rated much more highly, despite numerous failures at that level as well, especially in hotel quarantine and notably in Victoria. In Western Australia in July 2020, 99 per cent of respondents rated the state Labor government's performance either very well (83 per cent) or fairly well (16 per cent) (Markus, 2021a).

Those figures – amounting to an increase in political trust – raise wider questions about whether the pandemic might be a turning point in the nation's history, carrying the kind of burden that major events had in the past in the transformation of public expectations and government policy. The last great pandemic, Spanish Influenza, seemed to offer little hope of major change. Australia's gross domestic product had shrunk during World War I, and it grew in the wake of the Spanish flu (McLean, 2012). The flu, with its absenteeism, closure of businesses, and state border and port restrictions, certainly disrupted economic activity, as did industrial conflict during 1919, some of it related to workers' concerns about the flu itself. But much of life went on as before. Neither the war nor the flu unleashed any burst of policy creativity among progressives, although it did lead to the formation of a Commonwealth Department of Health (Roe, 1976). The Labor Party moved leftward, adopting a socialisation objective in 1921, but the lean interwar years saw no great advance in social protection, as distinct from efforts to protect Australian urban and rural industries with tariffs and subsidies. Australian society had been divided by the war and its aftermath, and policy innovation of an enduring kind in this country has generally emerged out of policy consensus, not fierce contestation (Bongiorno, 2022).

The Great Depression struck just as dramatically. Australia's unemployment rate peaked at perhaps 25 per cent in the early 1930s, and the economy again shrank. Joan Beaumont has pointed to how collective memory of the Great Depression, with its mass economic deprivation, would be deployed in public discourse in 2020 (Beaumont, 2022a). When long queues formed outside Centrelink offices, they immediately recalled for many an economic experience to which only a tiny minority of very elderly Australians could have had any direct access 90 years on.

Australia's economy was very simple in 1930. Exports then were dominated by wool and wheat; the crisis for Australia, to a great extent, arose from the plunge in prices for those commodities, with an accompanying retreat of overseas loan funds. The growing manufacturing sector, developing behind a rising tariff wall, was mainly engaged in import replacement. Few married women were in paid work. The household economy usually comprised a man engaged in employment, a breadwinner, and a woman in unpaid labour in the home, understood as a dependent. The macroeconomic capacity of the federal government in 1930 was much weaker than today. So, too, was the monetary capacity of the central bank of the day, the Commonwealth, in stark contrast with the kind of liquidity that the Reserve Bank of Australia – like other of the world's central banks – was able to release during the more recent crisis. Australia, following Britain, observed the gold standard when the crisis hit in 1929–30, which also limited room for manoeuvre in the monetary sense until it was abandoned in 1931. The welfare state of today has many deficiencies, but it was rudimentary in 1930, lacking an unemployment benefit, for instance, leaving aside a new and very basic system of insurance in Queensland. Australians of the COVID era demanded and received more protection from their government than those of the Great Depression (Beaumont, 2022b).

The COVID-19 crisis was obviously different, but no less potentially devastating for that. Jobs in the services sector were extremely vulnerable to social distancing measures. Moreover, today's export sector depends on services (e.g. education and tourism) to a much greater degree than a century ago. The economy is integrated and interconnected globally, through movements of people, capital and goods, in more complex ways than in 1930. Australia had accepted many immigrants in the 1920s, but it was arguably more vulnerable to the drying up of immigration in 2020. In the 1930s, Australia's economic recovery was shaped, to a great extent, by that of Britain. During the COVID-19 pandemic, Australia looked nervously to China, with whom its relations deteriorated drastically, including over the issue of the origins of COVID-19 itself. But iron ore exports continued, protected by Western Australia's isolation and severe and longstanding restrictions on interstate movement that kept the state safe.

Especially early in the pandemic, those optimistic about what might be achieved in its wake looked hopefully to the lessons of postwar reconstruction after 1945. In 2020, federal Labor shadow ministers formed a reading group that studied Stuart Macintyre's monumental history, *Australia's Boldest Experiment: War and Reconstruction in the 1940s* (Macintyre, 2015). The turn to postwar reconstruction indicated a desire for something other than 'snapback': the idea that government policy should be directed to restoring the status quo ante. The difficulty for those with such ambitions, however, was that the impulse to return to normality is such a powerful one, and Australia's policymakers have, to a great extent, felt the need to acquiesce in it – to acknowledge the public weariness with lockdowns, masks and other disruptions to normal life. Interestingly, that was how a lot of people also felt after World War II. Tired of its restrictions and austerity, and having felt rather isolated and alone, they hoped something like the world they had known before could be restored. The extent to which people in this country wanted to leave behind the world of the 1930s for a new order has been greatly exaggerated (Bongiorno, 2022).

That very likely also forms part of the explanation for what many have found perplexing about government handling of COVID-19 once the period of travel restrictions, border closures, lockdowns, mask mandates and vaccination certificates wound down – mostly during 2022. Government and people now seemed remarkably relaxed about rising levels of infections and an alarming number of deaths. At media conferences during the height of the pandemic, grim-faced state premiers would announce infections and deaths in rituals that seemed to draw the attention of vast audiences. Theirs became among the most widely recognised faces in the nation. Even the names of senior health officials became familiar to millions; some achieved celebrity status, rather as generals have done in wars. And then: nothing. Politicians stopped talking about COVID-19. The health officials returned to their desks. COVID-19 animated a minority of libertarian opinion with a taste for conspiracy theories, and it continued to worry another minority, of varying levels of zeal, who argued that governments needed to reimpose restrictions to bring down the infection and death rates. Most, however, got on with their lives.

The paradox of Australian governments imposing, and most Australians accepting, stringent restrictions, followed by an apparent laissez-faire approach, has attracted little commentary. The best explanation, I think, lies in the basic utilitarian patterning of the country's political culture (Collins, 1985). If the appeal is to a 'greatest good for the greatest number' defined by government with a large measure of popular consent, it becomes easier to understand how the same culture could produce two seemingly contrasting results in two very different contexts. Before vaccination became widespread, and while Australians were able to see the bodies piling up in other places such as northern Italy, the balance of policy moved sharply towards restriction. That process was always negotiated and contested – Morrison himself was much less enamoured of restriction than state premiers – but a consensus emerged that gained wide acceptance. However, once the calculus of risk shifted – through vaccination, especially – the balance moved, uncertainly at first, and then sharply, away from restriction. No doubt public weariness with restrictions played a role in this transition, but the social mood cannot alone explain government behaviour. The latter was conditioned by the political culture.

To recognise these dynamics, it must be emphasised, is not to celebrate them or their effects. It has been a feature of this utilitarian approach to government that it is poorly equipped to protect the marginalised and vulnerable. The most powerful generally do very well in such a system, and a large majority do well enough to be satisfied. The physically strong benefited from the relaxation of restrictions with minimal risk to their welfare; the ill, frail, poor and old have been much more exposed. 'Consensus' tends to rest on that foundation of inequality. But the vulnerable struggle to have their voices heard, or to exercise agency, in a system that seems so well calibrated towards finding a middle way. Australians sometimes celebrate the capacity of their system to achieve this kind of equilibrium. They are less inclined to reflect on those who lose in this scenario. And they certainly do not wish to pause for too long over those who lose their lives.

In such ways, the Australian response to the COVID-19 pandemic reached back into the country's settler history and deep into its cultural roots. The late historian John Hirst liked to tell newly arrived overseas students at his university that Australians are an obedient people, despite their self-image as anti-authoritarian larrikins. As he explained: 'The Australian people despise politicians, but the politicians can extract an amazing degree of obedience from the people, while the people themselves believe they are anti-authority' (Hirst, 2004, para. 7). 'Australians', he considered, 'are suspicious of persons in authority, but towards impersonal authority they are very obedient' (para. 66).

Hirst's use of the term 'obedient' slightly blurs the reality here of a people whose obedience is never blind but considered, negotiated and conditional. But his analysis has much to offer, and certainly much more than both local and overseas observers who saw some deep deficiency in the country's people and democracy in their willingness to accept stringent regulation of their lives. It is certainly superior to the claim made by critics of the severe and extended Victorian lockdowns that its people were suffering from Stockholm syndrome – the tendency of hostages to form emotional bonds with their captors. Nor did ignorant United States–based analysis of the decline of Australian democracy cut much ice, even if you ignore the deep crisis in that country's own electoral democracy that finds barely even faint echoes in Australia's robust version (Friedersdorf, 2021; Lee, 2021).

What COVID-19 exposed was not the absence of democracy in Australia, or even its weakness, but something of its distinctive character. And, for all its flaws, that system proved itself well adapted to the challenges of the greatest crisis in the country's history since World War II, and the greatest health crisis for a century.

References

Australian Government. (n.d.). *Weekly COVID-19 reporting*. Retrieved 5 March 2023, www.health.gov.au/health-alerts/covid-19/case-numbers-and-statistics.

Beaumont, J. (2022a). Governing during economic crisis: The importance of memory. In C. Holbrook, L. Megarrity & D. Lowe (Eds), *Lessons from history: Leading historians tackle Australia's greatest challenges*. NewSouth.

Beaumont, J. (2022b). *Australia's Great Depression: How a nation shattered by the Great War survived the worst economic crisis it has ever faced*. Allen & Unwin.

Belich, J. (2022). *The world the plague made: The Black Death and the rise of Europe*. Princeton University Press. doi.org/10.1515/9780691222875.

Benedictow, O. J. (2005). The Black Death: The greatest catastrophe ever. *History Today, 55*(3). www.historytoday.com/archive/black-death-greatest-catastrophe-ever.

Bongiorno, F. (2022). *Dreamers and schemers: A political history of Australia*. La Trobe University Press.

Cameron, S. & McAllister, I. (2022). *Trends in Australian political opinion: Results from the Australian election study 1987–2022*. The Australian National University. australianelectionstudy.org/wp-content/uploads/Trends-in-Australian-Political-Opinion-Results-from-the-Australian-Election-Study-1987-2022.pdf.

Chavez, J. (2023, 3 March). Long Covid is associated with significantly increased risk of death, heart and lung problems, study finds. *CNN*. edition.cnn.com/2023/03/03/health/long-covid-health-consequences/index.html.

Collins, H. (1985). Political ideology in Australia: The distinctiveness of a Benthamite society. *Daedalus, 114*(1), 147–169.

Conifer, D. (2021, 2 November). At least $38b in JobKeeper went to companies where turnover did not fall below thresholds, data finds. *ABC News*. www.abc.net.au/news/2021-11-02/38b-in-jobkeeper-went-to-companies-where-turnover-did-not-fall-/100586310.

Elias, N. (1994). *The civilizing process: The history of manners and state formation and civilisation*. Blackwell.

Finnane, M. (2021). Governing in a pandemic: Law and government in Australia, 1919. *Australian Historical Studies, 53*(2), 266–283. doi.org/10.1080/1031461X.2021.1920990.

Friedersdorf, C. (2021, 2 September). Australia traded away too much liberty. *Atlantic*. www.theatlantic.com/ideas/archive/2021/09/pandemic-australia-still-liberal-democracy/619940/.

Hancock, W. K. (1930). *Australia*. Ernest Benn.

Hirst, J. (2004). The distinctiveness of Australian democracy. *Papers on Parliament, 42*. Parliament of Australia. www.aph.gov.au/binaries/senate/pubs/pops/pop42/hirst.pdf.

Hirst, J. (2014). *Australian history in 7 questions*. Black Inc.

Kehoe, J. (2020, 9 April). Lives matter but at what cost? *Australian Financial Review*. www.afr.com/politics/federal/lives-matter-but-at-what-cost-20200407-p54hox.

Lee, J. (2021, 22 January). The risks to Australia's democracy. *Brookings*. www.brookings.edu/articles/the-risks-to-australias-democracy/.

Macintyre, S. (2015). *Australia's boldest experiment: War and reconstruction in the 1940s*. NewSouth.

Markus, A. (2021a). *Mapping social cohesion 2020*. Scanlon Foundation. scanloninstitute.org.au/report2020.

Markus, A. (2021b). *Mapping social cohesion 2021*. Scanlon Foundation. scanlon institute.org.au/mapping-social-cohesion-2021/.

McLean, I. W. (2012). *Why Australia prospered: The shifting sources of economic growth*. Princeton University Press. doi.org/10.23943/princeton/9780691154671.001. 0001.

O'Donnell, J. (2022). *Mapping social cohesion 2022*. Scanlon Foundation. scanlon institute.org.au/mapping-social-cohesion-2022.

Oster, E. (2020, 10 December). How the pandemic will end: Not with a bang, but with a whimper. *Slate*. slate.com/technology/2020/12/pandemic-end-with-a-whimper.html.

Roe, M. (1976). The establishment of the Australian Department of Health: Its background and significance. *Historical Studies*, *17*(67), 176–192. doi.org/ 10.1080/10314617608595546.

Roth, D. T. (2023). The efficiency of bacterial vaccines on mortality during the 'Spanish' Influenza pandemic of 1918–19. *Social History of Medicine*, *36*(2), 219–234. doi.org/10.1093/shm/hkad012.

Taksa, L. (1994). The masked disease: Oral history, memory and the influenza pandemic 1918–19. In K. Darian-Smith & P. Hamilton (Eds), *Memory and history in twentieth-century Australia* (pp. 77–91). Oxford University Press.

Thomson, A. (1994). *Anzac memories: Living with the legend*. Oxford University Press.

Toole, M. & Crabb, B. (2022, 28 July). Australia's response to COVID in the first 2 years was one of the best in the world. Why do we rank so poorly now? *The Conversation*. theconversation.com/australias-response-to-covid-in-the-first-2-years-was-one-of-the-best-in-the-world-why-do-we-rank-so-poorly-now-187 606.

Williams, J. F. (1995). *The quarantined culture: Australian reactions to modernism, 1913–1939*. Cambridge University Press.

3

Public value science outcomes: Lessons from the COVID-19 pandemic

Barry Bozeman

Introduction

One must search long and hard to find an institution not affected by the COVID-19 pandemic, but in some cases the effects seem transient. Restaurant and entertainment businesses punished by the pandemic now thrive. Many of the same airlines (e.g. American Airlines, Delta Airlines, Qantas) that required massive government bailouts to avoid pandemic-induced bankruptcy now have record profits. At the same time, some of the businesses spurred by the pandemic are in retreat. Amazon has announced large layoffs. Share prices for Zoom have dropped. One way to think of these changes, both good and bad, is that a post-pandemic status quo ante is well underway.

Science is arguably one of the institutions that has reverted to its pre-pandemic normal. During the pandemic we witnessed a great many changes in scientists' work and home lives, in their research processes and collaboration modes, and in the urgency and rapidity of application of their work. Overall, science and scientists have now returned to c. 2019. True, there are likely to be some long-term effects. For example, videoconference-based research collaboration, near universal in the pandemic, has proven to be a viable medium (Bozeman & Gaughan, 2023) and much less expensive than flying people around the globe. Those sponsoring long-distance people movement (e.g. universities, government funding agents, professional associations) have taken note. Likewise, some climate change advocates provided evidence that perhaps the pandemic showed us how to slow down greenhouse gas emissions just a bit. But, overall, as mentioned, science today is more like 2019 science than 2021 science. Scientists who work in the field are back in the field: entomologists are collecting species samples, polar scientists are drilling polar ice rather than only running computer simulations, and others are meeting face-to-face with their postdocs and graduate students rather than struggling with mentoring by Zoom.

This chapter presents a two-country comparison between the United States and Australia. While this book focuses chiefly on Australia, there are good reasons why I focus more on the US. First, this is the context I know best, having been born in the US and having studied its government, politics and economy during my entire professional career. Second, the US experience offers some cautionary notes for Australia, a country that has many similarities to the US but some significant differences, including ones manifested in policies for COVID-19 and science policy in general. Similarly, the relative success of Australia in coping with the pandemic provides some lessons for the US.

A key component of the paper is the analysis of 'public value science' – an approach to science that is not (only) about the normal expectations for productivity and innovation but (also) about equitable impacts and social benefit. Before moving to the pandemic experience, it is best to clarify some of these key concepts and theoretical frameworks.

Normal science and public value science

In so many respects, the post-pandemic 'back to normal' is a good thing for science. But not in every way. One thing that has not changed post pandemic is the gap between quality science and *public values* outcomes. Before discussing public value science and its meaning, it seems a good idea to introduce the concept of public values employed in much of public value theory and throughout this paper. Since I discuss public values in a variety of contexts in this paper, an early definition seems helpful. Public values are:

those providing normative consensus about (a) the rights, benefits, and prerogatives to which citizens should (and should not) be entitled; (b) the obligations of citizens to society, the state, and one another; and (c) the principles on which governments and policies should be based.

(Bozeman, 2007, p. 13)

This conception of public values was introduced more than 20 years ago (Bozeman, 2002), but it seems not so ancient when we consider its antecedents. From Aristotle's Lyceum, to the 1787 Constitutional Convention in Philadelphia, to the 1978 Belmont Report on ethics of human subjects research and beyond, there has been continual discussion of concepts linked closely to public values, often using those exact words, but in other cases using terms such as 'public interest' and 'common good', concepts that are never far removed from the standard lexical meaning of *public* as 'concerning the public as a whole'. In recent political theory, the closest concept to public values is public interest and, indeed, public interest theory is the taproot from which public value theory sprang. In the early decades of the twentieth century, during the period in which political science first emerged as a recognised scholarly discipline, public interest theory was at its centre, perhaps reaching its apex when Pendleton Herring, an academic whose speeches and written work featured public interest, was elected president of the American Political Science Association. For the first half of the twentieth century, writings on public interest theory were published in major journals and occupied the minds of many of the best-known academics in political science. The work began to be recognised in law, such as with admonitions that newly developed regulatory agencies would regulate in 'the public interest'.

In the 1960s, the political science discipline began to take the *science* part of its name more seriously. A discipline that had previously been dominated by history and public law began to favour quantitative data and statistics and to embrace a positivist philosophy of science. Public interest theory was attacked as having nothing to do with these new criteria and was not only out of fashion but also out of the journals. Indeed, one interested in precision, explanation and measurement would find little of value in public interest theory, which was dismissed as a set of myths (Shubert, 1957) and 'fables about the political process' (Sorauf, 1957, p. 638). As neoliberal economics began to take hold at the centre of public policy analysis, public interest theory began to seem even more *passé*, especially given the lack of clarity of its concepts, the absence of hypotheses and its disdain for data. The collective interest babies were thrown out with the conceptually muddy bathwater.

My own work in public value theory started as an effort to resurrect the core notions of public interest theory, but with more precise concepts, operationalisation, criteria and indicators. In my earliest contribution to this conceptualisation of public values, I developed 'public failure criteria' designed on a model somewhat resembling market failure criteria (Bator, 1958, 1995), which had guided so much public policy decision-making (Dollery & Worthington, 1996; Marciano & Medema, 2015; Weimer & Vining, 2017). Some of these criteria were 'looking glass reflection' concepts. Thus, 'monopolies' in market failure theory became 'imperfect monopolies', meaning an abridgement of government's monopoly authority, and 'externalities' or spillover effects became 'benefit hoarding'.

Various frameworks and criteria developed as part of public value theory (Bozeman, 2002, 2007; Bozeman & Crow, 2021) have been widely and diversely applied, including topics such as adoption of artificial intelligence (Schiff et al., 2022), higher education policy (Anderson & Taggart, 2016), geothermal energy (Ruef & Ejderyan, 2021), digital transformation in government (Scupola & Mergel, 2022), disaster recovery (Chandra & Paras, 2021) and even valuation of Australian museums (Grüb & Martin, 2020). The conceptualisation has proved adaptable.

The focus here, however, is on public values in the context of science and science policy or, shorthand, public value science (Bozeman, 2002). Much of the work on public value science has involved employing concepts and indicators (Nelson, 2021; Ribeiro & Shapira, 2020; Shin & Lee, 2017) first developed as 'public value mapping' (Bozeman & Sarewitz, 2011). But, aside from measures, mapping and indicators, what is at the core of public value science? How does one move from the broad and nearly universal applicability of public value theory to public value science and science policy?

Public value science policy

The basis of public value science (and science policy) is straightforward: that science produced with public funds should serve public values, which, let us remember, are the rights, benefits and prerogatives of all citizens – not only affluent citizens, or politically powerful citizens, or male citizens, or adult citizens, or citizens with papers, but also citizens with residence. This is the standard by which science investments and outcomes should be measured – not (primarily) according to the number of articles published, citations, patents or awards.

How do we even begin to determine what is and is not a 'public value' that science is to serve? One approach is to ask scientists about the public values they hold (Bozeman, 2019; Vaandrager & Marks, 2022), but there are other useful approaches, such as distilling them from public policy and public documents. Such elicitation is not as difficult as it might seem. We know that people cherish public and personal health and are concerned about climate change, gun control and space exploration, even though the latter has no immediate effect on them. Much publicly funded research focuses on these topics but often in ways that do not meet the requirements for public value. Thus, COVID-19 vaccines, while not perfect in their distribution in the US or Australia, were widely available at little or no cost. Conversely, the US and many other nations have invested much in fertility research, which tends to advantage the affluent, and in highly effective medical technologies that are lifesaving for people who have good health insurance.

Public value science requires that science policymakers, from the outset of science and technology development, pay attention not only to knowledge and technology products and their effectiveness but also to the distribution of their costs and benefits. Public value science is as simple and as complex as that. *Simple*: people in the US overwhelmingly favour gun control provisions. *Complex*: until recently, recipients of public research funds were prohibited from conducting research that might give rise to data or evidence on gun control. The 1997 'Dickey Amendment', named for Representative Jay Dickey who campaigned explicitly as 'a point man for the NRA [National Rifle Association]', worked indirectly by providing budget cuts for persons doing research on gun violence (Bonne et al., 2021). US agencies such as the Centers for Disease Control and Prevention (CDC) and the National Sanitation Foundation risked budget cuts if they funded any research related to gun violence and, thus, grants and contracts often included language stating that any funded work could not relate to gun violence. What does this anecdote have to do with science policy? Just about everything. It shows that 'public failures' in public policy can translate as public failures in scientific research (Rosenberg, 2019). Science and public values are inextricably linked.

Public funding does not ensure public value. The linear model of innovation espoused in the US favours public investment in science and technology; however, the private sector is expected to underinvest in research because inefficient markets cannot fully capture the benefits from those investments. To put this another way: a major rationale for government funding of science is to remedy inefficiencies in market capitalism. In the US, perhaps more than most nations, this justification, especially as applied to public support for basic research, has been embraced by political leaders from all major parties and coalitions.

Many contemporary science policies do not pertain directly to public values, assuming that public values will be achieved through the rising tide of economic growth. When does scientific research serve public values and what factors mitigate public values outcomes from research, especially publicly funded research? This paper examines that question, focusing on the answers suggested by the experiences during the COVID-19 pandemic of the mixing of science and social needs.

The (usual) disconnect between science and outcomes

The core assumption of this paper is largely undisputed: quality science does not necessarily lead to quality social outcomes or enhanced public values. Here is a simple, familiar example. US citizens often ask: how can the United States spend more money and conduct more research on medicine and health care than any other nation, yet lag behind in health outcomes for its citizens? Let us consider a comparison, noting that national comparisons require caveats. For example, both Cuba and Denmark have much better health outcomes than the US and at a lower cost, but they also have an utterly different government structure and political culture. So, let us compare the US to Canada, its neighbour and a nation with a similar economy and government structure as well as quality research institutions, and to Australia. The US spends 16.8 per cent of its GDP on health care, while Canada spends 10.8 per cent. More jarring, in the US, per capita adult expenses on health care are more than double (US$10,948) those in Canada (US$5,370). Canadians' life expectancy exceeds US citizens (82.2 years compared to 78.5 years) (Health Systems Facts, 2023).

With respect to Australia, the differences are similarly stark. During the 2019–20 period, Australia spent about US$202 billion on health, an average of US$7,926 per adult and about 10.2 per cent of GDP. Australia has one of the highest life expectancies in the world – 83 years for men and women when taken together, which is well ahead of the US. Indeed, for the first time in more than 100 years, average life expectancy in the US has recently begun to fall. Gaps in health and longevity outcomes are the result of numerous factors, but 'quality' or 'highly productive' science cannot plausibly be listed among them. The US spends vastly more than Canada and Australia on public (and private) funding of research and design (R&D) and retains substantial returns: research publications in the US exceed those in both Canada and Australia by more than 500 per cent, as do citations. While this does not imply a high level of input–output efficiency, it does suggest that the US is a world leader in science, and, if we consider patents, in applications of science.

Comparing health outcomes in the US with Australia and Canada is dicey. We know that many factors contribute to such differences, including ones that have nothing to do with science or research. But unravelling health care systems is not my point; rather, my objective is simply to point out that much social distance must be traversed to link up science outcomes and public value outcomes. We need to better understand the relationships between science and public values if we are to improve the ability of public values–focused science to have beneficial impacts. Moreover, we can learn from the COVID-19 pandemic, which matched extraordinary science outcomes to decidedly mixed public values outcomes.

Mythology to the contrary, much scientific research and its resultant technology impinges little, if at all, on public values. My focus is on enhancing public value science, research and technology that seeks positive impacts on collective (public) values, but much research has motives unrelated to public values. We would not expect industrial research to pursue public values. Industrial research focuses on profits; however, profit-motivated industrial research can sometimes, incidentally, have positive effects on public values. Such examples are legion, from improved medical devices to sustainable housing materials. But there are many more examples where profit does nothing to enhance public values, such as the development of food colours with longer shelf lives (Dai et al., 2014; Hutchings, 2011) or research on how consumers' self-concept relates to colour choices in automobiles (Lee, 2009). Much industrial research centres on objectives that actively thwart public values, such as studies focused on ways to offload administrative tasks from companies to robotics, often to the detriment of workers or clients (Collier, 1983; Papageorgiou, 2018).

In most cases, we do not expect industrial research to achieve public value, except, perhaps, when industrial research depends strongly on public funding. But what of government-funded science? Is it not reasonable to expect that tax-supported science and technology will serve public values? The expectation that public science will lead to public value is often not realised, in part, I argue, because of a tendency to confuse economic growth with public values.

Public values failure and the failures of Schumpeter

For decades, many nations have taken as an article of faith that one of the most important rationales for government investment in science is that research is the engine of innovation and, thus, economic development. This argument was fostered in Vannevar Bush's *Science, The Endless Frontier*, but has been expressed in many different ways, both in leading Western democracies (Bilbao-Osorio & Rodríguez-Pose, 2004; Scherer, 1986) and in countries at all tiers of economic development (Akinwale et al., 2012; Grazzi & Pietrobelli, 2016). Why do we so often hear this engine-of-the-economy metaphor? Largely because there is a good deal of truth to the claim. The best estimates of the contribution of research and innovation to growth provide solid evidence supporting this rationale for public investment (Aghion & Howitt, 1990; Griliches, 1979).

Oftentimes, science policies encourage research that is regressive, especially in inequitable societies. Ironically, we can look to Schumpeter for support of this regressive science notion. For years, economists have embraced the idea of 'creative destruction' – that is, the notion that technological change in a free-market economy, made possible in part through public investment in research, will destroy some industries and give rise to new ones that will power economic growth. Less attention has been given to the creative destruction of human lives – those who pay the costs through loss of employment, declining economic fortunes and social displacement. Thus, creative destruction celebrates the reality that many innovations lead to the displacement of workers with technology (Romer, 1990). To be sure, business owners often pay a price, as do shareholders who bet on the wrong company; however, the number of workers who lose when businesses are creatively destroyed is far higher and the impacts are often more grievous.

Another argument in favour of the regressive science thesis is the following simple proposition. Industry will tend to develop technologies perceived as maximising profits and, in many cases, the best way to do this is to develop technologies that are not only in high demand but also can command high prices. Related to this, some technologies and goods have economic and technological prerequisites that diminish their use by less wealthy consumers. A simple example, and one relevant to the COVID-19 pandemic, is educational innovation. When learning becomes increasingly distributed and technology based, many resultant innovations will be denied to those who do not have the wherewithal to purchase 'entry technologies' such as personal computers, software and internet connectivity. Similarly, medical technology development is rife with examples where the less wealthy become less healthy because they cannot afford access to costly devices and accoutrement. Again, this reflects the close ties between research, innovation and the structures of a nation's economy. More equitable nations tend to have widespread access to such technologies due to universal health care, whereas nations that are less equitable suffer disparities.

With this theory prologue, let us turn now to the objective of assessing the implications of COVID-19 research outcomes to help us understand the (limited) ability of science to contribute to public values.

COVID-19 implications for public value science

If there was ever a time in recent history when the need for public value science was apparent it was the COVID-19 pandemic. No-one debated whether there was a need for research aimed at producing an effective vaccine that would stem the progress of the coronavirus surge. Who would benefit? Everyone. Thus, production of a vaccine provides the paradigmatic case for analysing the critical importance of public value science, as well as its limitations. The pandemic shows that the successes and failures of even the most significant advances in science remain dependent on the fabric of politics, government and culture. With respect to the effects of science policy on the pandemic, one can identify two outcome categories – 'vaccine development' and 'everything else', neither of which followed typical science policy routines.

By most accounts, vaccine development, at least if we confine ourselves to the two or three most efficacious vaccines, was a resounding success. But, as we shall see, that is a bit of an overstatement.

The SARS-CoV-2 virus, which causes the disease that came to be known as COVID-19, was first isolated in late 2019 (World Health Organization [WHO], n.d.-a). While some elements of COVID-19 could be compared to previous epidemics, such as earlier SARS outbreaks, the rapidity and universality of its spread had not been witnessed since the 1917 influenza epidemic. Thus, the problem in the case of COVID-19 was not about *identifying* the best available scientific knowledge and applying it, but, rather, about rapidly *developing* scientific knowledge for a condition that had not previously existed.

The vaccine development was greatly accelerated by a unique collaboration between several national governments, international organisations and multinational pharmaceutical corporations. By agreement, the largest amount of research funding was provided to North American (40 per cent), Asian and Australian (30 per cent), and European (26 per cent) organisations, with the remaining funding spread among smaller projects in South America and Africa.

After just 11 months, safe and effective vaccines had been developed, well ahead of the projected 18–24 months time frame, and more rapidly than previous international collaborative vaccine development efforts. Indeed, as Thanh Le et al. (2020) observed, no other vaccine effective at treating infectious disease had been produced in one year's time and most had taken several years. The rapid development of the vaccines was due not only to the massive amounts of funding and organisation dedicated to the endeavour but also to recent breakthroughs in genetic research; specifically, the development of mRNA knowledge and applications (Park et al., 2021), which essentially served as the platform for the most effective vaccines (Vitiello & Ferrara, 2021).

Not all COVID-19 vaccines were mRNA based, but the most successful ones, including the Pfizer-BioNTech and Moderna vaccines, were. In addition, several vaccines were developed using adenovirus vectors – that is, a shell containing DNA that produces antigens eliciting a systemic immune response (Jacob-Dolan & Barouch, 2022). The Oxford-AstraZeneca, Sputnik V and Janssen vaccines were all of this type. While each of these vaccines proved effective, their rate of effectiveness was well below the leading mRNA vaccines (Zinatizadeh et al., 2022).

A third major type of vaccine was based on the inactive form of the virus. Virus particles were grown in cultures and then teamed with heat or formaldehyde to eliminate their ability to produce disease while still maintaining the ability to stimulate an immune response. Well-known vaccines of this type include China's CoronaVac (Baraniuk, 2021) and India's Covaxin (Thiagarajan, 2021). While estimates of the efficacy of these vaccines vary considerably, the rates are apparently considerably lower than the mRNA vaccines. Due to the population base where these vaccines were used – the two most populous nations in the world – and the hesitancy of China and India to distribute mRNA vaccines, this is the vaccine type that the majority of the world's population has received. The use of these non-mRNA vaccines is not simply a matter of national pride in research and development but also cost. For example, one dose of the Covaxin vaccine costs about 10 per cent as much as one dose of either the Moderna or Pfizer vaccines. The vaccine also requires normal refrigeration only, not the extremely low temperatures of the mRNA vaccines, a significant issue in India.

In November 2020, results of large-scale clinical trials of the Moderna and Pfizer vaccines were announced, with each having a 95 per cent effectiveness rate. By that time more than 1.2 million deaths had been reported worldwide. It is impossible to know how many lives and infections were avoided due to the development and distribution of effective vaccines; however, by any historical measure, the time required for developing the vaccine and the overall level of efficacy was remarkable. With this, we can conclude the more positive efforts of public value science and science policy.

There was some effort to develop a 'home-grown' COVID-19 vaccine in Australia, but this was relatively short-lived. There were several reasons for the retreat from an Australian-produced vaccine, the most important of which was timing. Australian research was still at the preliminary stage when results started coming in for the Moderna, Pfizer, Johnson and Johnson, and Astra-Zeneca vaccines, and there was every expectation that they would be available to Australian residents. Nonetheless, Australia's retreat from vaccine development resulted in a good deal of criticism. The former secretary of the federal Department of Health, Professor Jane Halton, led a review of the procurement plans, as well as vaccine and treatment plans, with Minister Mark Butler (2022) quoted as saying that the 'Morrison Government [was] caught flat footed in protecting Australians through vaccinations and treatments'.

Despite Australia's relatively successful COVID-19 outcomes, Prime Minister Scott Morrison lost political support. Far be it for this author to claim, from more than 9,000 miles (15,000 kilometres) distance, any knowledge of the forces impinging on elections in Australia. But I can quote others, who suggest that, despite rave reviews for Morrison's pandemic policies and outcomes in the *New York Times*, 'voters don't care about the Times. Instead, they care about Morrison's egregiously bad vibes and an unpleasantness that is so palpable he has remained Labor's strongest electoral asset'; the 'early days of vaccine rollout, the abrogation of leadership during the bushfires and floods and the omicron wave … made [Morrison] an obvious punching bag' (Napier-Raman, 2022). Who am I to question such analysis? Still, I wonder if the prime minister's comments about the Trump administration and Australia being 'best of mates', working to improve international responses to the pandemic, did not also play a role, especially in light of Trump's attack on WHO (not to mention the CDC and US Public Health Service).

COVID-19 policy: When science knowledge and innovation are not enough

As of April 2023, nearly 7 million COVID-related deaths had been reported worldwide (WHO, n.d.-b). Most observers viewed this official figure as underreporting the true scale of deaths, which may be at least twice as high (Bager et al., 2023; Msemburi et al., 2023). Comparing the US and Australia, the US experienced 103,436,829 confirmed cases of COVID-19 and 1,227,152 deaths. Australia experienced 11,299,954 cases and 20,553 deaths. The differences are notable. The US experienced about one fatality per 100 cases, whereas Australia experienced about one fatality per 6,000 cases. Therefore, from a per capita standpoint, the death odds in the US were much higher. With a current US population of about 340 million and a current Australian population of about 27 million, it is clear that population proportions are not reflected in COVID-19 numbers. The US's population is about 12 times larger than Australia's, but its deaths from COVID-19 were about 55 times higher – a huge discrepancy. There are many explanations for this difference, including geographic location, immigration patterns and political leadership – but *not* science. If nothing else, this comparison shows that highly effective science is socially and politically mediated, and that 'world-class science' does not necessarily yield world-class health and medical outcomes. We can take this further to say that assessing science apart from social determinants and social outcomes, an approach common in many parts of the world, makes about as much sense as boasting about one's ability to run 100 metres in 10.5 seconds while – oh, by the way – being chained to a wall. It is easy enough to have one's eye on the wrong prize.

Despite gross differences, we see some generalisations applying to both the US and Australia. For example, it makes a difference which part of the nation one inhabits. In Australia, the COVID-19 death rate per 100 stands at 0.114 in Victoria, but 0.039 in Western Australia. In the US, the gaps also widen, with Texas, Alabama and Oklahoma having death rates almost three times the rates of Massachusetts, Connecticut and Washington. Is the science different in the respective places? No, but some factors related to public health may be somewhat different and the political leadership is, in some cases, substantially different. But politics follows voter preference. In the US, one of the strongest predictors of death from COVID-19 has been partisanship. In some states, the COVID-19 death rate has been more than 70 per cent higher among Republicans than Democrats and these differences cannot be explained away by geography or characteristics of local public health systems (as we are talking about in-state comparisons) or by income and education (as, in many instances, the aggregate for Republicans is higher than for Democrats). When disease and treatment become strong political symbols, science provides little remedy.

Australia and the US have much in common with respect to inequitable outcomes for minorities. The COVID-19 outcomes for different races and ethnicities have been more complicated than one might expect. Typically, and generally, minorities experience considerably worse health outcomes, even controlling for income. However, during the COVID-19 pandemic, the trends were not unidirectional. As reported by Ndugga et al. (2022), early in the pandemic, disparities narrowed once overall infection rates began to fall. In the US, during the Omicron surge in winter 2022, disparities widened once again with Hispanic (4,341 per 100,000), indigenous (3,818 per 100,000), African American (2,937 per 100,000) and Asian (2,755 per 100,000) people having higher age-adjusted infection rates than white people (2,693 per 100,000). Then, once the surge waned, infection rates fell in spring 2022, but they remained high for African American and Hispanic people (192 per 100,000 for each group). Since late summer 2020, there have been some periods when death rates for white people have been higher than, or similar to, some groups of people of colour. Death rates are complicated by the fact that white people tend to have longer life spans, which means that there are more old people around to be vulnerable. Thus, age-adjusted data show that indigenous, African American and Hispanic people have experienced higher rates of death compared with white people over most of the pandemic and particularly during surges. As of April 2023, there was little difference between case incidence and death rates by race, with more than 66 per cent of deaths being white, non-Hispanic persons (who make up 59.3 per cent of the US population).

After acknowledging the great scientific successes of vaccine development, let us consider the diverse factors that contributed to the COVID-19 calamities and the connections among scientific research, science policy, and broader politics and policy. We already know enough recent history to see what is meant by 'science is not enough', but a review of recent history still seems merited. Then we will turn to a less explored question: how can those seeking public value science begin to cope with the many and diverse political and policy obstacles that blunt even the greatest scientific successes? There are no obvious answers. Much of the analysis below focuses on the US, not only because the author is intimately familiar with the US context, but also because the public values failures faced by the US are many, illustrating that being a world research leader, and a leader in COVID-19 vaccine research, does not ensure leadership in quality outcomes for citizens. Some consideration is also given to the case of Australia – a nation that, relatively speaking, has no 'COVID-19 calamities' to explain, only successes to emulate.

Inept and malevolent political leadership

We begin with the 'conspicuous exception'. When a political leader suggests that taking a vaccine may not be manly (Bolsonaro), or that drinking bleach may suffice as a coronavirus cure (Trump), or that a markedly inferior vaccine must be used exclusively because it is home-produced (Xi), then solutions potentially flowing from scientific research are blunted.

Since we are focusing on the case of the US, let us examine that nation's inept and malevolent political leadership, beginning, of course, with then president Donald Trump. Incompetent, malevolent political leaders are common enough in the US, but, for a period of more than 150 years, none had been elected to the US presidency – not until 2016. To be sure, the election of Donald Trump was a reflection of a degree of political rancour and discord not often seen in the US; however, it was also a reflection of structural public failures in the US's legal systems. His re-election even more so.

In the US, the experience of policymaking in the wake of COVID-19 is, to a significant extent, an account of the president's behaviour. This is necessarily the case when an executive chooses to ignore or argue contentiously with advisers and set off in unexpected directions. Thus, while many of President Trump's clashes over science and with scientists have been criticised for detrimentally affecting the public's interest in maintaining health and safety in the wake of the pandemic, such behaviour is not out of character for Trump. Moreover, Trump's clashes often reinforced the views of those citizens with limited faith in advisers and executive branch specialists, especially ones advising on science or health issues. Many of President Trump's responses to the pandemic were exaggerated forms of typical political responses: they were not, in any sense, unique. For example, 'happy news' is commonplace among politicians, especially those facing re-election contests.

In Australia, as in perhaps every nation, there were some pandemic missteps that can be subject to post-mortem. As mentioned, there were racial and regional inequities, but these were more modest than those experienced in many other nations. There was the sudden conclusion of the nation's work on vaccine development, but this can easily be explained as an effort to avoid duplication. There was some dissatisfaction with social distancing and closures, but that would likely yield some conflict regardless of the position taken. More interesting is what we can learn from Australia's political leadership. When I say 'political leadership', I am not only referring to the prime minister, the parliament or elected officials, but also to leaders in government agencies, especially public health and education, as they are often quite important to outcomes.

New technologies for information and misinformation

While President Trump's leadership and political style have been crucial to understanding the US response to the pandemic, other factors are also quite important. The rise of social media as a news source and the decline of traditional media (Street, 2011) has played a role, as has the lack of general trust in any media source (Fink, 2019; Jones, 2004). That mistrust is, to a large extent, understandable. In an environment in which social media is deployed for, variously, hoaxes, literal fake news, illicit and disguised commerce, and, in some cases, just to gain status as an 'influencer' by getting a tally of 'likes', mistrust seems well warranted. When the paid influencer role affects medicine and health choices (Díaz-Martín et al., 2020; Thomas, 2019), scepticism implies sound judgement.

When one also considers that, for most persons under the age of 40, social media comprises the main source of news, one sees a change in the environment in which scientific knowledge is evaluated (Anspach, 2017; Feezell, 2018). Doubtless, new media approaches to acquiring news, including health news (Bujnowska-Fedak et al., 2019; Eysenbach et al., 2002; Powell et al., 2003), have affected the use of scientific knowledge in the case of COVID-19. Posts on social media have sought to sell air purifiers, vitamins, teas, essential oils and colloidal silver as 'cures' for COVID-19 and, of course, have found many thousands of buyers (Lallie et al., 2021). Perhaps even more troubling, some social media posts peddling misinformation were presented on mocked-up facsimiles of UNESCO, WHO and the Canadian Department of Health letterheads.

The lack of trusted mass media and the balkanisation of news leaves a crisis in institutional vetting of science and science-related public issues. When one-half of a nation feels that any coverage on CNN is fake news and the other half thinks the same about Fox News, there are (at least) two truths, even in the case of science-intensive issues. The fragmentation is evidenced in the fact that, in one poll (Gramlich, 2020), Fox News was reported as the source *most trusted* by Republicans for political news (65 per cent), and the *least trusted* news source for all respondents (49 per cent) and especially Democrats (61 per cent). Perhaps not surprisingly, among those who say they regularly tune into Fox News, 63 per cent feel that President Trump's response to the COVID-19 outbreak was 'excellent', a sentiment shared by only 7 per cent of CNN regulars and 1 per cent of those who regularly read the *New York Times* (Gramlich, 2020). Understanding of current events, including the pandemic, is increasingly dominated by social enclaves and echo chambers (Flaxman et al., 2016; Garrett, 2009).

Fragmentation of authority: States as laboratories of life and death

Even when groups such as WHO sought to bring some degree of order to the chaos of an uncoordinated national response, the COVID-19 case illustrates the near impossibility of doing so. In the US, federalism played a role in responses to the pandemic and also shows how and why different political jurisdictions took very different approaches. While the federal government has the ability to initiate policies to which state governments must conform, the US Constitution, not to mention historical precedent, provides a good deal of autonomy for the states in the development, and especially the use, of scientific knowledge with regard to public health. While it is not clear that each of the US state governments embody all of the 13 socio-technical governance roles identified by Borrás and Edler (2020), they certainly embody most of them, often simultaneously and, indeed, one might add a fourteenth role, namely negotiator. The COVID-19 case highlights the extent to which, even after more than 230 years, the relative powers of federal v. state government are a matter of dispute and sometimes negotiation.

Since the states play a relatively minor role in funding and guiding the development of research and scientific knowledge, they have little input in determining issues pertaining to directions of research. However, the states have considerable autonomy, and discretion, in terms of how they use such research, including public health guidelines and associated data. Some governors have received a good deal of praise for their leadership, including the governors of Washington, Hawaii, New Jersey and California – all states that were quick to adopt a series of policy guidelines relating to COVID-19 and to enforce them. By contrast, other states and their governors evinced puzzling responses, some even displaying a dispiriting degree of ignorance about the pandemic and its causes. One of the most quoted cases of being out of touch was Governor Brian Kemp of Georgia who stated in April 2020: 'We didn't know that [the virus could be spread by people who were asymptomatic] until the last 24 hours. This is a game changer for us.' This suggests that, perhaps, the governor and his followers were not listening closely, since public health agencies and the President's Coronavirus Task Force had announced some months earlier that the disease could be transmitted by those who had the virus but were asymptomatic.

Many other governors (including those in Alabama, Mississippi and Oklahoma) refused to take any significant action limiting social gatherings or requiring business closures until well after the time their state might have had a chance of containing the COVID-19 virus. For example, Governor Reeves of Mississippi provided this guidance: 'If you feel that a statewide lockdown should be occurring, then you should put yourself on individual lockdown.'

The failed leadership of many of the US state governors stands in contrast to political leadership in Australia. Perhaps one lesson is the importance of having sub-national leaders whose policies are not entirely at odds with one another. Some argue that Australia's pandemic successes were not because of Prime Minister Morrison but despite him. State premieres made hard decisions about closures and lockdowns, often putting their political careers in peril. Arguably, this contrasts with the 'finger in the wind' policies of most governors in the southern US states, none of whom resisted the unfortunate views of Republican-controlled legislatures and their perceived voter base. One searches for profiles in courage but comes back empty-handed.

It is worth noting that state governments in the US had different levels of access to scientific knowledge during the pandemic, and that the quality of state public health resources, and state and regional political culture was also different. The basic point is that, when discussing the use of scientific knowledge in public policy, one can expect vast differences across public policy jurisdictions, and politics and government structures. In a nation as politically and culturally polarised as the US, these factors can have huge consequences. COVID-19 deaths and hospitalisations differed greatly in the US. For example, per capita COVID-19 fatalities in Alabama, Kentucky, Louisiana, Mississippi and West Virginia, each having conservative Republican legislatures and Republican governors who were, for the most part, loyal Trump acolytes, were about 2.5 times greater than in Hawaii, Massachusetts, Minnesota, Oregon and Vermont. Bumper sticker analysis: 'Live Free and Die.'

To be sure, it is much too glib to say that party politics is the only or even the primary determinant of regional differences in COVID-19 deaths. Other factors, such as age of population, existing health conditions before COVID-19 exposure, level of education and cultural heritage, must also be considered. However, the basic point remains: for a paradigmatic example of the dependence of science and health incomes on policy and politics, one needs to look no further than COVID-19.

How can public value science policy co-exist with political and social fracture?

Having spent a good deal of time and energy outlining and advocating public value science (e.g. Bozeman, 2020; Bozeman & Sarewitz, 2011; Bozeman & Youtie, 2017), my purpose here is to show some of the limits of public value science. The limits are well illustrated by the COVID-19 pandemic. Science is not a panacea. Science does not fix problematic government structures, corrupt politicians or deep-seated cultural beliefs. Indeed, sometimes scientific knowledge has the opposite effect of hardening positions (Sarewitz, 2010).

My question: how can public value science provide benefits in the midst of social fragmentation, economic inequities and, especially, political fractiousness? *Snarky answer*: it cannot, because you cannot fix stupid. *Better – not quite so snarky – answer*: in a nation divided with respect to political values, religion, belief systems, information sources, trusted leaders and even views about human life, science of any sort is unlikely to have uniform effects. Public value science strives to work for the collective interest, but it is good to be realistic about the fact that, at least in the US, one struggles to identify even a semblance of collective interest. One might think that it would be agreed upon that seeking available treatment that will likely ameliorate harm from a virus known to have killed millions of people would be the consummate collective interest. Alas, such is not the case. For some, tribal allegiance proved more important than collective interest. This is clearly shown by the fact that less educated white people were disproportionately infected by COVID-19; that their morbidity and mortality rates have been growing steadily since 2020 (Case & Deaton, 2021) might also be a symptom of this.

Best answer: we cannot expect to change the foundational social problems highlighted by COVID-19 in a hurry, but we can have some greater hope of reforming science institutions. People notice when science seems to have little to do with them, not only when it focuses on 'knowledge for its own sake', or results in poorly communicated social and economic outcomes, but also when they cannot afford the medical technology and drugs developed from research. However, an underlying theme relates to the idea that a 'rising tide lifts all boats'. I will refrain from citing the voluminous studies addressing the question of wealth v. equity in the US, partly because I alluded to some of the issues above (see the section on regressive science).

It seems clear enough that even when some of the most productive (in terms of published articles and accumulated prizes) scientists in the world are engaged in research about a particular topic (in this case COVID-19), large swathes of people are not much affected, at least not in a positive way.

A science policy reform that could address some of these issues would involve a reorientation towards public value science. In much of the US, but not everywhere, science funding is rationalised in terms of a sort of magical return on investment dynamic. The idea is that, in an efficient market economy, investment in scientific research will produce innovative technologies that will produce economic growth that will lead to universal benefits. Part of this is quite correct. Investments in science often yield economic growth and social benefits. The 'magical' part is in the following assumptions: that markets are efficient, that economic growth provides benefits to everyone and that innovations have at least net neutral effects on individuals' wellbeing.

Scholars around the world (Birch, 2020; Mazzucato, 2018; McNie et al., 2016; Ulnicane, 2016; Uyarra et al., 2019) have begun to question the aims of innovation and to focus on science policy approaches that reinforce not only economic but also social benefits, including 'responsible innovation' (Hartley et al., 2019; Stilgoe et al., 2013). Public value science policy complements these ideas and approaches. It focuses on ways to ensure universal, or at least shared, net benefit to the citizens who are effectively financing (through tax dollars or other subsidies) the research. Thus, public value science is necessarily progressive in its structure and impacts. The claim is that public investment in science should be redeemed in terms of public value, just as private investment should lead to private benefit to producers, investors and consumers.

I argue that the relationship between investment in research and economic impact is strongly affected by the fundamental structures of a nation's economy. Absent 'government intervention', aggregate research outcomes will tend to closely reflect the character of an economy, particularly, though not exclusively, as pertaining to concentrations of wealth and technological innovation and production strategies.

In the realm of COVID-19, science 'worked its wonders' in terms of vaccine development (Saag, 2022). An admirable achievement. However, broader experiences during the pandemic clearly show that science, even public value science, cannot suffice. One conclusion (my interpretation) is that public value science should be installed within the structure of nations' political and economic systems, as well as their social structure. As organisation theorists might analogise, a society with extremes in hierarchical differentiation cannot hope to successfully deploy public value science even when it successfully generates it. An aspiration, perhaps not a realistic one, is that science policymakers – those on the frontlines in providing resources for science – may be able to take steps that lessen the likelihood that science will conform to the inequities pervading society.

Australia as a COVID-19 success story: What can we learn?

Many people in the US have asked, and some continue to ask: where did the US go wrong with the COVID-19 pandemic and why did Australia respond so well? Here I examine some of the opinions about why Australia fared so well, especially compared to the US. I begin with an article in the *Washington Post* (Glover, 2021) that provided 10 explanations.[1] Below, I not only list the chief points in the article but also provide my own running comments as a sort of one-person Greek Chorus.

> **1. The bush fire experience:** Just before COVID-19 struck, Australia suffered its worst-ever bush fire season … In March last year [2020], international borders were closed, and returning Australians were forced into hotel quarantine.

We know that history often provides idiosyncratic and perverse outcomes. Maybe this is such a case. No significant public policy implications here.

> **2. First Nations people must be given power to run their own response:** Indigenous Australians have a life expectancy of around 8 years fewer than non-Indigenous Australians. But they were six times *less* likely to contract COVID-19… The reason: Indigenous leaders insisted that they should drive the response and – for once – they were listened to. Remote communities were closed to outsiders, food was supplied to limit travel, and information campaigns were created full of Indigenous humour and values. At the heart of the campaign was a First Nations passion for protecting their elders.

---

1   There are quite a few such articles, signalling that this is a topic of considerable interest among US readers. I focus on the *Washington Post* article because it has most of the same points as other such analyses (e.g. Haseltine, 2021; O'Sullivan et al., 2021).

I certainly do not take issue with this, but this observation needs amplification to be of much use. In the US, indigenous Americans have a good deal of autonomy. The tribe with which I am most familiar is the Navajo (Dine), which has approximately 332,000 members. As one who travelled extensively in Navajo territories during the pandemic, I saw many signs of autonomous policy that, in my view, had positive effects. The mask rules were stricter than in most other communities and social aggregation rules were strong and detailed. Despite often living in quite remote areas, the Navajos' completion rate for primary vaccination was about the same as the general population (71.8 per cent). However, their death rate (0.0064) was double that of the general population (0.0033). Autonomy, and good decision-making and implementation, while surely beneficial, cannot overcome centuries of neglect and the limited availability of timely health care.

> **3. States matter:** Like the United States, Australia has three levels of government – federal, state and local ... Suddenly, though, we've discovered the virtues of states. The most populous, New South Wales (NSW), has elevated contact tracing to an art form. The ability to close borders also turned Australia into eight small nations – an advantage in a world in which smaller countries have generally done best in the pandemic.

Indeed! I would genuinely like to know why so many American governors can best be described with one word. No, I am not thinking of 'stupid', but 'craven'. In my view, more than a few intelligent, well-educated, so-called leaders made decisions that advanced their short-term political careers and perhaps cost many lives.

> **4. It helps if people follow the rules:** Australians love to think of themselves as rebels but, in truth, we're a compliant lot. There were few anti-mask protests, and when people were told to wear masks, they immediately obeyed. And though some complained about the tough lockdowns, swelling approval ratings greeted the leaders who imposed them.

The US also prides itself in its rebellious history; however, in recent times, the rebels have become know-nothing nihilists. This has always been a component of the US citizenry. What has happened recently to increase their rate of propagation? There is a theory that such people are 'no longer under the rock', which suggests that they have been waiting for a sufficiently authoritarian fearmonger to appear, as happened in 2016. But that is too simple. National character theories are out of date. Nevertheless, for an interesting take on national characters, I recommend Charles Dickens's *American Notes*, which chronicles his tour of America in 1842. After reading that, one is likely to ask: why did those people disappear for a while and then re-appear in 2016?

> **5. It's important to reach across the aisle:** Australian politics is highly combative, but when COVID-19 struck, a truce was called … The leader of the opposition, Labor's Anthony Albanese, largely backed the government's pandemic response. 'There are no blue teams or red teams', Morrison said early on … The truce didn't last forever, but it helped.

Spot on. This particular answer relates not only to COVID-19 but also to nearly every major social or economic problem currently facing the US: continual games of chicken regarding defaulting on the national debt, using LBGTQIA+ people as a punching bag to gain political favour with party Troglodytes, shirking from immigration policy in every way except incessantly blaming the Opposition. Politics with no quarter.

> **6. You don't have to choose between 'saving lives' and 'saving the economy':** Australia's tough lockdown had a shattering impact on business. Yet by controlling the pandemic, Australia has been able to reopen its economy.

Yes, a tragic false dichotomy. How many political leaders knew this but pretended not to?

> **7. People trust the health system:** For all the controversy over 'socialist medicine' in the United States, Australia's Medicare – a system of universal health care – is immensely popular. When people were told to get tested, the starting point was a health system people believed in. Nearly 15 million COVID-19 tests have been conducted, equivalent to more than half the country's population.

The public health system in the US has long been a cruel farce. To save Americans from 'socialized medicine', many have been saved from any medicine at all. Wealthy Americans enjoy excellent health care, poor Americans typically do not. Since 2004, the Commonwealth Fund has ranked national health care systems. Among the world's 11 wealthiest nations, the US has ranked last in each year's analysis. The criteria? Access to care, care processes, administrative efficiency, equity and health outcomes (Commonwealth Fund, 2021).

8. Make use of the police and military: Whether it was the army bringing its organisational skills to contact tracing in NSW, or the police and naval officers enforcing hotel quarantine, those in uniform won fresh levels of respect.

Here is an idea that the US can and should adopt. The US National Guard has been helpful in many civil emergencies and almost every city's police force could use some favourable public relations, especially after having killed more than 1,000 citizens in 2022, nearly 200 of whom carried no weapon.

9. Mobilise communities: The worst outbreak, which occurred in Victoria, occurred in migrant communities that had been inadequately served with information in their languages. It was a lesson we had to learn.

It is also a lesson the US must learn. In the US, 21.7 per cent of citizens predominately speak a language other than English.

10. Be an island: Australia is a very large island. It's not the whole story. But it helped.

The US is turning itself into several large islands, but not geographically. Still, it is worth thinking about how a nation can work towards an immigration policy that is both humane and rational and, at the same time, understands the relationship between immigration, travel and the dissemination of disease.

Beyond homage: Even a good story can improve

From any US vantage point, the Australian pandemic response seems an unblemished paragon. But it is possible to have a few blemishes and yet remain a paragon. Let us consider the findings from a systematic review of Australia's COVID-19 response authored by a distinguished multidisciplinary panel (Basseal et al., 2023). This panel concluded that the response was, overall, effective but that lessons remained. These included: 1) improvements in restrictions on movement, 2) limitations of national data systems and data modelling, 3) system weaknesses in residential care for elderly and 4) greater focus on the needs and interests of young people. The panel underscored the strengths of the nation's response, including consultative and transparent decision-making, regional collaboration and early recognition of novel vaccine technology.

Public value science policy: Implications

Perhaps the single most important implication of the foregoing is that science, either science-as-usual or public value–focused science, cannot solve social or economic problems that are systemic. This will not come as a surprise, probably not even to the giddiest science optimist. Thus, let us consider this question: if we assume that public value science is socially embedded and its ability to unilaterally solve problems is minimal, then what might those committed to public value science do to work within political systems that they, presumably, have little or no ability to affect directly? Here are some all-too-modest suggestions.

Scientists and, especially, leaders of science institutions need to be aware of the embeddedness of even their very best research and technology efforts and, if possible, understand that science outcomes may be regressive, especially if the economy is regressive and rife with inequality. Consider this: in the US the top 1 per cent of earners average more than 40 times the income of the bottom 90 per cent (World Population Review, 2023). Science 'products' (e.g. vaccines) and delivery systems (e.g. clinics, hospitals) have costs. In some nations, these costs are largely born collectively, provided by governments, usually with funds from progressive taxation. Other nations celebrate low taxes; prize tax systems that have little or no vertical equity; and celebrate the myth of the self-made person working in the 'land of opportunity', while ignoring generations of economic immobility. How can science outcomes, even the best of public value science, compete with a socio-economic system so designed?

A *proactive* public value science policy is a step in the right direction, albeit a small step. Thus, for example, if one is charged with, say, working with a National Science Foundation panel that is planning research that will have new socially and publicly relevant outcomes, such plans had best consider not only the scientific and technical success of such efforts but also who benefits from the successes and, in some cases, who pays any social costs associated with them. Forethought can help, especially if public value thoughts are those in the fore.

References

Aghion, P. & Howitt, P. (1990). *A model of growth through creative destruction.* National Bureau of Economic Research. doi.org/10.3386/w3223.

Akinwale, Y. O., Dada, A. D., Oluwadare, A. J., Jesuleye, O. A. & Siyanbola, W. O. (2012). Understanding the nexus of R&D, innovation and economic growth in Nigeria. *International Business Research*, *5*(11), 187. doi.org/10.5539/ibr.v5n 11p187.

Anderson, D. M. & Taggart, G. (2016). Organizations, policies, and the roots of public value failure: The case of for-profit higher education. *Public Administration Review*, *76*(5), 779–789. doi.org/10.1111/puar.12606.

Anspach, N. M. (2017). The new personal influence: How our Facebook friends influence the news we read. *Political Communication*, *34*, 590–606. doi.org/ 10.1080/10584609.2017.1316329.

Bager, P., Nielsen, J., Bhatt, S., Nielsen, L. B., Krause, T. G. & Vestergaard, L. S. (2023). Conflicting COVID-19 excess mortality estimates. *The Lancet*, *401*(10375), 432–433. doi.org/10.1016/S0140-6736(23)00115-0.

Baraniuk, C. (2021). What do we know about China's COVID-19 vaccines? *BMJ*, *373*(912). doi.org/10.1136/bmj.n912.

Basseal, J. M., Bennett, C. M., Collignon, P., Currie, B. J., Durrheim, D. N., Leask, J. & Marais, B. J. (2023). Key lessons from the COVID-19 public health response in Australia. *The Lancet Regional Health – Western Pacific*, *30*. doi.org/10.1016/ j.lanwpc.2022.100616.

Bator, F. (1958). The anatomy of market failure. *Quarterly Journal of Economics*, *72*(3), 351–379. doi.org/10.2307/1882231.

Bator, F. (1995). *The anatomy of market failure*. In S. Estrin & A. Marin (Eds), *Essential Readings in Economics* (pp. 129–158). Bloomsbury Academic. doi.org/ 10.1007/978-1-349-24002-9_7.

Bilbao-Osorio, B. & Rodríguez-Pose, A. (2004). From R&D to innovation and economic growth in the EU. *Growth and Change*, *35*(4), 434–455. doi.org/ 10.1111/j.1468-2257.2004.00256.x.

Birch, K. (2020). Technoscience rent: Toward a theory of *rentiership* for technoscientific capitalism. *Science, Technology, & Human Values*, *45*(1), 3–33. doi.org/10.1177/0162243919829567.

Bonne, S., Boxer, P., Gusmano, M., Sloan-Power, E., Ostermann, M., Centellas, A. & Hohl, B. (2021). Looking at the Second Amendment from the Tenth: Early experiences with a state gun violence research center. In M. Crandall, S. Bonne, J. Bronson & W. Kessel (Eds), *Why we are losing the war on gun violence in the United States* (pp. 223–232). Springer. doi.org/10.1007/978-3-030-55513-9_17.

Borrás, S. & Edler, J. (2020). The roles of the state in the governance of socio-technical systems' transformation. *Research Policy, 49*(5), article 103971. doi.org/10.1016/j.respol.2020.103971.

Bozeman, B. (2002). Public-value failure: When efficient markets may not do. *Public Administration Review, 62*(2), 145–161. doi.org/10.1111/0033-3352.00165.

Bozeman, B. (2007). *Public values and public interest: Counterbalancing economic individualism.* Georgetown University Press. doi.org/10.1353/book13027.

Bozeman, B. (2019). Public values: Citizens' perspective. *Public Management Review, 21*(6), 817–838. doi.org/10.1080/14719037.2018.1529878.

Bozeman, B. (2020). Public value science. *Issues in Science and Technology, 36*(4), 34–41.

Bozeman, B. & Crow, M. M. (2021). *Public values leadership: Striving to achieve democratic ideals.* JHU Press.

Bozeman, B. & Gaughan, M. (2023). The 'zoomification' of collaboration: How timely technology has affected academic research. *Minerva, 61*(4), 467–493. doi.org/10.1007/s11024-023-09500-4.

Bozeman, B. & Sarewitz, D. (2011). Public value mapping and science policy evaluation. *Minerva, 49*, 1–23. doi.org/10.1007/s11024-011-9161-7.

Bozeman, B. & Youtie, J. (2017). Socio-economic impacts and public value of government-funded research: Lessons from four US National Science Foundation initiatives. *Research Policy, 46*(8), 1387–1398. doi.org/10.1016/j.respol.2017.06.003.

Bujnowska-Fedak, M. M., Waligóra J. & Mastalerz-Migas, A. (2019). The internet as a source of health information and services. In M. Pokorski (Ed.), *Advancements and Innovations in Health Sciences* (pp. 1–16). Springer. doi.org/10.1007/5584_2019_396.

Butler, M. (2022, 30 June). *Review into COVID-19 vaccine and treatment purchases.* Department of Health and Aged Care. www.health.gov.au/ministers/the-hon-mark-butler-mp/media/review-into-covid-19-vaccine-and-treatment-purchases.

Case, A. & Deaton, A. (2021). *Mortality rates by college degree before and during COVID-19.* National Bureau of Economic Research. doi.org/10.3386/w29328.

Chandra, Y. & Paras, A. (2021). Social entrepreneurship in the context of disaster recovery: Organizing for public value creation. *Public Management Review, 23*(12), 1856–1877. doi.org/10.1080/14719037.2020.1775282.

Collier, D. A. (1983). The service sector revolution: The automation of services. *Long Range Planning, 16*(6), 10–20. doi.org/10.1016/0024-6301(83)90002-X.

Commonwealth Fund. (2021). *Mirror, mirror 2021: Reflecting poorly. Health care in the US compared to other high-income countries.* www.commonwealthfund.org/publications/fund-reports/2021/aug/mirror-mirror-2021-reflecting-poorly.

Dai, Y., Lu, Y., Wu, W., Lu, X-M., Han, Z-P., Liu, Y. & Dai, R-T. (2014). Changes in oxidation, color and texture deteriorations during refrigerated storage of ohmically and water bath-cooked pork meat. *Innovative Food Science & Emerging Technologies, 26*, 341–346. doi.org/10.1016/j.ifset.2014.06.009.

Díaz-Martín, A. M., Schmitz, A. & Yagüe Guillén, M. J. (2020). Are health e-mavens the new patient influencers? *Frontiers in Psychology, 11*, 779. doi.org/10.3389/fpsyg.2020.00779.

Dollery, B. E. & Worthington, A. C. (1996). The evaluation of public policy: Normative economic theories of government failure. *Journal of Interdisciplinary Economics, 7*(1), 27–39. doi.org/10.1177/02601079X9600700103.

Eysenbach G., Powell, J., Kuss, O. & Sa, E-R. (2002, 22–29 May). Empirical studies assessing the quality of health information for consumers on the World Wide Web: A systematic review. *JAMA, 287*(20), 2691–2700. doi.org/10.1001/jama.287.20.2691.

Feezell, J. T. (2018). Agenda setting through social media: The importance of incidental news exposure and social filtering in the digital era. *Political Research Quarterly, 71*(2), 482–494. doi.org/10.1177/1065912917744895.

Fink, K. (2019). The biggest challenge facing journalism: A lack of trust. *Journalism, 20*(1), 40–43. doi.org/10.1177/1464884918807069.

Flaxman, S., Goel, S. & Rao, J. M. (2016). Filter bubbles, echo chambers, and online news consumption. *Public Opinion Quarterly, 80*(S1), 298–320. doi.org/10.1093/poq/nfw006.

Garrett, R. K. (2009). Echo chambers online?: Politically motivated selective exposure among internet news users. *Journal of Computer-Mediated Communication, 14*, 265–285. doi.org/10.1111/J.1083-6101.2009.01440.X.

Glover, R. (2021, 15 March). 10 reasons for Australia's COVID-19 success story. *Washington Post.* www.washingtonpost.com/opinions/2021/03/15/10-reasons-australias-covid-19-success-story/.

Gramlich, J. (2020, 8 April). 5 Facts about Fox News. *Pew Research Center.* www.pewresearch.org/short-reads/2020/04/08/five-facts-about-fox-news/.

Grazzi, M. & Pietrobelli, C. (2016). *Firm innovation and productivity in Latin America and the Caribbean: The engine of economic development.* Springer Nature. doi.org/10.1057/978-1-349-58151-1.

Griliches, Z. (1979). Issues in assessing the contribution of research and development to productivity growth. *The Bell Journal of Economics, 10*(1), 92–116. doi.org/10.2307/3003321.

Grüb, B. & Martin, S. (2020). Public value of cultural heritages – Towards a better understanding of citizen's valuation of Austrian museums. *Cultural Trends, 29*(5), 337–358. doi.org/10.1080/09548963.2020.1822142.

Hartley, S., McLeod, C., Clifford, M., Jewitt, S. & Ray, C. (2019). A retrospective analysis of responsible innovation for low-technology innovation in the Global South. *Journal of Responsible Innovation, 6*(2), 143–162. doi.org/10.1080/23299460.2019.1575682.

Haseltine, W. A. (2021, 24 March) What can we learn from Australia's COVID-19 response? *Forbes.* www.forbes.com/sites/williamhaseltine/2021/03/24/what-can-we-learn-from-australias-covid-19-response/?sh=19a72d903a01.

Health Systems Facts. (2023, 14 April). *Comparison of National Health Systems.* health systemsfacts.org/comparisons-of-health-systems/comparing-several-national-health-systems/?_gl=1*8zmknj*_up*MQ..*_ga*OTMzNzgxMDQ0LjE3NDM1NTQ2NTM.*_ga_SDY74B5S30*MTc0MzU1NDY1MS4xLjEuMTc0MzU1NDcyNi4wLjAuMA...

Hutchings, J. B. (Ed.). (2011). *Food colour and appearance.* Springer Science & Business Media.

Jacob-Dolan, C. & Barouch, D. H. (2022). COVID-19 vaccines: Adenoviral vectors. *Annual Review of Medicine, 73*, 41–54.

Jones, D. A. (2004). Why Americans don't trust the media: A preliminary analysis. *The International Journal of Press/Politics, 9*(2), 60–75. doi.org/10.1177/1081180X04263461.

Lallie, H. S., Shepherd, L. A., Nurse, J. R. C., Erola, A., Epiphaniou, G., Maple, C. & Bellekens, X. (2021). Cyber security in the age of COVID-19: A timeline and analysis of cyber-crime and cyber-attacks during the pandemic. *Computers & Security, 105*, 102248. doi.org/10.1016/j.cose.2021.102248.

Lee, J. W. (2009). Relationship between consumer personality and brand personality as self-concept: From the case of Korean automobile brands. *Academy of Marketing Studies Journal, 13*(1), 25–44.

Marciano, A. & Medema, S. G. (2015). Market failure in context: Introduction. *History of Political Economy*, *47*(Suppl 1), 1–19. doi.org/10.1215/00182702-3130415.

Mazzucato, M. (2018). Mission-oriented innovation policies: Challenges and opportunities. *Industrial and Corporate Change*, *27*(5), 803–815. doi.org/10.1093/icc/dty034.

McNie, E. C., Parris, A. & Sarewitz, D. (2016). Improving the public value of science: A typology to inform discussion, design and implementation of research. *Research Policy*, *45*(4), 884–895. doi.org/10.1016/j.respol.2016.01.004.

Msemburi, W., Karlinsky, A., Knutson, V., Aleshin-Guendel, S., Chatterji, S. & Wakefield, J. (2023). The WHO estimates of excess mortality associated with the COVID-19 pandemic. *Nature*, *613*(7942), 130–137. doi.org/10.1038/s41586-022-05522-2.

Napier-Raman, K. (2022, 20 May). For Scott Morrison, this should have been the unloseable election. *Crikey*. www.crikey.com.au/2022/05/20/should-have-been-unloseable-election-for-morrison/.

Ndugga, N., Hill, L. & Artiga, S. (2022, 17 November). COVID-19 cases and deaths, vaccinations, and treatments by race/ethnicity as of fall 2022. *Kaiser Family Foundation*. www.kff.org/racial-equity-and-health-policy/issue-brief/covid-19-cases-and-deaths-vaccinations-and-treatments-by-race-ethnicity-as-of-fall-2022/.

Nelson, J. P. (2021). Public value promises and outcome reporting in advanced research projects agency – energy. *Minerva*, *59*(4), 493–513. doi.org/10.1007/s11024-021-09444-7.

O'Sullivan, D., Rahamathulla, M. & Pawar, M. (2021). The impact and implications of Covid-19: An Australian perspective. *The International Journal of Community and Social Development*, *2*(2), 134–151. doi.org/10.1177/2516602620937922.

Papageorgiou, D. (2018). Transforming the HR function through robotic process automation. *Benefits Quarterly*, *34*(2), 27–30.

Park, J. W., Lagniton, P. N. P., Liu, Y. & Xu, R-H. (2021). mRNA vaccines for COVID-19: What, why and how. *International Journal of Biological Sciences*, *17*(6), 1446–1460. doi.org/10.7150/ijbs.59233.

Powell, A. (2003). Satellites, the internet, and journalism. In K. Kawamoto (Ed.), *Digital journalism: Emerging media and the changing horizons of journalism* (pp. 103–113). Rowman and Littlefield.

Ribeiro, B. & Shapira, P. (2020). Private and public values of innovation: A patent analysis of synthetic biology. *Research Policy*, *49*(1), 103875. doi.org/10.1016/j.respol.2019.103875.

Romer, P. M. (1990). Endogenous technological change. *Journal of Political Economy*, *98*(5, Part 2), S71–S102. doi.org/10.1086/261725.

Rosenberg, M. L. (2019). Let's bring the full power of science to gun violence prevention. *American Journal of Public Health*, *109*(3), 396–397. doi.org/10.2105/AJPH.2018.304912.

Ruef, F. & Ejderyan, O. (2021). Rowing, steering or anchoring? Public values for geothermal energy governance. *Energy Policy*, *158*, 112577. doi.org/10.1016/j.enpol.2021.112577.

Saag, M. (2022). Wonder of wonders, miracle of miracles: The unprecedented speed of COVID-19 science. *Physiological Reviews*, *102*(3), 1569–1577. doi.org/10.1152/physrev.00010.2022.

Sarewitz, D. (2010). World view: Curing climate backlash. *Nature*, *464*(7285), 28–29. doi.org/10.1038/464028a.

Scherer, F. M. (1986). *Innovation and growth: Schumpeterian perspectives*. MIT Press.

Schiff, D. S., Schiff, K. J. & Pierson, P. (2022). Assessing public value failure in government adoption of artificial intelligence. *Public Administration*, *100*(3), 653–673. doi.org/10.1111/padm.12742.

Scupola, A. & Mergel, I. (2022). Co-production in digital transformation of public administration and public value creation: The case of Denmark. *Government Information Quarterly*, *39*(1), 101650. doi.org/10.1016/j.giq.2021.101650.

Shin, D-H. & Lee, M-K. (2017). Public value mapping of network neutrality: Public values and net neutrality in Korea. *Telecommunications Policy*, *41*(3), 208–224. doi.org/10.1016/j.telpol.2016.12.012.

Shubert, G. A. (1957). 'The public interest' in administrative decision-making: Theorem, theosophy, or theory. *American Political Science Review*, *51*, 346–368. doi.org/10.2307/1952196.

Sorauf, F. J. (1957). The public interest reconsidered. *The Journal of Politics, 19*(4), 616–639. doi.org/10.2307/2126954.

Stilgoe, J., Owen, R. & Macnaghten, P. (2013). Developing a framework for responsible innovation. *Research Policy*, *42*(9), 1568–1580. doi.org/10.1016/j.respol.2013.05.008.

Street, J. (2011). *Mass media, politics, and democracy* (2nd ed.). Springer.

Thanh Le, T., Andreadakis, Z., Kumar, A., Gómez Román, R., Tollefsen, S., Saville, M. & Mayhew, S. (2020). The COVID-19 vaccine development landscape. *Nature Reviews Drug Discovery, 19*(5), 305–306. doi.org/10.1038/d41573-020-00073-5.

Thiagarajan, K. (2021). What do we know about India's Covaxin vaccine? *BMJ, 373*. doi.org/10.1136/bmj.n997.

Thomas, K. (2019). Key opinion leaders supercharged by the internet: paid doctor and patient influencers on social media. *BMJ, 365*. doi.org/10.1136/bmj.l2336.

Ulnicane, I. (2016). 'Grand challenges' concept: A return of the 'big ideas' in science, technology and innovation policy? *International Journal of Foresight and Innovation Policy, 11*(1–3), 5–21. doi.org/10.1504/IJFIP.2016.078378.

Uyarra, E., Ribeiro, B. & Dale-Clough, L. (2019). Exploring the normative turn in regional innovation policy: Responsibility and the quest for public value. *European Planning Studies, 27*(12), 2359–2375. doi.org/10.1080/09654313.2019.1609425.

Vaandrager, D. & Marks, P. (2022). Disclosing public values: Citizens' perspectives based on group model building. *Public Performance & Management Review, 45*(2), 282–307. doi.org/10.1080/15309576.2022.2034655.

Vitiello, A. & Ferrara, F. (2021). Brief review of the mRNA vaccines COVID-19. *Inflammopharmacology, 29*(3), 645–649. doi.org/10.1007/s10787-021-00811-0.

Weimer, D. L. & Vining, A. R. (2017). *Policy Analysis: Concepts and Practice*. Taylor & Francis. doi.org/10.4324/9781315442129.

World Health Organization. (n.d.-a). *Timeline: WHO's COVID-19 response*. Retrieved 27 April 2020, www.who.int/emergencies/diseases/novel-coronavirus-2019/interactive-timeline.

World Health Organization. (n.d.-b). *WHO COVID-19 dashboard*. Retrieved 12 April 2023, data.who.int/dashboards/covid19/cases?n=c.

World Population Review. (2023). *Gini coefficient by country 2023*. worldpopulation review.com/country-rankings/gini-coefficient-by-country.

Zinatizadeh, M. R., Zarandi, P. K., Zinatizadeh, M., Yousefi, M. H., Amani, J. & Rezaei, N. (2022). Efficacy of mRNA, adenoviral vector, and perfusion protein COVID-19 vaccines. *Biomedicine & Pharmacotherapy, 146*, 112527. doi.org/10.1016/j.biopha.2021.112527.

4

JobKeeper: A critical analysis

Rohan Pitchford and Rabee Tourky

Introduction

In 2020, Australia conducted a large-scale policy experiment, introducing a hastily designed wage subsidy scheme to address the economic shock caused by the unexpected appearance and spread of COVID-19. Below, we consider the effectiveness of JobKeeper as economic policy.

The first cases of COVID-19 in Australia were reported on 25 January 2020. The first COVID-19 death occurred on 1 March that year. State and territory governments responded with restrictions on 'non-essential business' such as pubs and clubs, gyms, cinemas, restaurants, schools and religious gatherings. In conjunction, essential businesses and activities were advised to adopt physical distancing measures and non-essential workers were advised to stay at home (Storen & Corrigan, 2020).

COVID-19 had an impact unlike 'standard' economic shocks. In restricting interactions between people, it placed constraints not only on people's ability to consume, but also limited businesses' ability to produce. The greater an industry's reliance on face-to-face interaction, the worse the impact of COVID-19 restrictions. Labour mobility was severely impacted: it was difficult for employees to move to other – perhaps less restricted – industries, and almost impossible to obtain jobs within industries that were heavily impacted, in part due to restrictions on such movement.

The situation had policymakers very worried, not just because both supply and demand sides of a wide range of economic activities were restricted, but also because the duration of the constraints was uncertain. How long such restrictions would be in place would depend on the severity profile of the virus and its mutations, as well as how long it would take to develop effective vaccines and treatments. Added to this was the fact that similar restrictions in the rest of the world would impact demand for Australian products as well as supply to Australians of internationally produced items, both consumption goods and inputs to production. This uncertainty was reflected in a statement issued by the Australian government on 12 March 2020:

> There remains considerable uncertainty around the potential economic implications of the Coronavirus for the June quarter and beyond. The economic shock is likely to be significant. There are a wide range of potential paths for the spread and containment of the virus globally and in Australia. In addition, there is uncertainty around the impact on confidence, people's ability to work and business cash flow. The global spread of the virus and its global economic impact will also flow through to demand for Australia's exports and the availability of inputs into domestic production and imported consumption goods.

JobKeeper introduced

At the end of March 2020, the Australian government introduced a wage subsidy scheme, JobKeeper, as a primary economic instrument for addressing the unusual economic shock that COVID-19 entailed. Originally given a very large budget of A$130 billion, the scheme was premised on the idea of 'preserving the match' between employers and their workers:

> 'We will give millions of eligible businesses and their workers a lifeline to not only get through this crisis, but bounce back together on the other side', the Prime Minister said.

> 'This is about keeping the connection between the employer and the employee and keeping people in their jobs even though the business they work for may go into hibernation and close down for six months.'

> 'When the economy comes back, these businesses will be able to start again and their workforce will be ready to go because they will remain attached to the business through our JobKeeper payment.'

> (Morrison & Frydenberg, 2020)

JobKeeper paid a wage subsidy, not directly to the employee, but to the business in the first instance, thereby leaving open negotiation about subsequent conditions for eligible employees. The amount was A$750 per week per eligible retained employee regardless of hours worked. Qualifying businesses were deemed eligible based on turnover and their *self-reported* estimate that anticipated GST turnover would experience a sufficiently large drop.[1] All eligible employees of a business had to be part of the scheme if any single employee was approved – a 'one-in, all-in' principle. The scheme was administered by the Australian Tax Office. Employees had to be on the payroll as of 1 March, in the job continually while the subsidy was paid and have had 12 months of employment with that employer. The subsidy was initially for six months (to the end of September 2020) but was extended a further six months at reduced rates with new requirements on hours worked.

The coverage of JobKeeper was wide. From nearly 30 per cent of Australian workers in the first six months of its operation, it dropped to around 13 per cent after its extension and modification. Outlays were initially A$70.9 billion, falling to A$18.4 billion in the second phase (Borland & Hunt, 2023). This represented the highest outlay of any of the government's pandemic policies, the total of which was one of the largest emergency fiscal expenditures in Australian history (Treasury, 2020b).

Treasury evaluates its policy

In its three-month review of JobKeeper, Treasury (2020b, p. 7) made the claim that the policy had met its primary objectives: 'JobKeeper had three objectives: supporting business and job survival, preserving the employment relationship, and providing needed income support. It has met these objectives.' The evidence cited for this was take-up by 920,000 businesses and payments of some A$20.3 billion. Treasury asserted that the payments were well targeted, because:

---

1   A fact sheet put out by the Australian government advised that:
     Employers (including not-for-profits) will be eligible for the subsidy if:
     •   their business has an aggregated turnover of less than $1 billion (for income tax purposes)
         and estimate their GST turnover has fallen or will likely fall by 30 per cent or more; or
     •   their business has an aggregated turnover of $1 billion or more (for income tax purposes)
         and estimate their GST turnover has fallen or will likely fall by 50 per cent or more.
                                                                              (Treasury, 2020a)

the payment went to businesses that experienced an average decline in turnover in April of 37 per cent against the same month a year previous (compared with a 4% decline for other businesses).

(Treasury, 2020b, p. 7)

Further, it asserted that there was no evidence of large-scale closure of businesses and that this was due to JobKeeper as well as other policies such as bank forbearance. The three-month review also flagged concerns about adverse effects on labour market incentives, including labour mobility and possibly keeping some unviable businesses open.

In its 2021 review, Treasury proclaimed that JobKeeper, along with other significant fiscal and monetary policies, had had both an immediate and lasting positive effect on the economy. GDP outcomes exceeded earlier forecasts. The (measured) unemployment rate was much lower than expected. Treasury estimated that unemployment without JobKeeper would have peaked at 15 per cent, but instead hit only 5 per cent (Treasury, 2021). Household balance sheets were strong, and recipient businesses experienced muted falls in job losses and increased worker hours for subsidised employees. The claim was that this was all due to the stimulus effect as well as a boost from reduced uncertainty. Before the policy, businesses subsequently receiving JobKeeper experienced a decline of 20 per cent in jobs. Afterwards, the decline was limited to around 10 per cent (Treasury, 2021).

Critique

Wage subsidies are not a new idea. Kaldor (1936) was an early proponent, arguing that such policies are better suited to addressing general reductions in unemployment than other means (such as public projects or monetary policy). More modern approaches to subsidies, such as those analysed by Katz (1996), saw these policies as a way to increase low-wage workers' total earnings and to encourage the hiring and training of the disadvantaged. Recently, and during the COVID-19 crisis, wage subsidies and other more sophisticated variants – such as the German Kurzabeit short-term work schemes that subsidise 'hours not worked' – have been shown to improve the ability of firms to retain jobs as an economy emerges from recession (see OECD, 2020). JobKeeper, in contrast to the German scheme, was crude. As will be argued below, this led to a wide array of adverse outcomes.

After the initial proclamations of success, concerns began to emerge about firms gaming the policy's eligibility requirements. A significant fraction of JobKeeper outlays went to businesses that did not meet the turnover criterion. Indeed some businesses receiving JobKeeper even experienced a rise in turnover. According to Treasury:

> Analysis of turnover data indicates that $11.4 billion and $15.6 billion in the June and September quarters 2020 was paid to businesses whose turnover did not decline by 30 per cent (or 50 per cent) compared with a year earlier. JobKeeper payments to these businesses covered on average around 1.45 million individuals. Around $6.8 billion and $6.4 billion in the June and September quarters was paid to businesses whose turnover fell, but not by 30 per cent (or 50 per cent), and $4.6 billion and $9.2 billion, respectively, was paid to businesses with a turnover increase compared with a year earlier.
>
> (Treasury, 2021, p. 2)

There was no public register of businesses receiving the subsidies, making independent tracking of the recipients difficult. JobKeeper did not include a clawback mechanism – that is, a stipulation that funds be returned if businesses failed to experience a reduction in turnover matching their reported reduction. Despite this outcome, Treasury argued that it was an appropriate policy at the time because something had to be done quickly and that a guarantee of support was meant to provide certainty to recipients of the subsidy even though this led to the risk of overpayment. A policy of clawback was not included, it was argued, because such a scheme might have muted the recovery (Treasury, 2021, p. 1). Treasury explained that eligibility was based on expected turnover, which according to the legislation, was self-assessed. As a consequence, it was argued, there could be no inference that any of the businesses receiving funds on this basis were, in fact, *not* eligible for the subsidy (Treasury, 2021, p. 3). One of the biggest critics of this feature of JobKeeper was Andrew Leigh (2021), who, although amenable to wage subsidies as an idea, publicly shamed businesses for accepting payments despite rising revenues (Wright, 2021). Towards the end of 2021, the Parliamentary Budget Office reported that at least A$38 billion in JobKeeper subsidies went to companies that would have been ineligible if the subsidies were based on actual declines in turnover (Conifer, 2021).

To date, there has not been a comprehensive statistical analysis of the impact on employment and the cost-effectiveness of JobKeeper. Authors of some preliminary studies (i.e. not published in peer-reviewed journals) have argued that it was successful on both these metrics. Bishop and Day (2020) claim that JobKeeper saved 700,000 jobs over the period from April to July 2020. Watson et al. (2022) put the figure at 812,000 over the 12-month period of the policy. The first study extrapolated to the entire economy from a very small sample (i.e. as a fraction of the 3.5 million recipients) of less than 500 people, in both the treatment and control groups it used for its estimates. Further, the external validity[2] of their results depends on whether the data for the control group (ineligible casual employees) yield estimates that can be extended to the differently constituted treatment group (those eligible for JobKeeper) – a debatable contention (see Borland & Hunt, 2023). The robustness of the results to alternative statistical strategies relied on a sample of only 53 individuals in the treatment group (Bishop & Day, 2020), throwing further doubt on the results. Watson et al.'s (2022) study suffered from an analogous external validity critique, in this case because of its assumption that firms with verified declines in revenue were the same as firms without such declines, where both received the subsidy. However, perhaps the biggest problem with these studies is that both counted recipients as employed even if they worked for zero hours.[3] Thus, an employee who stayed at home while receiving JobKeeper was weighted equally as a full-time employee in their analysis. The evidence of the effectiveness in saving jobs is weak and certainly worthy of further study should better data become available.

Another metric for the effectiveness of policy aimed at retaining employment is the annualised cost per job saved. The studies cited above estimate the annual cost per job saved by JobKeeper to be around A$100,000. After the removal of those nominally employed but working zero hours, this cost would be significantly higher. The level of outlays per job saved is consistent with findings in US studies of similar schemes implemented there. Using much higher quality data than any available in Australia, Chetty et al. (2020) estimate the cost of the US 'Paycheck Protection Program' per job saved was an astounding US$377, 000.

---

2   The external validity criterion is met if the population subject to the policy (the treatment) depends on the same underlying factors as the population that was not subject to the policy (the control), in ways that cannot be corrected (e.g. through methods such as comparing differences before and after the policy). Selection bias is a leading problem for external validity.

3   See Borland and Hunt (2023), who are sceptical of both the external validity of these studies and the inclusion of zero-hour employment.

If match preservation was a target of JobKeeper, then a fair reading of outcomes is that the arrow landed at best halfway short of its mark. Borland and Hunt (2023) estimate that 50 per cent of JobKeeper's impact was due to zero-hour employment. Further, those on zero hours did not, in fact, quickly retain positive hours once the economy started to improve, as the 'preserving the match' logic argued that they would. Increases in employment were dominated by inflows, not by retention. Borland and Hunt (2023, p. 18) conclude that 'workers who maintained a connection with their employer through JobKeeper did not return to positive hours faster than individuals who left the labour market entirely'.

The popularity of modern wage subsidy schemes belies the lack of rigorous empirical or even theoretical support for match preservation when workers are on very low or zero hours. As shown in the data, JobKeeper did not work as advertised to preserve job matches. Indeed, there is reason to believe it might have impeded labour market adjustment in Australia at least in the latter part of its implementation (see Andrews et al., 2021; Borland & Hunt, 2023). Empirical evidence against its effectiveness at preserving job matches is significant. Why did JobKeeper dominate unemployment benefits for workers on zero hours for extended periods? Government could pay a generous benefit, though less than the full A$750 per week, and then reward a firm some amount, say A$1,000, if it kept in regular contact or chose to re-employ one of its old workers for a minimum period, resulting in significant savings. The idea of retention seems fundamentally different for a worker on zero hours to one who can only be gainfully employed for 50 per cent of the time. Some form of job insurance for people who work half the time keeps 'on the job' skills honed; however, for the zero hours employee, there are few such benefits.

A key feature of JobKeeper was that it locked employees into the firm they found themselves working for when the pandemic hit. If employees quit the likelihood of them obtaining a job in a similar industry was zero, because such workers would lose access to the subsidy. A crucial bargaining tool that employees otherwise have – the threat to leave – was, thus, removed. The subsidy was paid directly to the firm, and along with suspension of some provisions of the *Fair Work Act 2009* (Fair Work Commission, 2021), this meant a substantial reduction in bargaining power was dealt to employees. Employees could be directed to take annual leave. The quality of their work environment, their work classification and pay, or the tasks they undertook, could change. This reduction in bargaining power increased the share of the subsidy that firms extracted from their JobKeeper-subsidised workers. Although A\$750 per week went to these people, it was, for some, at the cost of the removal of holiday leave and other working conditions (Baker, 2020).

The reason why economists focus on helping unemployed workers during a recession is that private insurance markets for lost earnings provide insufficient coverage. Unemployed workers would suffer great hardship otherwise. The case for providing some analogous kind of direct 'unemployment insurance' for firms, such as was effectively done by JobKeeper through direct subsidies, is weak. A principal risk to businesses is having to pay recurring costs, such as interest on loans and rent while revenue is low during episodes like the COVID-19 lockdowns. Government policy rightly included moratoria on such fixed payments. Wealthy owners of businesses can ride out the shock; less wealthy small business owners or owner-managers can themselves access unemployment benefits. The important point is that it is human beings who need to be helped in such crises, whether they are workers or management, not firm owners who are either diversified shareholders or wealthy investors. The design of JobKeeper contradicted this basic economic conception.

JobKeeper was overly generous to wealthy owners of firms, both through firms' ability to extract the subsidy from their workers and by allowing ineligible firms to keep subsidy payments totalling billions. Basic macroeconomics tells us that stimulus payments are best made to those with high 'marginal propensities to consume', that is, to those who spend a high fraction of each dollar they receive. At least A\$38 billion in JobKeeper went to firms that were not subsequently eligible, whose owners consume far less per dollar than the typical worker. As a tool of aggregate demand stimulus, JobKeeper was very poorly designed.

In summary, JobKeeper had myriad adverse outcomes. First, many firms appear to have taken advantage of the fact that eligibility was based only on self-reported estimates of revenue reductions. This is hardly surprising: with no clawback facility, why would a business *not* accept a large subsidy that comes with little obligation? Wasteful spending is economically costly because taxpayer funds are scarce and could have been used for more worthy policies. As a tool of economic stimulus, it gave too much to people who would have undertaken little consumption expenditure. Second, many employees obtained relatively high JobKeeper payments despite working for zero hours, and despite the fact that they were *not* ultimately re-employed (i.e. their match was not preserved). These lucky workers obtained funds that could have otherwise been used to increase unemployment benefits for a broader range of people. JobKeeper was expensive due to both of these forms of mis-targeting. Many of these problematic features were apparent in advance, not just in hindsight.

Even in terms of the goals Treasury set for itself, JobKeeper did not meet its most important objectives. Treasury's first objective was 'supporting business and job survival'. Putting aside business support for the moment, the data tell a story of a high unemployment rate disguised by a semantic definition of employment, namely being counted as employed if connected to an employer by the job subsidy despite working zero hours (Australian Bureau of Statistics, 2020). The real unemployment rate, accounting for zero hours employment, would have been a lot higher than the peak of 7 per cent suggested by Treasury (2021). The second objective – preserving the employment relationship – is also unsupported by the data, as Borland and Hunt (2023) demonstrated. The final objective – 'providing needed income support' – was met for employees, though the cost of this support was extremely high, at least A$100,000 per job, an amount, we conjecture, that was likely well above the average annual wage of recipients.

The goal of 'supporting business survival' is reasonably interpreted as giving funds to businesses that would otherwise have been viable if not for COVID-19. It is difficult to obtain statistics to evaluate this counterfactual situation, although this is an important issue that should be studied. We can point out that some A$27 billion in expenditure initially went to firms that did not even experience a reduction in turnover and so were literally at no risk of disappearing.

US experience

Wage subsidies – and related schemes of payments to businesses that were conditional on employee retention – were used all around the world as pandemic policy, although they differed markedly in their design (OECD, 2020). An extensive review is beyond the scope of this piece; however, it is worth discussing the US experience because of the uniquely high-quality data used to assess the scheme.

Chetty et al. (2020) constructed a database that tracked consumer spending, jobs, employment, business revenue and so on at a very fine level, which they used to analyse the impact of direct stimulus payments on American consumers. They also evaluated aspects of the US's Paycheck Protection Program (PPP). They found that low- and high-income workers differed markedly in their spending of stimulus cheques. Initially (April 2020), both groups spent substantially after receiving the funds; however, some nine months later (January 2021), wealthy households saved virtually all their payments whereas low-income households spent a large fraction.

The PPP made loans to eligible businesses (fewer than 500 employees) that were forgivable if the business maintained employment (payroll) costs. Up to 40 per cent of the loan could also be used for non-payroll items. Along with other researchers, Chetty et al. (2020) found that the scheme had a very small impact on employment of some 2 percentage points. The cost per job saved was extremely high, estimated to be US$377,000, or US$359,000 if unemployment benefits were netted out. They concluded:

> PPP had modest marginal impacts on employment in the short run, likely because the vast majority of PPP loans went to inframarginal firms that were not planning to lay off many workers.
>
> (Chetty et al., 2020, p. 33)

The US experience supports two contentions. One is that such schemes tend to pay funds to wealthy recipients who are less likely to spend them and, hence, less likely to provide stimulus to the economy. The second is that employment subsidy schemes can be very expensive and have limited impact on employment. The former contention is backed up by Australian research; the latter is still an open question.

Alternatives

The real test of a policy is how it performs relative to a set of available 'counterfactual' options – that is, alternative policies that might have been undertaken. Many of the problems of JobKeeper appear to have stemmed from the fact that it locked the support of workers and the support of firm owners together. Economic policy usually argues in favour of the decoupling of economic instruments because they can be adjusted to suit their targeted outcomes more effectively. A key example is to decouple the provision of income insurance to workers from provisions to help keep firms viable. The traditional remedy for job loss is unemployment benefits or some other form of income insurance. All laid-off workers could have received unemployment benefits directly at a much lower cost than A$100,000 per job saved. If match preservation really was a thing for zero-hour workers, then those let go by eligible firms could have carried with them a reward that accrued to any eligible firms that re-employed them.

Decoupling means that firms should only get relief for fixed payments because these are the only impediments to a firm's survival – all other things being equal. (If the economic environment changes post-COVID, firms should adapt to these changes on their own.) Those who would otherwise receive fixed payments from firms, such as landlords, can be supported by government – for example, through moratoria on loan repayments. Banks, in turn, can be supported by government by underwriting any losses through the mechanism of the monetary system. In this scenario, building owners who would otherwise receive rents above interest payments on their loans would need to 'take a haircut', as they would with any other economic downturn.

Conclusion

The use of wage subsidies as a catch-all device for employment and business insurance, as well as a tool of stimulus, is far from a settled remedy for a sudden economic downturn, such as experienced with COVID-19. Treasury's JobKeeper experiment achieved a few of its goals – notably transferring funds to workers – but did so at an extremely high cost. Some of this experimental policy's aims were, themselves, questionable: paying funds directly to businesses appeared to benefit wealthy owners of firms rather than provide properly targeted insurance. Other aspects of the policy, such as basing firm eligibility on self-reporting without clawback, were obviously due to bad design. We conjecture that well-understood policy alternatives such as direct unemployment insurance, moratoria for fixed business costs and central bank support of lending institutions would have been better.

Our arguments are far from definitive – there is plenty of room for debate about the role of well-designed wage subsidies versus more traditional remedies. However, we would argue that with every experience, the goal should be to improve policy. The only way to do this is through extensive scrutiny. We argue that if Treasury proposes a policy, then it should be required to articulate the following: 1) the goals of the policy, 2) discussion of why the goals are desirable and 3) the measurable outcomes through which the policy should be regarded as effective. The first and second of these will help discipline thinking regarding policy objectives. The third should be regarded as a grading criterion for Treasury performance. Measuring outcomes will likely require the collection of relevant data. Public scrutiny also requires that such data be made available to all. In this, it appears, Treasury is in full agreement. According to Treasury:

> Beyond this review, it is imperative that a program of this magnitude and novelty should be studied and evaluated very closely. The Treasury, the Australian Taxation Office and the Australian Bureau of Statistics will work with the academic community and others to make de-identified program administration data available for research purposes. An independent evaluation should be conducted at the completion of the program.
>
> (Treasury, 2020b, p. 8)

The Australian government should keep Treasury to its word.

References

Andrews, D., Hambur, J. & Bahar, E. (2021). The COVID-19 shock and productivity-enhancing reallocation in Australia: Real-time evidence from Single Touch Payroll. *OECD Economics Department Working Papers, 1677*. www.oecd-ilibrary.org/docserver/2f6e7cb1-en.pdf?expires=1698037539&id=id&accname=guest&checksum=52B4811CB8C0B4E1E586E8A9896FDE62.

Australian Bureau of Statistics. (2020, 15 June). *Classifying people in the Labour Force Survey during the COVID-19 period.* www.abs.gov.au/articles/classifying-people-labour-force-survey-during-covid-19-period.

Australian Government. (2020, 12 March). *Economic response to the coronavirus* [Media release]. parlinfo.aph.gov.au/parlInfo/download/media/pressrel/7234791/upload_binary/7234791.PDF;fileType=application%2Fpdf.

Baker, E. (2020, 21 May). Worker claims unfair dismissal after questioning cleaning requirement for JobKeeper. *ABC News.* www.abc.net.au/news/2020-05-21/customs-house-worked-sacked-over-jobkeeper-cleaning-extra-hours/12273712.

Bishop, J. & Day, I. (2020). How many jobs did JobKeeper keep? *Reserve Bank of Australia, Research Discussion Paper RDP 2020–07.* doi.org/10.47688/rdp2020-07.

Borland, J. & Hunt, J. (2023, March). JobKeeper: An initial assessment. *Australian Economic Review, 56*(1), 109–123. doi.org/10.1111/1467-8462.12503.

Campbell, K. & Vines, E. (2021, 23 June). COVID-19: A chronology of Australian government announcements (up until 30 June 2020). *Parliamentary Library, Research Paper Series, 2020–21*.

Chetty, R., Friedman, J. N. & Stepner, M. (2020, June [revised April 2023]). The economic impacts of COVID-19: Evidence from a new public database built using private sector data. *NBER Working Paper, 27431*. doi.org/10.3386/w27431.

Conifer, D. (2021, 2 November). At least $38b in JobKeeper went to companies where turnover did not fall below thresholds, data finds. *ABC News*. www.abc. net.au/news/2021-11-02/38b-in-jobkeeper-went-to-companies-where-turnover-did-not-fall-/100586310.

Fair Work Commission. (2021, 29 March). *JobKeeper disputes benchbook. Overview of the coronavirus economic response provisions in the Fair Work Act*. www.fwc.gov.au/overview-coronavirus-economic-response-provisions-fair-work-act.

Kaldor, N. (1936, December). Wage subsidies as a remedy for unemployment. *Journal of Political Economy, 44*(6), 721–742. doi.org/10.1086/254994.

Katz, L. F. (1996, July). Wage subsidies for the disadvantaged. *NBER Working Paper, 5679*. doi.org/10.3386/w5679.

Leigh, A. (2021, 13 October) *JobKeeper overpayments hit $20 billion* [Media release]. www.andrewleigh.com/jobkeeper_overpayments.

Morrison, S. & Frydenberg, J. (2020, 30 March). *$130 billion JobKeeper payment to keep Australians in a job* [Media release]. ministers.treasury.gov.au/ministers/josh-frydenberg-2018/media-releases/130-billion-jobkeeper-payment-keep-australians-job.

OECD. (2020, 12 October). *Job retention schemes during the COVID-19 lockdown and beyond*. www.oecd.org/en/publications/2020/10/job-retention-schemes-during-the-covid-19-lockdown-and-beyond_5002bb9f.html.

Storen, R. & Corrigan, N. (2020, 22 October). COVID-19: A chronology of state and territory government announcements (up until 30 June 2020). *Parliamentary Library, Research Paper Series, 2020–21*.

Treasury. (2020a, 11 April). *JobKeeper payment – Frequently asked questions*. treasury. gov.au/sites/default/files/2020-04/JobKeeper_frequently_asked_questions_2.pdf.

Treasury. (2020b, 29 June). *The JobKeeper payment: Three-month review* [Executive summary]. treasury.gov.au/sites/default/files/2020-07/jobkeeper-review-executive-summary.pdf.

Treasury. (2021, 11 October). *Insights from the first six months of JobKeeper*. treasury. gov.au/publication/p2021-211978.

Watson, T., Tervala, J. & Sainsbury, T. (2022, 9 May). The JobKeeper payment: How good are wage subsidies? *CAMA Macroeconomic Analysis Working Paper no. 36/2022*. doi.org/10.2139/ssrn.4103865.

Wright, S. (2021, 28 August). Australians want JobKeeper overpayments given back to taxpayers. *Sydney Morning Herald*. www.smh.com.au/politics/federal/ australians-want-jobkeeper-overpayments-given-back-to-taxpayers-20210827-p58mff.html.

5

Bioethics after COVID-19: Should we embrace a political turn?

Nathan Emmerich

This chapter examines the field of bioethics and offers a commentary on some recent developments, particularly those that have been given further impetus by the COVID-19 pandemic. The discussion concerns the tensions generated when a normative or evaluative discipline is involved in political and policymaking processes, specifically with the provision of advice, guidance and *expertise*. Questions are raised about the way in which the field can or should engage with the world around it, particularly when questions about justice or, more pertinently, social justice are being brought to the fore. I argue that care should be taken to distinguish between what is an appropriate undertaking for an academic and what others might pursue on the basis of insights generated within the field.

***

After completing an undergraduate degree in philosophy and the history and philosophy of science, and a master's degree in healthcare ethics, and before undertaking a PhD, I studied for a master of research in social science research methods. One of the questions we were presented with towards the beginning of the course concerned the sociopolitical role of the social sciences: are they tools for bringing about modernist utopian visions and were we, those undertaking the course, therefore setting out to pursue such ends? Can the social sciences be applied in such a way as to permit social engineering and, if so, could we become social engineers?

As someone who had recently been convinced by Bauman's (1991) analysis of modernity, I was – and am – sceptical of such ideas and, in particular, the underlying utopian impulse they and the idea of social engineering represent. At least in part, this scepticism stems from the fact that bringing about and maintaining – or *continuing to bring about* – a utopia will inevitably require some degree of political *imposition*. No entirely modernist, or totalising, vision can be grassroots, bottom up or *democratic*, at least not in any fulsome sense. The point is not merely that the end does not justify the means or even that the end is incompatible with the seemingly required means. Nor is it that there is no democratic pathway that can lead us to utopia, or even that a utopia brought about by undemocratic means seems unworthy of the name. Rather, it is that the only way to maintain a utopia is to bring it about continuously, something that would seem to require non-utopian – and quite possibly dystopian – means. The term utopia was coined with double meaning for good reason. There is no place in which the perfect society can flourish; contradiction is central to the concept. Societies are as imperfect as the individuals whose existence and practices bring them about.

***

At the time I formed these views, and more so now, I was and am a bioethicist – or, at least, bioethics is the field I primarily work within. I suspect that there is a central irony to my intellectual endeavours. The core of the field I work in is constituted by applied philosophical ethics, and while other disciplinary approaches make their own contribution, bioethics is – and arguably must continue to be – a fundamentally modernist enterprise. Although the point is generally allowed to remain implicit, the mainstream of the field seems to be organised around the idea of a systematised, generalised and universal account of normative ethics in which bioethics can and *should* be set out. These kinds of suppositions have, of course, been subject to criticism, including from feminist perspectives, for example. Nevertheless, this does not challenge the point I am trying to make. I am not suggesting that all bioethicists advance or even accept this picture, simply that it forms the core of the discipline's imaginary. Indeed, it certainly seems to do so for those who actively seek to work against bioethics as they see it, a point that is arguably well illustrated by Franklin's (2019) anti-bioethical stance on research ethics. Consequentially, and much like applied ethics and analytic philosophy more generally, the field's central 'mode of thought' can feel like it has more in common with scientific discourse than with those found in the arts, the humanities and even the social – or, perhaps, *human* – sciences.

One should, of course, acknowledge that bioethics has undergone an empirical turn since (at least) the millennium (Borry et al., 2005; Hurst, 2010). However, it is arguably the case that, even if bioethics has taken up certain social scientific tools or methods, the empirical turn remains theoretically and methodologically untethered. On the one hand, one might point out that bioethics has not embraced the kind of critical and interpretive standpoint one finds in the human sciences. On the other, one might also note that those working in disciplines such as sociology, anthropology and (to a degree) history – and who therefore embrace this kind of standpoint – are generally reluctant to consider their work as contributing to the field of bioethics or to frame themselves as bioethicists. This point is particularly pertinent with regard to Franklin's article in *Nature*; the validity of the perspective she advances assumes that her own work – and that contributed by authors working from a similar standpoint on a great variety of topics relating to medicine and the life science – is not taken to be 'bioethics'. The obvious response is to suggest that we should consider this kind of work to be part of the field of bioethics and, as a result, do more to engage with such perspectives, particularly at the level of theoretical debate.

Putting such matters to one side, the presupposition of applied philosophical ethics that exists at the core of bioethics, which suggests that a full – or, at least, reasonably comprehensive – account of what one should and should not do is not only something that can be produced but also should be implemented, is a rather utopian idea. However, it seems misguided to suppose that the conclusions drawn by bioethicists or from within the (academic) field of bioethics can, without significant further effort, determine what ought to be done or how something ought to be done. Of course, a not dissimilar problem attends scientific advice. Factual testimony alone cannot tell us what we ought to do. Our values and the ends we – or our elected representatives – adopt determine, structure or shape what course of action we will pursue. Scientific advice provides input into the decision-making process, which can then be placed in service to such values or ends. The obvious question is, of course, what broader role should bioethics play in the sociopolitical life of a national, international or global polity? Is bioethics a technocratic endeavour, one that can be used to socially engineer the moral or normative aspects of medicine, healthcare and the life sciences, or should the field be pursuing a role that is more dialogical or critical or one that is facilitative and democratic?

The idea that bioethics raises these kinds of questions is not new. However, placed alongside topics such as climate change and racism, the pandemic has given them new significance and impetus. Existing responses raise the possibility of there being a political turn within the field. The following two sections examine the nature and scope of any such turn. The first concerns the role of bioethics and bioethicists within the sociopolitical infrastructure that not only sought to manage national pandemic responses but also, by extension, their role in the management and delivery of (public) health (care) more generally. The second considers ongoing developments within the field of bioethics that, since the millennium, have seen interest in justice being renewed. In the context of the pandemic and other events of global significance – notably climate change and Black Lives Matter – this is being transmuted into a concern for social justice. When it comes to a possible political turn, such thinking represents an interesting and perhaps irresolvable problem for bioethics as an academic endeavour.

***

Given the contributions made by scholars working in science and technology studies (STS) and the social studies of science (SSS), it is clear that the *ideal* of value-neutral or objective scientific advice cannot be guaranteed. Nevertheless, as long as we wish to be governed in a manner that is factually, which is to say scientifically, informed, such advice – and, for that matter, the *scientific enterprise* as a whole – must be defended (Lusk, 2021). As this allusion to Foucault's text *Society Must be Defended* implies, any defence of science and its value cannot simply adopt the scientific point of view or take the tales it tells of itself uncritically. As responses to the crisis of expertise amply demonstrate, critical engagement with science as a sociopolitical institution is indispensable if its value is to be safeguarded. While the same might be said of bioethics, it is also clear that what it is to do bioethics entails setting forth the case for particular values, perspectives and ends. Further, if they are to accord with disciplinary norms, the justifications offered for specific values and particular ends should be objective and, somewhat ironically, articulated from a value-neutral standpoint or perspective. Of course, no standpoint is truly value neutral, not least because objectivity is itself a value. Nevertheless, there is good reason to suppose that knowledge generated by those who more or less successfully adopt the epistemic values embedded within the scientific (or scholastic) standpoint has greater credence and should play a privileged role in our collective sociopolitical life. Thus, when it comes to regulating the life sciences and biomedicine, bioethics would seem to increase the degree to which technocracy – or, more accurately, epistocracy – might be thought of as a realistic possibility. Indeed, studies of the European project suggest that this is not merely a possibility but also something of a reality (Littoz-Monnet, 2020). However, such work tends to be focused on relatively technical issues and concerns and, given it might be compared to the kind of effort civil services have engaged in since the inception of the modern state, it is perhaps not overly concerning. Nevertheless, in the context of COVID-19, some bioethicists seemed to become more vocal about their role in directing policy and public health responses.

An example of this can be found in a *BMJ* editorial published by a number of UK bioethicists in late May 2020. Writing at a time when it was becoming increasingly self-evident that the UK government was mishandling the pandemic while repeatedly claiming to be 'following the science', the authors set out the 'need to follow the ethics [and] not just the science' (Fritz et al., 2020). To this end they called for 'an ethical plan' that, at minimum, should consist of national ethical guidance that can provide assistance in 'all healthcare and policy settings'; the development of formalised ethics support structure that can 'support the interpretation and application of national guidance' as an embedded part of the health and social care system; and research that can 'inform and support the development of ethical policy and guidance, and the interpretation of both' (Fritz et al., 2020, para. 7, 9).

Even in the context of the UK government's misguided response to the first few months of the pandemic, such calls might be seen as suggesting that what is already being done should be done better. Certainly, effort has been expended in planning for pandemics at both national and international levels and ethics support structures are already a feature of health and social care, not least in the form of clinical and research ethics committees. Further, research informs and supports policy and guidance, and has been drawn on in the aforementioned national and international plans, as well as in the creation, implementation and practices of ethics committees. However, this call (and others like it) would seem to go further. It did not simply respond to the mishandling of the pandemic by the UK government and present a substantive alternative or remedy. What was being put forth might be thought of as significant structural reform, this being a more formally established role for bioethics, bioethical knowledge and the expertise of bioethicists. Such a role would go beyond the use of scientific expertise and knowledge to frame or, perhaps, constrain political decision-making in a manner similar to the role played by scientific knowledge and expertise. Bioethicists would no longer merely be providing advice: some would arguably be placed in key positions where they would be directly involved in determining and implementing policy. However, as more recent analysis has shown (Jamrozik, 2022), the value and impact of various public health responses to the pandemic were uncertain, indicating that it would have been inappropriate for epistocrats to shoulder this kind of burden; responsibility for such decisions must remain with elected representatives, with those who are charged with taking an holistic or overarching – rather than a narrow or singular – perspective (Jamrozik & Heriot, 2020).

While the idea of bioethicists becoming responsible for what are, or should be, political decisions seems to be a step too far, the parameters of bioethicists providing advice to decision-makers also seem uncertain. As noted, bioethical advice is unlike scientific advice. Even if fields such as STS and SSS have shown the distinctions to be blurred in practice, scientific facts and political values can at least be conceptually distinguished (Collins & Evans, 2017). Such a principled distinction is not possible when it comes to the values that are embedded in bioethical (and political) discourses. Bioethics is an *evaluative* discourse. Therefore, and in contradistinction to scientific experts, bioethicists cannot claim to provide a fixed resource (a body of factual knowledge) that can inform both political debate and public policy. While bioethicists might legitimately cast themselves in the role of moderator, facilitator or even setter of argumentative standards, it is inevitable that they will also be seen as participants in such debates in a way that is not necessarily true of scientific advisers.

Of course, scientific advisers can and do step outside their role as advisers, and it is not uncommon for them to participate in broader *public* debates. Nevertheless, those advising the government may be well advised to exhibit greater caution than academics who do not (directly) do so. Aspects of the career of Professor David Nutt might be instructive in this regard. A scientist at the University of Bristol, Nutt was a long-term adviser to the UK government and, ultimately, became chair of the Advisory Council on the Misuse of Drugs. While in this role he became directly entangled in the politics of drug policy. In the first instance, this related to an academic article in which he compared the dangers associated with the drug ecstasy to those of horse riding (Nutt, 2009). Later that year, Nutt gave a public lecture to the Centre for Crime and Justice Studies at King's College London in which he set forth a policy framework that substantively differed from the established approach and the view of the government. The appearance of this lecture as a pamphlet reignited media discussion of Nutt and his role as the chair of a governmental advisory body. While this resulted in his dismissal, it is arguably the case that, in both his article and his lecture, Nutt was fulfilling his role as an academic scientist and that neither was in direct conflict with his role as an adviser as he did not directly criticise the government's position. Nevertheless, it is also clear that politics does not always respect such delineations. The position of an academic and scientific adviser can be difficult to maintain, as their scholarly activities can sometimes be drawn into the broader political context of an adviser even when the individual concerned may not explicitly be seeking to do so.

That bioethics has a *political* role to play is unavoidable. As such, the field or its contributors cannot hope to definitively set the terms of the debate and should not hope to determine the outcome. The implication is that bioethics cannot hope to provide '*the* ethics' and that seeking to fulfil roles in which 'the ethics' are determined and implemented is likely to prove challenging. In short, even in a pandemic, 'the ethics' is not something bioethics should purport to offer, at least not in the sense of something that politicians should (or should claim to be) follow(ing), as was said of 'the science'.

***

Calls for bioethics and, perhaps more pertinently, *bioethicists* to better attend to matters of justice in health and healthcare certainly predate the pandemic, as do calls for a greater degree of political engagement. For example, for some time there have been calls for bioethics to address questions of public health (Brock, 2000; Dawson & Verweij, 2008), global health (Nussbaum, 2013; Ruger, 2010; Venkatapuram, 2013), as well as to engage with environmental concerns and climate change (Brown, 2013; Pierce & Jameton, 2004; Richie, 2019). There is also an ongoing debate about whether or not bioethicists should adopt an activist role (Draper et al., 2019; Kaebnick, 2021) and the pandemic has clearly given such concerns further impetus (King et al., 2022). The reasons for this debate are numerous. However, of particular importance is the way in which 'health' is increasingly seen to be 'the highest law, and the highest policy objective' (Middleton, 2023); as a virtually unassailable ethico-political imperative. In this context, the differential impact of the pandemic and the clarity with which its relationship to pre-existing inequalities and associated social determinants of health was established is of particular significance (Bambra et al., 2020; Fiske et al., 2022).

It is also noteworthy that the pandemic coincided with the murder of George Floyd in the US and the subsequent emergence of the Black Lives Matter protests and movement. Of course, as King et al. (2022, p. 137) point out:

> It shouldn't have taken a pandemic or the murder of George Floyd … to recognize how neglected justice has been in medicine, human research, and bioethics … but … it did.

Although a coincidence, an additional resonance between the progression of SARS-CoV-2 that had a disproportionate effect on the US African American population was provided by Floyd's final words: 'I can't breathe.' Within bioethics, the overlap between the pandemic and questions of race and racial discrimination in the US has led to – or significantly amplified – calls for the field to more fully address and engage with matters of social justice, particularly as it relates to health and healthcare, as well as for the development of a 'Black Bioethics' (Ray, 2021; Vo & Campelia, 2021). Equally, while such calls may not have directly motivated its publication, a recent article entitled 'Racial Justice Requires Ending the War on Drugs' (Earp et al., 2021) – something that is, of course, hardly a novel point of view in sociological and criminological circles – can be taken as indicating that bioethics seems to have already been moving in the kind of direction the field is advocating for itself following the pandemic.

The turn to justice has been given significant further impetus by concerns about climate change (or the climate *emergency*), racial politics (albeit primarily American racial politics) and, most significantly, the way the pandemic unfolded. In effect, the pandemic highlighted the way these phenomena intersect and, alongside other social categories such as educational attainment and socio-economic status, resonate and reinforce each other, particularly in their contribution to social inequalities of health. The result is that the turn to justice in bioethics has recently morphed into a concern for *social justice* (Powers & Faden, 2008). The difference is that, whereas the notion of justice tends to be focused on matters of procedural fairness, or how a society or its institutions should be structured, the notion of social justice leads to concerns about the way society and its institutions are in fact structured and the consequences of those structures. Crudely, where a concern for justice would seek to ensure (structural) racism is eliminated, a concern for social justice seeks to address the consequences of racism as a structurally embedded phenomenon. While these need not be seen as mutually exclusive endeavours, the latter undertaking might say something about the scale of the former.

In the context of bioethics, much of the motivation for attending to matters of social justice is the way in which health can be linked to such concerns. Indeed, to varying degrees, topics such as climate change, racism and the war on drugs are rendered within the scope of bioethics precisely because of this link. The point here is that bioethical concern for racism, social inequalities and (even) climate change, and the fact that such phenomena impact health, is not only instrumental but also licences a specifically bioethical interest in or analysis of them. Two points are worth making here. First, the degree to which health has become a – and perhaps the – singular moral and ethico-political imperative of the present time. Appealing to health and, in particular, the way in which whatever one wants to argue for (or against) will positively (or negatively) impact the health of some population or group is among the most powerful and effective claim one can make in the contemporary political landscape. Second, the moral valorisation of 'health' reflects an inherent anthropocentricism, a common critique of bioethics advanced within environmental ethics (Ferguson, 2020; Gardiner, 2022). The result is that bioethical arguments regarding racism, social inequalities and climate change are arguably not engaging with such matters as phenomena in their own right. Rather, they are treated instrumentally: the problem with them is that they negatively impact health, at least insofar as bioethical analysis is concerned. The potential, and untenable, implication is that discrimination and so forth is only a social issue if it impacts on (public or population) health.

On the face of it, the idea that health is a guiding moral imperative for both bioethics and more generally would not seem obviously problematic. However, not only is it the case that health should be seen as one value among many, but also that bioethics has often demonstrated that other ethical commitments, such as respect for autonomy, may take priority. Once again, the question seems to be about the sociopolitical role of bioethics and bioethicists. The turn to (social) justice is certainly consistent with recent discussions of the relationship between bioethics and activism (Draper et al., 2019; Meyers, 2021) as well as broader social changes, such as the tendency to focus on the notion of equity rather than equality, often without clear delineation between these terms. Nevertheless, it is also clear that not everyone is entirely comfortable with the idea of active political engagement being something that bioethicists might legitimately undertake

(Benatar, 2006; Cribb, 2010; van der Vossen, 2014). Some of those who have addressed themselves to this issue of activism in bioethics have, of course, sought to chart a third way, one that makes room for both contemplative and politically active approaches to bioethics. Perhaps the same is inevitably true of my own position. After all, I am not seeking to conclude that academics are above politics or that they should simply eschew it. Rather, the point I am seeking to make is that academics and, by extension, bioethicists (or, at least, those of us who are – or who are *primarily* – academics) occupy a specific (anti)political position that circumscribes the kind or mode of political engagement we pursue when speaking as academics.

Part of the problem with the idea of bioethics undergoing a turn towards politics or 'the political' is that it may become increasingly difficult to contain academic divisions within scholarly (or scholastic) norms, particularly when such activities are coupled with calls to give primacy to the pursuit of social justice and for the field to engage in a greater degree of activism. As such, there is a risk that disagreements between academics will become increasingly partisan, the inevitable result being the politicisation – or, perhaps, further politicisation – of an intellectual field that is already proximate to the so-called culture wars, particularly in the US. Of course, academia, academics and academic debates have always been susceptible to a degree of factionalisation. However, the point and purpose of academia is to remove the pursuit of truth from economic and sociopolitical necessity: from influences that can produce conflicts of interest and exert forms of epistemic influence that can often go unrecognised. Of course, this is not to say that splendid isolation is ultimately achievable (or even that achieving, rather than simply aiming for, splendid isolation should necessarily be seen as desirable). Nor is it to say that we should not be reflexive about our social position and how it might condition and inform our inquiries and perspectives. It is, however, to say that academic 'interest in disinterestedness' (Bourdieu, 1989, pp. 101, 110; 2004, p. 94) has a distinctive value and a too-ready embrace of (political) interestedness will have consequences for academic bioethics and the sociopolitical positioning that is fundamental to establishing and maintaining trust in scholars and the value of scholarship.

***

In a previous section I compared bioethics to science, particularly in relation to the role it plays in providing input into political and policymaking processes. However, it might be fruitful to examine an alternative comparison, one that might facilitate a fuller evaluation of bioethics in its broader context. Perhaps the most obvious parallel that might be made is with medicine and the healthcare professions more generally. Indeed, insofar as ethics consultation is a part of clinical practice and a full-time occupation (at least for some, and albeit predominantly in the US), one might think of logical, secular and friendly clinical ethics consultants (Bosk, 1999) as being involved in the practice of yet another allied health profession. As such, one might take the view that at least some part of bioethics is part of medicine or healthcare. Indeed, some critics of medicine have argued that 'bioethics has taken up residence in the belly of the medical whale' (Rosenberg, 1999, p. 38); others consider it an exercise in public relations undertaken on behalf of medicine and the life sciences (Mayes, 2022; cf. Turner, 2009). Of course, we expect the healthcare professions and, in particular, medicine to engage with relevant political and public policy debates. While we also expect such contributions to aim at the common or greater good, managing conflicts of interest and other sources of bias is not easy. Equally, the contributions medicine and the healthcare professions make to such debates come from a particular standpoint that, while valuable, is never the only relevant perspective. As such we might expect bioethics to offer critical insight into healthcare, developing knowledge in the life sciences and emerging biotechnologies. Nevertheless, bioethics is not institutionalised as a profession. Indeed, the field does not have a clearly defined sociopolitical role and, in any event, lacks the degree of internal agreement that would be required for it to speak as a singular body. Questions therefore remain about the nature of any contribution that bioethics or bioethicists might be asked to provide.

In the first instance, however, we might contrast the way in which the medical and healthcare professions involve themselves in different kinds of questions. Certainly, they advocate for both better healthcare and better public health. It is not unusual to see interventions about service provision (and, inevitably, funding) as well as campaigns regarding the use of tobacco and, more recently, consumption of alcohol and sugar, as well as campaigns defining healthy diets and minimum levels of exercise more generally. However, a slightly different approach arguably obtains when the discussion turns towards matters of morality, ethics and conscience. Generally speaking, while a position might be adopted, the medical and healthcare professions tend to be more circumspect when it comes to matters like abortion and assisted dying. Certainly, they seek to represent the facts and they also seek to ensure the interests of their members are represented. Nevertheless, the positions they set forth are often less directive. In these cases, the primacy of democratic processes undertaken by elected representatives is recognised implicitly. Of course, some professionals can and do band together to put forward more substantive views, yet such groups commonly exist outside of established professional institutions while also focusing on a single issue. In this regard, they are no different to any other grassroots organisation that a group of citizens might choose to form.

There is, then, a tacit distinction between different sorts of policy proposals or reforms that healthcare professions might collectively pursue and those that individual or ad hoc groups of professionals might campaign for. Of course, in both cases, bioethics might provide a resource to advance, oppose, or (more likely) both advance *and* oppose the positions being put forward. However, it is far from clear that this kind of approach can be replicated within bioethics itself. The social institutionalised organisations of the healthcare professions can legitimately advocate in the interests of both patient and population health. Can the same be said of bioethics? First, bioethics does not seem to be institutionalised in such a way that it can legitimately set forth policies of any kind. Second, it is not clear that bioethics can be thought of as being able to pursue any sort of overriding value comparable to the way health (or the public's interest in health) operates for the healthcare professions as, in a sense, stewards of both public and individual health. Certainly, bioethics may have both positive and negative (or critical) contributions to make to various of the ethico-political pursuits the healthcare professions might engage in. But they – we – are underlabourers.

***

At the outset of this chapter, I indicated my sense of disquiet at the idea of social scientists and, indeed, bioethicists being positioned as utopian engineers. While I am not alone in my reticence, there are certainly others who seem better disposed to the idea. Equally, this chapter has presumptively considered a certain type of bioethics, and a particular kind of bioethicist, namely academic bioethics, and bioethicists who are academics. Yet, one might think that there are many other ways to do bioethics and, therefore, multiple ways to be a bioethicist. Consider, for example, those who work for Nuffield Bioethics in the UK or those employed as clinical ethicists in the US. Indeed, consider all those who are involved in the normative regulation of health, the life sciences and biotechnology, areas that will encompass a wide range of organisational contexts – public, professional, corporate and (non-)governmental. It seems clear that those who might be thought of as 'doing' bioethics in some way occupy an expansive array of structural positions and are located within a variety of social fields. Finally, consider the fact that all medical and healthcare professionals will find themselves engaging with the ethical dimension of their practice at various points in their careers. Such activities and undertakings can be considered a form of (non-academic) bioethics. While I might be reluctant to suppose that the *academic* pursuit of social scientific or bioethical research should have social engineering at its heart, this does not mean that collectively seeking to shape and reshape the societies we live in is misguided or that social scientific and bioethical research are not resources for those who endeavour to do so. Rather, it is to suggest that there should (continue to) be a division of labour and that the social structures that distance academics from other areas of society should in some way be productive.

Something of this can be seen in Bourdieu's analysis of the role of intellectuals in the modern world. In his view, academics have an 'interest in disinterestedness' and engage in an 'anti-political politics' (Bourdieu, 1989, pp. 101, 110; 2004, p. 94). It is this, and the broader 'social relations of intellectual life' that provides academic knowledge production with its 'universalizing power' and the ability of disciplines to produce 'transhistorical truths' (Bourdieu, 2004, p. 69; Emmerich, 2021; Medvetz, 2018, p. 456). If it is to retain its ability to produce the kind of knowledge it is associated with, the academy – and, by extension, its academics – must be able to maintain a degree of insulation from the kinds of necessities society imposes and, more importantly, from politics, or what Bourdieu calls the field of power. Bourdieu (1990) should not, however, be read as simply rejecting the scholastic point of view. Rather, he offers a warning against its (and *our*) tendency to mistake the things of logic for the logic of things and, consequentially, to not comprehend the logic of practice (Bourdieu, 1992).

At least on the face of it, the idea of academic bioethicists becoming activists is in contradiction with the social (or sociopolitical) foundations of intellectual labour, at least to some degree. The point is not that academics are apolitical, or that they or their work is value neutral; rather, it is that their position within the social structure entails a certain set of values and a circumscribed approach to political engagement. Given Bourdieu's association with the idea of sociology being *un sport de combat*, it might seem odd to use his thought to oppose academic activism. However, the phrase can be taken to mean either 'combat sport' or 'martial art' and it is interesting to reflect on the different implications. The former seems more aggressive, violent and oppositional whereas the latter seems more consistent with the idea of sociology as a discipline – and as a disciplined mode of thought. Martial arts commonly involve maintaining one's own equilibrium while using an opponent's excesses against them. The difference would seem to highlight a distinction between joining the fray as an activist and engaging as an academic who remains committed to disciplinary and intellectual ideas.

Of course, none of this is to say that bioethics should not pursue this, that or the other topic – although what constitutes the scope of the field remains an interesting question. Nor is it to say that continuing the turn to (social) justice would be a mistake. Rather, the issue remains one of the sociopolitical role(s) of academic bioethics and bioethicists, particularly in the post-COVID context. If the question is whether or not bioethics should undergo a political turn, and if what is meant by that is that academics who work in the field should pursue a greater level of activism, then my answer is that we should not. Our contributions should remain academic – if not in nature, then in tone. The example of Professor David Nutt shows that what this might mean is not necessarily clear. Indeed, what might legitimately be said as an academic may not be tenable to say as an academic who provides advice to government or other institutions. The conclusion is not without irony. If, as seems fundamental to its inception and continued practice, academic bioethics is to engage with and, ideally, change the world, it cannot employ overtly political means. The ethical pursuit of bioethics means restricting oneself to an ethical, rather than political, register, at least for those of us who wish to be and remain academics.

References

Bambra, C., Riordan, R., Ford, J. & Matthews, F. (2020). The COVID-19 pandemic and health inequalities. *Journal of Epidemiology & Community Health*, *74*(11), 964–968. doi.org/10.1136/jech-2020-214401.

Bauman, Z. (1991). *Modernity and the holocaust*. Polity Press.

Benatar, D. (2006). Bioethics and health and human rights: A critical view. *Journal of Medical Ethics*, *32*(1), 17–20. doi.org/10.1136/jme.2005.011775.

Borry, P., Schotsmans, P. & Dierickx, K. (2005). The birth of the empirical turn in bioethics. *Bioethics*, *19*(1), 49–71. doi.org/10.1111/j.1467-8519.2005.00424.x.

Bosk, C. L. (1999). Professional ethicist available: Logical, secular, friendly. *Daedalus*, *128*(4), 47–68.

Bourdieu, P. (1989). The corporatism of the universal: The role of intellectuals in the modern world. *Telos, 81*, 99–110. doi.org/10.3817/0989081099.

Bourdieu, P. (1990). The scholastic point of view. *Cultural Anthropology, 5*(4), 380–391. doi.org/10.1525/can.1990.5.4.02a00030.

Bourdieu, P. (1992). *The logic of practice.* Polity Press.

Bourdieu, P. (2004). *Science of science and reflexivity.* Polity Press.

Brock, D. W. (2000). Broadening the bioethics agenda. *Kennedy Institute of Ethics Journal, 10*(1), 21–38. doi.org/10.1353/ken.2000.a18635.

Brown, D. A. (2013). *Climate change ethics: Navigating the perfect moral storm.* Routledge.

Collins, H. M. & Evans, R. (2017). *Why democracies need science.* Polity Press.

Cribb, A. (2010). Translational ethics? The theory–practice gap in medical ethics. *Journal of Medical Ethics, 36*, 207–210. doi.org/10.1136/jme.2009.029785.

Dawson, A. & Verweij, M. (2008). Public health ethics: A manifesto. *Public Health Ethics, 1*(1), 1–2. doi.org/10.1093/phe/phn009.

Draper, H., Moorlock, G., Rogers, W. & Scully, J. L. (2019). Bioethics and activism. *Bioethics, 33*(8), 853–856. doi.org/10.1111/bioe.12680.

Earp, B. D., Lewis, J., Hart, C. L. & with Bioethicists and Allied Professionals for Drug Policy Reform. (2021). Racial justice requires ending the war on drugs. *The American Journal of Bioethics, 21*(4), 4–19. doi.org/10.1080/15265161.2020.1861364.

Emmerich, N. (2021). Ethos and eidos as field level concepts for the sociology of morality and the anthropology of ethics: Towards a social theory of applied ethics. *Human Studies, 44*, 373–395. doi.org/10.1007/s10746-021-09579-2.

Ferguson, K. (2020). The health reframing of climate change and the poverty of narrow bioethics. *The Journal of Law, Medicine & Ethics, 48*(4), 705–717. doi.org/10.1177/1073110520979381.

Fiske, A., Galasso, I., Eichinger, J., McLennan, S., Radhuber, I., Zimmermann, B. & Prainsack, B. (2022). The second pandemic: Examining structural inequality through reverberations of COVID-19 in Europe. *Social Science & Medicine, 292*, 114634. doi.org/10.1016/j.socscimed.2021.114634.

Franklin, S. (2019). Ethical research – The long and bumpy road from shirked to shared. *Nature, 574*(7780), 627–630. doi.org/10.1038/d41586-019-03270-4.

Fritz, Z., Huxtable, R., Ives, J., Paton, A., Slowther, A. M. & Wilkinson, D. (2020). Ethical road map through the Covid-19 pandemic. *BMJ, 369*. doi.org/10.1136/bmj.m2033.

Gardiner, S. M. (2022). Environmentalizing bioethics: Planetary health in a perfect moral storm. *Perspectives in Biology and Medicine, 65*(4), 569–585. doi.org/10.1353/pbm.2022.0048.

Hurst, S. A. (2010). What 'empirical turn in bioethics'? *Bioethics, 24*(8), 439–444. doi.org/10.1111/j.1467-8519.2009.01720.x.

Jamrozik, E. (2022). Public health ethics: Critiques of the 'new normal'. *Monash Bioethics Review, 40*(1), 1–16. doi.org/10.1007/s40592-022-00163-7.

Jamrozik, E. & Heriot, G. S. (2020). Pandemic public health policy: With great power comes great responsibility. *Internal Medicine Journal, 50*(10), 1169–1173. doi.org/10.1111/imj.15038.

Kaebnick, G. E. (2021). Ethicists and activists. *Hastings Center Report, 51*(4), 2. doi.org/10.1002/hast.1261.

King, N. M. P., Henderson, G. E. & Churchill, L. R. (2022). *Bioethics reenvisioned: A path toward health justice*. UNC Press Books.

Littoz-Monnet, A. (2020). *Governing through expertise: The politics of bioethics*. Cambridge University Press. doi.org/10.1017/9781108921060.

Lusk, G. (2021). Does democracy require value-neutral science? Analyzing the legitimacy of scientific information in the political sphere. *Studies in History and Philosophy of Science Part A, 90*, 102–110. doi.org/10.1016/j.shpsa.2021.08.009.

Mayes, C. (2022). Co-producing bioethics: How biomedical scientists and applied philosophers established bioethics in Australia. *Social History of Medicine, 35*(4) 1310–1333. doi.org/10.1093/shm/hkab133.

Medvetz, T. (2018). Bourdieu and the sociology of intellectual life. In T. Medvetz & J. J. Sallaz (Eds), *The Oxford handbook of Pierre Bourdieu* (p. 454). Oxford University Press. doi.org/10.1093/oxfordhb/9780199357192.013.20.

Meyers, C. (2021). Activism and the clinical ethicist. *Hastings Center Report, 51*(4), 22–31. doi.org/10.1002/hast.1269.

Middleton, J. (2023). Happy 175th birthday to public health. *BMJ, 382*, 2001. doi.org/10.1136/bmj.p2001.

Nussbaum, M. C. (2013). *Creating capabilities: The human development approach*. Harvard University Press. doi.org/10.2307/j.ctt2jbt31.

Nutt, D. J. (2009). Equasy – An overlooked addiction with implications for the current debate on drug harms. *Journal of Psychopharmacology, 23*(1), 3–5. doi.org/10.1177/0269881108099672.

Pierce, J. & Jameton, A. (2004). *The ethics of environmentally responsible health care.* Oxford University Press. doi.org/10.1016/j.scitotenv.2004.03.034.

Powers, M. & Faden, R. (2008). *Social justice: The moral foundations of public health and health policy.* Oxford University Press. doi.org/10.1093/oso/9780195375138.001.0001.

Ray, K. S. (2021). It's time for a black bioethics. *The American Journal of Bioethics, 21*(2), 38–40. doi.org/10.1080/15265161.2020.1861381.

Richie, C. (2019). *Principles of green bioethics: Sustainability in health care.* Michigan State University Press. doi.org/10.14321/j.ctvhrd1wq.

Rosenberg, C. E. (1999). Meanings, policies, and medicine: On the bioethical enterprise and history. *Daedalus, 128*(4).

Ruger, J. P. (2010). *Health and social justice.* Oxford University Press. doi.org/10.1093/acprof:oso/9780199559978.001.0001.

Turner, L. (2009). Anthropological and sociological critiques of bioethics. *Journal of Bioethical Inquiry, 6*(1), 83–98.

van der Vossen, B. (2014). In defense of the ivory tower: Why philosophers should stay out of politics. *Philosophical Psychology, 28*(7), 1045–1063. doi.org/10.1080/09515089.2014.972353.

Venkatapuram, S. (2013). *Health justice: An argument from the capabilities approach.* John Wiley & Sons.

Vo, H. & Campelia, G. D. (2021). Antiracist activism in clinical ethics: What's stopping us? *Hastings Center Report, 51*(4), 34–35. doi.org/10.1002/hast.1271.

6

The disruption of consumption

Sally Wheeler

It is hard to find anything across the globe – individuals, institutions, businesses or practices – that was not affected in some way by COVID-19. It was a multidimensional crisis with interlocking impacts. For example, while interventions such as lockdowns to suppress the spread of the virus harmed the economy and relaxing them boosted productivity, those returning to the workplace risked contracting COVID-19 and spreading it (Fetzer, 2022). It was a crisis unlike other health-related events, such as the SARS outbreak of 2003; it rapidly became clear that, although COVID-19 had the potential to 'close' the world, closure was not actually going to happen. The closest parallel is the rather less global but considerably more deadly influenza outbreak of 1918. Both pandemics produced an economic shock, but there are key differences: the demographics of the population affected, the degree of pre-existing global economic integration and the level of governmental control asserted over individual freedoms to prevent the spread (Beach et al., 2022). Global disruption and the recovery from COVID-19 have been exacerbated by different infection rates and profiles across countries and different policy settings to counter the virus (Strange, 2020).

The focus of this paper – the supply chain and its successor, the global value chain (GVC) – is certainly no stranger to these disruptions. It is estimated that, globally, 97 per cent of firms suffered supply chain difficulties by May 2020 (Institute for Supply Management, 2021). During COVID-19, end of supply chain consumers were surprised to find basic grocery goods, such as toilet paper, in short supply and commodities they needed to purchase rather less often, such as garage doors and bicycles, also very difficult to obtain (Dempsey, 2021). Shortages of goods and increased prices for available goods plagued economies around the world for some time after even the most conservative nation-states reopened their borders. Those working in supply chains, usually located thousands of kilometres from the finished item's point of use, found themselves suddenly without employment as multinational enterprises (MNEs) recalibrated what supply and demand shocks might be during the disruption of consumption to which there was no forecasted end date, and cancelled contracts or refused delivery of finished goods. MNE is not used as a term of art here to denote firms of any minimum size or particular jurisdictional incorporation, but, rather, to indicate businesses engaged in international trade with multiple overseas suppliers. Contractors and subcontractors in developing countries saw their firms become insolvent as payment terms were extended or reneged altogether. In the informal economy, suppliers that were dependent on MNEs (Narula, 2019) but did not have an underlying contractual relationship faced abandonment.

COVID-19 illustrated the importance of geography to MNEs engaged in global trade. The scale of trade in numbers is confronting: Contractor (2020) cites global trade figures from the United Nations Conference on Trade and Development's (UNCTAD's) 2013 report that suggest that, in 80 per cent of world trade transactions, an MNE was either an importer or exporter or otherwise participated as the creator of the supply chain; then there is the frequently cited but rather misleading comparator of national GDP versus MNE turnover that sees corporate turnover exceed national GDP in 69 out of 100 cases (Global Justice Now, 2018). However, numerical descriptions alone cannot reveal the crucial importance of geographic linkage, regional concentration and specialisation across many different nation-states in the same way. The shape, rather than volume, of international trade is created by nation-states and their economic policies and by the activities of MNEs that work within and around those policies to maximise their profits. The reworking of supply chains to embrace pan-global production opportunities as GVCs has been the poster child of neoliberalism. During COVID-19, the idea within developed market economies of nation-state control over business activity, something that was deemed impossible during the previous 30 years or so, underwent something of a resurgence (Chernilo, 2021). These nations (e.g. Australia, Japan, the UK and the US) placed restrictions on domestic economic activity and labour migration flows across borders, reconsidered protectionist policies in light of populist nationalism and the emergence of interest in country of origin issues from consumers (Felix & Fuat Firat, 2019), and offered business domestically through tax breaks and stimulus packages (Capano et al., 2020; Kaplan et al., 2020). Post-COVID, these nation-states have embarked on policies or inquiries designed to lead to policies that offer an alternative narrative to globalisation.

This chapter looks at GVCs under COVID-19, particularly in relation to the activities of MNEs. It then turns to consider what the emergence from COVID-19 might bring for the design of supply chains in the future. It concludes by examining the position taken by developed market economies like Australia in advocating the re-engineering of domestic manufacturing capability to try to create supply chain resilience in light of GVC failure.

From supply chains to global value chains

Harvey offers a definition of neoliberalism as a political and economic ideology that sees wellbeing as best served by setting individual entrepreneurial skills 'within an institutional framework characterised by strong private property rights, free markets and free trade' (Harvey, 2005, p. 2). Within this ideology, the role of the nation-state is pared back to the enforcement of contracts and the securing of private property rights within an economic system that it is structured to privilege both. The idea that governance of MNE activity has been ceded at the national level comes from the involvement of the Bretton Woods institutions – the International Monetary Fund and the World Bank – and the World Trade Organization in creating, incentivising and supporting this settlement within individual nation-states. Nations approach the successful achievement of neoliberalism through the privatisation of public assets, the abandonment of subsidies and tariffs that supported and protected national 'champions', the adoption of fiscal conservatism (triggered by regimes of low taxation) in relation to public spending on welfare and aspects of regulation, and the promotion of foreign direct investment. For those nation-states that have a poor balance of payments, supra-state financial assistance is often available subject to the adoption of these types of policies (Kalderimis, 2004; Parker & Kirkpatrick, 2005). For nation-states in stronger financial positions, this explains the proliferation of bilateral investment treaties, free trade agreements and the creation of trading blocks, such as RCEP (Regional Comprehensive Economic Partnership) and APEC (Asia-Pacific Economic Cooperation) (Nizamuddin, 2008). In Australia, the successive Labor governments of

Hawke and Keating moved towards neoliberalism as an operating paradigm by inter alia floating the dollar, encouraging foreign investment and restructuring industrial relations (Collins & Cottle, 2010).

A bold proposition is that, as a key player in neoliberalism, MNE has embraced three roles: sponsor, inhibitor and provider. It has sought to sponsor some arrangements, particularly in relation to trade agreements; it has acted to inhibit the creation of rules around labour and environmental standards, and human rights more generally, unless clearly to its benefit; and it has provided, instead, deliberately crafted private regulation in the form of international standards in areas such as corporate social responsibility (CSR), safety and technical product specification (Bartley, 2018). At the operational level, MNE has organised its activities so that, rather than emphasising vertical integration, it now slices production into segments located in different nations where it can access the cheapest and, often, well-educated labour; the lowest environmental regulations; the most efficacious tax regime; the availability of raw materials at source; and technical expertise and specialisation. Sole country production of a final product for export is no longer the norm. The mechanism for executing production is through a non-equity mode of agreement (UNCTAD, 2011), most often through contractual arrangements that are then underpinned by webs of subcontracts (Gereffi, 2005). Further support for organising production in this way comes from technological developments around digital communication that shorten distance and overcome time issues, allowing segments of production to be located far away from eventual intended markets. The focus is not just on the product per se but also on the task in each segment. Theoretically, this allows specialised functions, if they are required by the individual GVC, to grow in particular geographic areas, and aids development in those economies (Pietrobelli et al., 2021) – until it does not, such as during COVID-19. Each segment-based task delivers value in and of itself, hence the name given to this form of organisation – GVC (Gereffi, 2018; Hameiri, 2021).

Prior to COVID-19, notwithstanding the 'slowbalisation' of globalisation (Irwin, 2020) due to successive, repeated local and regional economic and political shocks from the GFC of 2008 onwards (e.g. the US–China trade war, the collapse of the Trans-Pacific Partnership Agreement, BREXIT and the rise of populism [Kobrin, 2020]), GVCs were very successful, if by successful we mean the incurring of costs in low-cost economies and the realisation of profits in higher cost, more developed economies. In a context in which world trade has fallen as a percentage of national GDP since the

GFC, trade within GVCs between 2011 and 2019 still accounted for 70 per cent of world trade (Jaax et al., 2023). Alongside the obvious advantages for MNEs in adopting GVCs, there are several negative features for nation-states of production organised this way. There has been a lack of wage growth in many developed economies as domestic manufacturing capacity has declined that, arguably, in some countries (e.g. the US and the UK), has fuelled the rise of populist politics. In terms of the decline of domestic manufacturing, Australia is a very good example. This decline is considered later in this chapter. Many developed economies have become ones that both lack skilled artisanal and technical labour workers and current opportunities for employment in those sectors. Instead, they provide employment opportunities only in low-paid service sectors. With economies structured in this way, the profits from GVC organised production have been realised by corporate shareholders not by employees through higher wages.

There are obvious reasons why COVID-19 would cause a seismic disruption to the operation of GVCs, notwithstanding the different design characteristics of individual GVCs. They might require very little by way of technology and specialised infrastructure and labour, being configured instead for highly standardised products (e.g. textile and clothing manufacture), but they are in locations where scale is available. Alternatively, they might require access to considerable specialised labour and specific components, the production of which is co-located or located nearby (e.g. the electronics and computing sector). In all cases though, even if we consider only the supply-side risks of GVC activity (Christopher & Peck, 2004), goods need to be sourced, moved from one location to another during production and delivered to their final market, and globally based production is likely to require the movement of staff from headquarters or regional bases to other places (Paul, Chowdhury et al., 2021). The closure of international borders and severe curtailment of air travel during COVID-19 made both prerequisites very difficult to satisfy (Strange, 2020). Sea routes and ports presented no lesser challenge, as they were subject to health measures and health checks exacerbating delays and labour shortages (Australian Competition and Consumer Commission, 2021). The depth and complexity of any GVC in terms of the time taken to uncouple it and source new locations for tasks, as well as the lack of domestic production infrastructure or technical expertise in many countries, explains the shortages of manufactured goods in many economies during COVID-19.

Multinational enterprises and COVID-19

MNEs such as Carrefour, Nike and Walmart manage huge chains of manufacturers linked by contract where there is often direct visibility for the lead MNE over only tier-one (direct) suppliers. Suppliers in subsequent tiers often have no idea where their products are ultimately destined for or which MNE stands at the head of the chain. The security that contractual relationships offer suppliers through all tiers of the chain has been called into question by the actions of MNEs during COVID-19. Any idea that contracts contain legally enforceable terms that can be relied upon has proved to be incorrect in many instances. The garment industry is a particularly good example of this (Majumdar et al., 2020). Fibres (either natural or artificial) are produced in one country but are often woven or knitted in another. Yarn produced in a third country is added to this process before the garment is sown. During the sowing process, the garment might be cut in one factory and sewn and trimmed (finished) in several others before it goes via a wholesaler to a retailer. These activities might span national borders as well as different factory locations. The closure of retail premises accompanied by stay-at-home instructions changed the supply and demand dynamic for clothing retailers and fashion brands (Goolsbee & Syverson, 2020).

Retailers and brands responded in a variety of ways. A small minority converted their manufacturing operations to support the COVID-19 response by making personal protective equipment (PPE) equipment to sell or donate (Kim & Woo, 2021). For the majority, however, their actions were to brutally leave loss wherever it fell in the GVC. One response was simply to cancel contracts for finished garments, dispatched garments or garments in the production process, sometimes justifying this by citing contractual provisions around frustration or force majeure. The US retailer Kohl's is a case in point. According to media reports, it cancelled contracts with factories in Bangladesh and Korea totalling US$150 million without notice, furloughed many of its US staff and closed all of its US retail outlets. Kohl's was still able, and its management thought it appropriate, to pay a dividend of US$109 million to shareholders in the same time frame (McNamara, 2020). Indicative of the populist nationalism that, while on the rise before COVID-19, became hugely significant during the pandemic is the Edelman Trust Barometer's (2020) finding that the general population in the US (where Kohls' retail outlets are located) expected that businesses would put employees and communities in their locality ahead of their contractual obligations further afield. Similar examples from Australia would be the retailers Country Road, R. M. Williams and Cotton On (Kaine et al., 2020).

Another response was to offer a much lower price for finished garments than the one that had previously been contractually agreed. Variations included demands for long extensions to previously agreed payment terms and demands to lower the number of garments purchased from what had been previously agreed (Roberts-Islam, 2020). Most fashion items are seasonal and are produced on a 'just in time' basis. From a retailer's perspective, although consumers were always going to return to buying clothes once restrictions were lifted, it is vital to have clothes available in shops and online to sell that are relevant (e.g. winter clothes in winter) to the consumer at the point of reopening. This explains the reluctance to stand by existing contracts and, in effect, to impose losses on those in the supply chain instead. In garment GVCs, like many other GVCs, none of the component parts of the supply chain are unique to any one provider. Trading partners are selected on price competitiveness and availability to supply or perform a particular task at scale within a specified time frame – not on their specialist skills. This substantially reduces the bargaining power of the component supplier in the event of dispute or disruption, even when a contract with detailed terms exists. Raw materials that suppliers have purchased and buyers refuse to pay for impose costs on factories at the bottom of the supply chain, as does the refusal to pay the production costs of part-worked garments. Garment factories cannot pay their workers in the absence of liquidity.

Manufacturers in garment production GVCs in East Asia were predicting turnover drops of 26 per cent on their 2019 figures. The predicted drops for South-East Asia and South Asia were more precipitous at 38 per cent and 31 per cent, respectively (International Textile Manufacturers Federation, 2020). By the end of the first few months of the pandemic, thousands of workers at the bottom of the supply chain had been laid off (Kabir et al., 2021). For manufacturers, regardless of their place on the GVC, and even if they had sufficient income to carry on production, containment measures such as social distancing and lockdowns reduced working capacity, making trading out of their difficulties almost impossible. In many jurisdictions, bank loans could only be accessed if garment factories could produce export documentation or contemporaneous promises from buyers to pay for finished items. In some countries, for example Cambodia and Vietnam, the garment trade, being the largest or second largest industry sector, anchors national economic development. Without taxation revenue and export receipts from this industry, together with the loss of consumer spending from laid-off workers, national economies suffered (Anner, 2020; Voss, 2020).

Supply chains are always going to be disrupted by local micro issues such as labour disputes or weather incidents. These are not novel situations for businesses to cope with. COVID-19, however, presented a challenge of a magnitude that could only be met with a coherent supply chain resilience strategy and plan. It is unfortunate then, from a consumer supply perspective, that, as research from the Australasian Supply Chain Institute (2020) tells us, prior to COVID-19, only 45 per cent of businesses had a business continuity plan and that, of those with a plan, reliance on legacy technology was considered to be the biggest risk. We should, perhaps, not be surprised by this. Supply chain management has long been about maximising profits and return on investment not about risk management – and certainly not about managing the risks of the unknown and the unimagined. Within supply chain studies, 'resilience' emerged as 'the' concept to discuss only after COVID-19 began (Pettit et al., 2019). Castillo (2023) reports that, in a bibliographic assessment of supply chain literature on resilience over the last 17 years, over half the articles were published during COVID-19, with much of the pre-COVID literature discussing organisational efficiency post disruption rather than what would be needed to cope with a disruption on the scale of COVID-19.

In 2018, the Advanced Manufacturing Growth Centre (AMGC), a not-for-profit organisation created and supported by the Australian government as part of its Industry Innovation and Competitiveness Agenda, recommended three resilience strategies for Australian companies to manage their supply chains: superiority, diversity (in terms of 'product segments, service offerings or geographically export markets') and flexibility (AMGC, 2018, p. 4). None of these suggestions would have been of much assistance in the pandemic because of its global nature. Post-COVID-19, we might wonder whether there is an opportunity to do things differently – to reconceive supply chains and their management so that unsustainable losses are not pushed onto those lower down the GVC. Perhaps supply chain membership might no longer just be based on cost, quality and timely delivery but also include genuine auditable measures around worker health, safety and support, fair wages and environmental standards.

A recent survey of experienced supply chain executives identified nine strategies for post-COVID-19 supply chain management. There was broad agreement that 'valuing sustainability not just compliance' was a key to effective and resilient design. In other words, it was agreed that only doing what is required to keep regulators and investors satisfied in the environmental and social space is not enough and that there needs to be proactive approaches to embedding sustainability in the supply chain (Paul, Moktadir et al., 2021). There has always been a business case for sustainability or, more broadly, CSR (Carroll & Shabana, 2010), and governments are beginning to take this more seriously by legislating on issues such as climate limits and greenwashing, in addition to the moral case. MNEs are aware of the importance of both of these drivers and often incorporate provisions on sustainability into their first-tier contracts. The difficulty comes in trying to implement this further down the GVC, in areas where they have little visibility. In jurisdictions with legislation against modern forms of slavery (e.g. Australia), there is a requirement to identify such risks in the supply chain. This requires mapping the supply chain; however, there is no requirement to include practices that are environmentally corrosive and socially undesirable, as these do not meet the definitions of modern slavery. There needs to be much greater awareness of what individual GVCs encompass and more comprehensive mapping, which includes the role of the informal economy, supported by cutting-edge technology for tracking and tracing components if sustainability activity is going to push back neoliberal efficiency in the post-COVID-19 world (Villena & Gioia, 2020).

Nation-states, COVID-19 and global value chains

Australia, in common with the US, UK and many other nations in the global north, entered the pandemic with a domestic manufacturing capacity that had been contracting for at least the previous three decades. The definition of domestic manufacturing used here is an activity that occurs within a given nation-state – this article does not look at taxation or incorporation issues. In a pandemic, and particularly a global pandemic, domestic capacity matters because there is little possibility of either self-sufficiency or redirection (towards, say, the production of PPE) without a strong domestic footprint of activity. In response to national governments' calls for assistance (Gibson et al., 2021), firms such as Ford, Dyson, Rolls Royce and a host of other manufacturers tried in various ways across their global locations to switch their car and electrical appliance manufacturing plants to ventilator production plants. Export bans imposed by nations (e.g. Germany) during COVID-19 would mean that the only nation-states able to benefit from this switch were those that hosted these companies (Nienaber, 2020).

Looking specifically at Australia, in March 2020, the Australian government put out a tender request to its domestic manufacturing base to ascertain what COVID-related supplies could be produced: testing kits, face masks and other PPE equipment, and ethanol for cleaning. It received a raft of positive responses (Black, 2020). However, the results of this tendering exercise should not disguise the fact that Australia's manufacturing capacity has declined substantially, both in terms of its contribution to GDP and employment. Manufacturing comprised 25 per cent of GDP throughout the 1960s but had declined to 6 per cent by 2020 (Connolly & Lewis, 2010; World Bank, n.d.). In the 1960s, 1.2 million people (25 per cent of the Australian workforce) were employed in manufacturing. By June 2018, that figure had dropped to around 840,000 people, representing just 6 per cent of the current workforce capacity, the lowest percentage of any OECD country (Pupazzoni, 2020). If we take the difference between Australia's output of manufactured products to Australians' use of manufactured products as a self-sufficiency measure, Australia has the lowest level of self-sufficiency in the OECD (Stanford, 2020). Medical equipment provides a good example of this imbalance: in 2019, Australia produced A$1.84 billion in medical equipment for export but imported the same to the value of A$4.43 billion (Stanford, 2020).

Neoliberal policy settings are not the only factor in Australia's declining manufacturing capacity. The turn to neoliberalism was compounded by the emergence within Australia of primary extractive industries around coal, iron ore and other minerals and metals. Australia's domestic economy then became structured around the demand for and pricing of these commodities in the global economy. When the political stability of Australia is added to its huge and comparatively accessible mineral resources, what results is a classic 'Dutch disease' scenario: the strength of the Australian dollar has made other exports expensive without subsidy support and imports cheap at the expense of domestically produced goods without tariff protection (Martinus et al., 2018). The saga of vehicle manufacture in Australia provides a case in point. Australia began to produce vehicles for the mass car market as part of its economic recovery from World War II. Subsequently, car manufacturing facilities for US, UK and South-East Asian MNEs were established in

Australia. While some of these were production plant facilities only (i.e. they assembled imported parts and structures), others engaged in the manufacture of, or purchased from others in the domestic Australian market, component parts and pursued vehicle build activity within Australia. From 1992 or so onwards, these MNE manufacturers started to exit Australia; for example, Nissan in 1992, Mitsubishi from 2004 to 2008 and Ford in 2013–14. These exits had knock-on effects on the viability of component manufacturing. In 2017, vehicle manufacture in Australia ceased when Holden closed both its assembly and build facilities. Beer (2018) provides a detailed analysis of the factors that produced this manufacturing collapse: neoliberal industrial policy in Australia, the emergence of lower-cost labour and regulation markets overseas, and structural economic changes in Australia brought about by a reorientation to primary industry.

The effect of supply chain issues and the shortage of consumer goods, medical supplies and components for a host of other sectors prompted national governments to think about boosting supply chain resilience through re-shoring activity, shortening supply chains and reducing exposure to single-country supply. Consideration was also given to the extent to which self-sufficiency or sovereignty capability in particular areas should become an issue of government policy (Free & Hecimovic, 2021) as opposed to being left solely to the profit and risk assessments of MNEs in a post-COVID-19 world (Barbieri et al., 2020; Basu & Partha, 2022). For some countries, this meant building on pre-existing policy choices. The UK and the US, for example, two countries that Australia now has close strategic defence ties to, had already embarked on this journey with varying degrees of success. In the UK, Reshoring UK began in 2014 as a taskforce between government and the peak manufacturing trade body to support firms in planning a re-shoring strategy, finding locations for operations activities and securing local suppliers (Gov.UK, 2014). In the US in 2012, the Obama administration launched a number of similar initiatives, such as production networks, tax breaks, clean energy schemes and support for foreign investment in manufacturing in the US (White House, 2012). A major plank of both Trump campaigns and subsequent presidencies is the re-shoring of manufacturing activity, albeit supported by protectionism rather than support for foreign investment (Vanchan et al., 2018). Australia's conversion to re-shoring did not occur until after the start of COVID-19.

In November 2020, Karen Andrews, then Australia's minister for industry, science and technology in the Morrison government, tweeted:

> If COVID-19 has taught us anything it is that we need to be on the front foot in times of a crisis. Our Supply Chain Resilience Initiative under our $1.5b Modern Manufacturing Strategy will help position Australia to respond in the future.
>
> (Andrews, 2020)

Andrew Liveris, chair of the National COVID Coordination Commission's Manufacturing Taskforce, referred to Australia as having drunk the 'free-trade juice for too long', and suggested that it needed to look at on-shoring key capabilities (Greber, 2020). This might seem something of a volte-face for an administration that, in November 2018, had been vigorously urging other world leaders to embrace free trade and reject protectionism (Packham, 2018). However, Prime Minister Morrison (2020, p. 5) was keen to stress that Australia would continue to take part in global supply chains that delivered 'the prosperity we rely on to create jobs, support incomes and build businesses'. What this meant was not a return to protectionism, but the establishment of 'economic sovereignty', which would be achieved by ensuring Australian industries were 'highly competitive, resilient and able to succeed in a global market' (Morrison, 2020, p. 5).

In October 2020, Australia launched its Modern Manufacturing Strategy – an initiative with three broad component parts as, essentially, a re-shoring project. It promised A$1.3 billion in support of six key industries (medical products, space, defence, recycling and clean energy, food and beverages, and resources technology and critical minerals processing) to build scale, harness research and create innovation partnerships around 'value rather than cost' (Australian Government, 2020, p. 7). There was A$107 million for supply chain resilience and A$52.8 million for investment into shovel-ready manufacturing modernisation projects. The supply chain resilience effort was supported by an agreement around regional cooperation with Japan and India. Coming to power in May 2022, the Albanese Labor government also made a commitment to supporting manufacturing, specifically high-tech manufacturing, in Australia with the creation of a A$15 billion fund promising to support industries such as defence and agriculture and to fund projects around technology development (Australian Government, 2022). The modalities might differ (Labor's fund is structured through an investment board and co-investment) but the intention to support re-shoring and develop Australian manufacturing is the same.

Australia's re-shoring strategy relies on harnessing technology for smarter manufacturing through using techniques such as three-dimensional printing, automation and digitisation to cut production costs and support logistics. While there might be an understanding of what these technologies offer in theory, utilising them across a firm's entire operating structure is some way away. The skills required to do this include coding, advanced computing, artificial intelligence (AI) and human-computer interaction around design thinking and blockchain possibilities (Pegoraro et al., 2022). The geographic scale of Australia means that local suppliers and skilled local labour forces are needed even if both are supplemented by imports and skilled inward migration. Creating a labour force with an appropriate skill level means funding technical education, both in terms of student support and financial encouragement for employers to invest in this (Stein, 2021). Investment in research and development and innovation is core to achieving the scale and synergies needed for genuinely modern manufacturing, even in areas where Australia should have commercial advantages (e.g. solar panels, batteries and wave technology). Financial support for research in universities is the most efficient way for this to occur. However, the funding relationship between government, universities and the private sector will need to change to become one that is much more cooperative if industrial reinvigoration is to become a reality. In terms of government support, Australia spends less on research than other comparable advanced economies. It ranks twenty-eighth in the OECD, with Japan spending more than three times and the US more than twice the amount Australia spends on research per million of the population (OECD, 2022). The A$50 million fund for university–industry cooperation created by the then minister for education, Alan Tudge, in 2021 does little to close this gap (Sinclair, 2021). Historically, the private sector in Australia has not been a funder of university research in any meaningful way (McCarthy & Jayasuriya, 2023).

Where are we now?

We can make many observations about the effect of the pandemic on trade, supply and demand for goods, patterns of consumption and so forth. What is clear is that there has not been an effective global response. Different countries have made their own calculations about the costs of economic shutdown versus healthcare. MNEs have made similar individual calculations around continuing production, shutting down, refusing to pay previously agreed prices for goods and so on (Enderwick & Buckley,

2020). What unites MNEs and developed economies is their retreat from neoliberalism in the face of COVID's reset. For MNEs, this has manifested itself in the search for supply chain resilience – taking faltering steps away from simple efficiency at the lowest cost and towards something that resembles a sustainability narrative. At the level of nation-states there are different degrees of urgency and readiness around re-establishing sovereign capabilities and manufacturing capacity through re-shoring policies. Pursuing this requires investing in new technologies and creating business ecosystems around skills, education, research and innovation. For some countries, such as Australia, only a major change in policy direction will deliver this.

References

Advanced Manufacturing Growth Centre. (2018). *Building resilience in Australian manufacturing.* www.amgc.org.au/news/amgc-releases-a-report-on-building-resilience-in-australian-manufacturing/.

Andrews, K. (2020, 10 November). *If COVID-19 has taught us anything it is that we need to be on the front foot in times of a crisis.* [Tweet].

Anner, M. (2020, 27 March). Abandoned? The impact of COVID-19 on workers and businesses at the bottom of global garment supply chains. *PennState Center for Global Workers' Rights.* www.workersrights.org/wp-content/uploads/2020/03/Abandoned-Penn-State-WRC-Report-March-27-2020.pdf.

Australasian Supply Chain Institute. (2020). *The state of supply chain management report 2020.* supplychainchannel.co/the-state-of-supply-chain-management-report-2020/.

Australian Competition and Consumer Commission. (2021). *Container stevedoring monitoring report 2020–21.* www.accc.gov.au/about-us/publications/serial-publications/container-stevedoring-monitoring-report/container-stevedoring-monitoring-report-2020-21.

Australian Government. (2020, 1 October). *Make it happen: The Australian government's Modern Manufacturing Strategy.* www.industry.gov.au/publications/make-it-happen-australian-governments-modern-manufacturing-strategy.

Australian Government. (2022, 27 October). *National Reconstruction Fund: Diversifying and transforming Australia's industry and economy.* www.industry.gov.au/news/national-reconstruction-fund-diversifying-and-transforming-australias-industry-and-economy.

Barbieri, P., Boffelli, A., Elia, S., Fratocchi, S., Kalchschmidt, M. & Samson, D. (2020). What can we learn about reshoring after Covid-19? *Operations Management Research, 13*, 131–136. doi.org/10.1007/s12063-020-00160-1.

Bartley, T. (2018). Transnational corporations and global governance. *Annual Review of Sociology, 44*, 145–165.

Basu, P. & Partha, R. (2022). China-plus-one: Expanding global value chains. *The Journal of Business Strategy, 43*(6), 350–356. doi.org/10.1108/JBS-04-2021-0066.

Beach, B., Clay, K. & Saaverda, M. (2022). The 1918 influenza pandemic and its lessons for COVID-19. *Journal of Economic Literature, 60*(1), 41–84. doi.org/10.1257/jel.20201641.

Beer, A. (2018). The closure of the Australian car manufacturing industry: Redundancy, policy and community impacts. *Australian Geographer, 49*(3), 419–438. doi.org/10.1080/00049182.2017.1402452.

Black, E. (2020, 23 March). Private companies join the war effort to produce crucial supplies. *The New Daily.* thenewdaily.com.au/finance/finance-news/2020/03/23/factories-war-effort-supplies/.

Capano, G., Howlett, M., Jarvis, D. S. L., Ramesh, M. & Goyal, N. (2020). Mobilizing policy (in)capacity to fight COVID-19: Understanding variations in state responses. *Policy and Society, 39*(3), 285–308. doi.org/10.1080/14494035.2020.1787628.

Carroll, A. & Shabana, K. (2010). The business case for corporate social responsibility: A review of concepts, research and practice. *International Journal of Management Reviews, 12*(1), 85–105. doi.org/10.1111/j.1468-2370.2009.00275.x.

Castillo, C. (2023). Is there a theory of supply chain resilience? A bibliometric analysis of the literature. *International Journal of Operations and Production Management, 43*(1), 22–47. doi.org/10.1108/IJOPM-02-2022-0136.

Chernilo, D. (2021). Another globalisation: Covid-19 and the cosmopolitan imagination. In G. Delanty (Ed.), *Pandemics, politics, and society* (pp. 157–170). De Gruyter. doi.org/10.1515/9783110713350-011.

Christopher, M. & Peck, H. (2004). Building the resilient supply chain. *International Journal of Logistics Management, 15*(2), 1–14. doi.org/10.1108/09574090410700275.

Collins, J. & Cottle, D. (2010). Labor neoliberals or pragmatic neo-Laborists? The Hawke and Keating Labor governments in office, 1983–96. *Labour History, 98*, 25. doi.org/10.5263/labourhistory.98.1.25.

Connolly, E. & Lewis, C. (2010). Structural change in the Australian economy. *Reserve Bank of Australia – Bulletin*, September. www.rba.gov.au/publications/bulletin/2010/sep/1.html.

Contractor, F. (2020, 6 April). *What does flattening the curve mean?* Academy of International Business. www.aib.world/news/what-does-flattening-the-curve-mean/.

Dempsey, H. (2021, 15 November). Covid turbulence still strains overextended supply chains. *The Financial Times*. www.ft.com/content/c8808515-7165-45b3-88de-a72e1c7aac92.

Edelman Trust Barometer. (2020). *Special report: Trust and the coronavirus*. www.edelman.com/sites/g/files/aatuss191/files/2020-03/2020%20Edelman%20Trust%20Barometer%20Coronavirus%20Special%20Report_0.pdf.

Enderwick, P. & Buckley. P. J. (2020). Rising regionalization: Will the post-COVID-19 world see a retreat from globalization. *Transnational Corporations, 27*(2), 99–112. doi.org/10.18356/8008753a-en.

Felix, R. & Fuat Firat, A. (2019). Brands that 'sell their soul': Offshoring, brand liquidification and the excluded consumer. *Journal of Marketing Management, 35*(11–12), 1080–1099. doi.org/10.1080/0267257X.2019.1604562.

Fetzer, T. (2022). Subsidising the spread of COVID-19: Evidence from the UK's Eat Out to Help Out Scheme. *The Economic Journal, 132*(643), 1200–1217. doi.org/10.1093/ej/ueab074.

Free, C. & Hecimovic, A. (2021). Global supply chains after COVID-19: The end of the road for neoliberal globalisation? *Accounting, Auditing and Accountability Journal, 34*(1), 58–84. doi.org/10.1108/AAAJ-06-2020-4634.

Gereffi, G. (2005). The global economy: Organization, governance, and development. In N. Smelser & R. Swedberg (Eds), *The handbook of economic sociology* (pp. 160–182). Princeton University Press.

Gereffi, G. (2018). *Global value chains and development: Redefining the contours of 21st century capitalism*. Cambridge University Press. doi.org/10.1017/9781108559423.

Gibson, C., Carr, C., Lyons, C., Taksa, L. & Warren, A. (2021). COVID-19 and the shifting industrial landscape. *Geographical Research, 59*(2), 196–205. doi.org/10.1111/1745-5871.12462.

Global Justice Now. (2018, 17 October). *69 of the richest 100 entities on the planet are corporations, not governments, figures show*. www.globaljustice.org.uk/news/69-richest-100-entities-planet-are-corporations-not-governments-figures-show/.

Goolsbee, A. & Syverson, C. (2020). Fear, lockdown, and diversion: Comparing drivers of pandemic economic decline 2020. *NBER Working Paper, 27432*.

Gov.UK. (2014, 24 January). *New government support to encourage manufacturing production back to the UK* [Media release]. www.gov.uk/government/news/new-government-support-to-encourage-manufacturing-production-back-to-the-uk.

Greber, J. (2020, 9 April). Liveris calls the start of the on-shoring era. *Australian Financial Review.* www.afr.com/politics/liveris-calls-the-start-of-the-on-shoring-era-20200408-p54i37.

Hameiri, S. (2021). COVID-19: Is this the end of globalization. *International Journal: Canada's Journal of Global Policy Analysis, 76*(1), 30. doi.org/10.1177/0020702020985325.

Harvey, A. (2005). *A brief history of neoliberalism.* Oxford University Press.

Institute for Supply Management. (2021). *COVID-19's global impact on supply chains* [White paper]. www.ismworld.org/globalassets/pub/research-and-surveys/white-papers/white_paper_coronavirus_round4_research.pdf.

International Textile Manufacturers Federation. (2023). *3rd ITMF-survey about the impact of the corona-pandemic on the global textile industry* [Press release]. itmf.org/images/dl/press-releases/2020/Corona-Survey-3nd-2020.04.29-Press-Release.pdf.

Irwin, D. (2020, 5 May). The pandemic adds momentum to the deglobalisation trend. *Centre for Economic Policy Research.* cepr.org/voxeu/columns/pandemic-adds-momentum-deglobalisation-trend.

Jaax, A., Miroudot, S. & van Lieshout, E. (2023). Deglobalisation? The reorganisation of GVCs in a changing world. *OECD Trade Policy Papers, 272*. doi.org/10.1787/b15b74fe-en.

Kabir, H., Maple, M. & Usher, K. (2021). The impact of COVID-19 on Bangladeshi readymade garment (RMG) workers. *Journal of Public Health, 43*(1), 47–52. doi.org/10.1093/pubmed/fdaa126.

Kaine, S., Payne, A. & Coneybeer, J. (2020, 28 May). What COVID-19 means for the people making your clothes. *The Conversation.* theconversation.com/what-covid-19-means-for-the-people-making-your-clothes-134800.

Kalderimis, D. (2004). IMF conditionality as investment regulation: A theoretical analysis. *Social and Legal Studies, 13*(1), 103–131. doi.org/10.1177/09646639 04040194.

Kaplan, G., Moll, B. & Violante, G. (2020). The great lockdown and the big stimulus: Tracing the pandemic possibility frontier for the U.S. *NBER Working Paper, 27794*. www.nber.org/papers/w27794.

Kim, S. & Woo, H. (2021). Global fashion retailers' responses to external and internal crises during the COVID-19 pandemic. *Fashion and Textiles, 8*, 32. doi.org/10.1186/s40691-021-00260-x.

Kobrin, S. J. (2020). How globalization became a thing that goes bump in the night. *Journal of International Business Policy, 3*, 280–286. doi.org/10.1057/s42214-020-00060-y.

Majumdar, A., Shaw, M. & Kumar Sinha, S. (2020). COVID-19 debunks the myth of a socially sustainable supply chain: A case of the clothing industry in South Asian countries. *Sustainable Production and Consumption, 24*, 150–155. doi.org/10.1016/j.spc.2020.07.001.

Martinus, K., Sigler, T. J., O'Neill, P. & Tonts, M. (2018). 'Global restructuring' two decades on: Australia's relational economy in the twenty-first century. *Australian Geographer, 49*, 341–348. doi.org/10.1080/00049182.2018.1446384.

McCarthy, G. & Jayasuriya, K. (2023). The pandemic and the politics of Australian research governance. *Higher Education Research & Development, 42*, 679–693. doi.org/10.1080/07294360.2022.2106947.

McNamara, M-L. (2020, 10 June). Anger at huge shareholder payout as US chain Kohl's cancels $150m in orders. *The Guardian.* www.theguardian.com/global-development/2020/jun/10/anger-at-huge-shareholder-payout-as-us-chain-kohls-cancels-150m-in-orders.

Morrison, S. (2020, 6 May). *Address, National Press Club* [typescript]. www.uensw.com.au/wp-content/uploads/2020/06/Address-National-Press-Club-_-Prime-Minister-of-Australia_26-May2020.pdf.

Narula, R. (2019). Enforcing higher labour standards within developing country value chains: Consequences for MNEs and informal actors in a dual economy. *Journal of International Business Studies, 50*, 1622–1635. doi.org/10.1057/s41267-019-00265-1.

Nienaber, M. (2020, 4 March). Germany bans export of medical protection gear due to coronavirus. *Reuters.* www.reuters.com/article/health-coronavirus-germany-exports/germany-bans-export-of-medical-protection-gear-due-to-coronavirus-id USL8N2AX3D9.

Nizamuddin, A. M. (2008). Declining risk, market liberalization and state-multinational bargaining: Japanese automobile investments in India, Indonesia and Malaysia. *Pacific Affairs, 81*(3), 339–359. doi.org/10.5509/2008813339.

OECD. (2022). *Main science and technology indicators*. www.oecd.org/en/data/datasets/main-science-and-technology-indicators.html.

Packham, C. (2018, 16 November). Australian PM urges global leaders to reject protectionism, embrace free trade. *Reuters*. www.reuters.com/article/us-apec-summit-ceo-australia/australian-pm-urges-global-leaders-to-reject-protectionism-embrace-free-trade-idUSKCN1NM013.

Parker, D. & Kirkpatrick, C. (2005). Privatisation in developing countries: A review of the evidence and the policy lessons. *Journal of Development Studies*, *41*(4), 513–541. doi.org/10.1080/00220380500092499.

Paul, S. K., Chowdhury, R., Moktadir, A. & Lau, K. H. (2021). Supply chain recovery challenges in the wake of COVID-19 pandemic. *Journal of Business Research, 136*, 316–329. doi.org/10.1016/j.jbusres.2021.07.056.

Paul, S. K., Moktadir A. & Ahsan, K. (2021). Key supply chain strategies for the post-COVID-19 era: Implications for resilience and sustainability. *International Journal of Logistics Management, 34*(4). doi.org/10.1108/IJLM-04-2021-0238.

Pegoraro, D., De Propis, L. & Chidlow, A. (2022). Regional factors enabling manufacturing reshoring strategies: A case study perspective. *Journal of International Business Policy, 5*, 112–133. doi.org/10.1057/s42214-021-00112-x.

Pettit, T. J., Croxton, K. & Fiksel, J. (2019). The evolution of resilience in supply chain management: A retrospective on ensuring supply chain resilience. *Journal of Business Logistics*, *40*(1), 56–65. doi.org/10.1111/jbl.12202.

Pietrobelli, C., Rabellotti, R. & Van Assche, A. (2021). Making sense of global value chain-oriented policies: The trifecta of tasks, linkages, and firms. *Journal of International Business Policy, 4*, 327–346. doi.org/10.1057/s42214-021-00117-6.

Pupazzoni, R. (2020, 23 July). Australian manufacturing has been in terminal decline but coronavirus might revive it. *ABC News*. www.abc.net.au/news/2020-07-23/coronavirus-pandemic-leads-to-australian-manufacturing-revival/12481568.

Roberts-Islam, B. (2020, 30 March). The true cost of brands not paying for orders during the COVID-19 crisis. *Forbes*. www.forbes.com/sites/brookerobertsislam/2020/03/30/the-true-cost-of-brands-not-paying-for-orders-during-the-covid-19-crisis/?sh=2ae6bad75ccc.

Sinclair, J. (2021, 7 June). Research commercialisation is top priority, says Tudge. *Research Professional News*. www.researchprofessionalnews.com/rr-news-australia-universities-2021-6-research-commercialisation-is-top-priority-says-tudge/.

Stanford, J. (2020). *A fair share for Australian manufacturing: Manufacturing renewal for the post-COVID economy*. The Centre for Future Work at the Australia Institute. australiainstitute.org.au/wp-content/uploads/2020/12/A-Fair-Share-for-Australian-Manufacturing-WEB.pdf.

Stein, J. A. (2021). *Industrial craft in Australia: Oral histories of creativity and survival*. Palgrave Macmillan. doi.org/10.1007/978-3-030-87243-4.

Strange, R. (2020). The 2020 Covid-19 pandemic and global value chains. *Journal of Industrial and Business Economics, 47*, 455–445. doi.org/10.1007/s40812-020-00162-x.

United Nations Conference on Trade and Development (UNCTAD). (2011). *World investment report, 2011*. unctad.org/publication/world-investment-report-2011.

Vanchan, V., Mulhall, R. & Bryson, J. (2018). Repatriation or reshoring of manufacturing to the U.S. and UK: Dynamics and global production networks or from here to there and back again. *Growth and Change, 49*(1), 97–121. doi.org/10.1111/grow.12224.

Villena, V. & Gioia, D. (2020). A more sustainable supply chain. *Harvard Business Review, 84*. hbr.org/2020/03/a-more-sustainable-supply-chain.

Voss, H. (2020). Implications of the COVID-19 pandemic for human rights and modern slavery vulnerabilities in global value chains. *Transnational Corporations, 27*(2), 113–126. doi.org/10.18356/1d28cbee-en.

White House. (2012, 25 January). *President Obama's blueprint to support U.S. manufacturing jobs, discourage outsourcing, and encourage insourcing* [Fact sheet]. obamawhitehouse.archives.gov/the-press-office/2012/01/25/fact-sheet-president-obama-s-blueprint-support-us-manufacturing-jobs-dis.

World Bank. (n.d.). *Manufacturing, value added (% of GDP)*. Retrieved 23 March 2023, data.worldbank.org/indicator/NV.IND.MANF.ZS.

7

The arts, music and the pandemic

Kim Cunio

Loss and grief

There is a lot of loss this chapter is not able to discuss: deforestation, our loss of biodiversity, the decimation of Aboriginal languages and the end of the myth of an egalitarian Australia. I start with the assumption that all of our losses have been amplified by the pandemic.

Early settler accounts offer something of an insight into our country and how we dealt with loss and death. Aboriginal death practices on the Murray are described as 'curiosities', with their physical artefacts becoming keepsakes for the colonialists:

> In 1838, Mr. Joseph Hawdon observed some skull-shaped caps, made of white plaster, which he thought was obtained by burning shells and grinding them into powder. They were laid on the grave of a native near Lake Bonnie on the Murray River. He says that inside the cap was a network of twine. Mr. Hawdon states that he also noticed a great quantity of crystallized lime or gypsum in the locality; it was in masses some tons weight.
>
> (Mathews, 1909, p. 318)

Putting aside the ethics of our time, this text describes our First Peoples as having deep practices that will be important as we strive towards reconciliation and truth telling. Aboriginal thinker Kim McCaul writes:

> More than 70 years later [than the writing of A. P. Elkin in the 1930s], traditional ritual practice has ceased in large parts of Australia but as this book [a collection of essays], demonstrates Aboriginal cultural beliefs about death continue and funeral practices, even if seemingly Anglo Australian, carry very distinct cultural markers. While death is a universal human experience, the manner in which death is experienced continues to represent a significant division between Aboriginal societies and the dominant culture in which many now find themselves embedded.
>
> (McCaul, 2009, p. 278)

As such I wish to reflect on the effect of colonisation on this country's ability to process loss. Let us imagine a country where sacred song, language and ritual are unencumbered by forced settlement, warfare and cultural destruction. How might the losses of COVID-19 have been responded to in such a country?

Contrast this to our contemporary experiences. In twenty-first-century Australia, death is often fashioned into a process that seeks to lessen its deadening pain. Most Australians do not die on country or at home with their families; they die alone in hospitals or nursing homes. In the last week of life, many Australians are given a cocktail of opioids to relieve the pain of passing. After death, the family has a short time with the body before it is cleaned up, removed, painted and packed in a wooden box. The White Lady company, which employs predominantly white women (no irony intended) as funeral celebrants symbolises a trend of moving away from ritual towards a type of monochromatic humanism:

> At White Lady Funerals, our philosophy is to – with a woman's understanding – help families reflect on and celebrate the life of their loved one, and to provide a funeral service of remembrance that is as unique as the individual the funeral service is created for. This is what sets us apart from other funeral service providers. Our female funeral directors gently guide you through the arrangement process. We understand that each family is unique, with their own traditions and personal requests. A woman's understanding of these matters can make all the difference to the precious memories that your family will have forever.
>
> (White Lady Funerals, 2023)

I have nothing against the funeral industry, but it is worthwhile to examine its assumptions.

Funerals such as this are possibly more artistic works than religious rituals. We might ask what is a 'woman's understanding'? We might also ask whether Australian women understand death better because they are less likely to be in full-time employment, have superannuation, or are more likely to suffer physical or sexualised violence.

To make sense of how we do loss in Australia, I need to compare the death industry to my own tradition. In my tradition of Mizrachi Judaism, described by my elders as being 2,500 years old, text and ritual are used to process grief. Death brings Mizrachi Jews back to the synagogue, no matter what they believe.

My father asked me to speak the central prayer of Judaism at the moment of his final breath years before his death. This is because he wanted to die like Rabbi Akiva, who had, according to Jewish tradition, recited the Sh'mah as a prayer on his final outward breath to release his soul from the body.

דהא ’ה ונ’אנולא ’ה לא’שי עמש
Sh'mah Yisrael Adonai Elohainu Adonai Ehad
Hear O Israel the Lord is God the Lord is One

While this is only the first line, I think you get the point. My father taught the Sh'mah to me so I could return the prayer to him at the time of his passing. When I sang the *Kaddish* (a memorial prayer) at his funeral, I felt thousands of years of collective grief behind me.

Then there are the rituals. There is the *K'riah*, the tearing of a shirt, a seven-day memorial candle that must never cease, the practice of sitting *Shiva*, which means that a mourner sits on low benches or stools. Men do not shave, women wear no make-up, mourners cover their mirrors and do not wear shoes if possible.

A. P. Benders wrote about Jewish death rituals in 1894. Focusing on the Ashkenazi Jews of Europe – and being aware of anti-Semitism and how easily a Jew can be seen as a primitive throwback – his tone looks to identify with the European Enlightenment. He describes a journey of the soul:

As the soul is leaving the body, a threefold call is heard from Heaven, 'O son of Adam, hast thou abandoned the world, or has the world abandoned thee; hast thou gathered of the world, or has the world gathered of thee; hast thou slain the world, or has the world slain thee?' In this moment the sound occasioned by the divorce of soul from body reaches from one end of the world to the other, but none hears it … [It is stated] that the sound is heard by the cock alone.

(Bender, 1894, p. 101)

White ladies and candle sticks

Contrast this to the White Lady universe. At a White Lady funeral, we are offered a mediated and safe process. A funeral will typically consist of relaxing music, curated readings from Christianity or the religion of the deceased, a slideshow and an ecumenical blessing. After that we get on with things, the body of the deceased is (usually) cremated and some time must pass before the scattering of the ashes.

We have structures that mostly work for us. We can navigate death until the time of our own reckoning, or the times we cannot see coming, such as war or pandemic. At these times, we need something more, because death is suddenly everywhere. If we are lucky, we might find a text to meditate on. I love this text of Donne (1571–1631):

Bring us, O Lord God, at our last awakening into the house and gate of heaven, to enter into that gate and dwell in that house, where there shall be no darkness nor dazzling, but one equal light; no noise nor silence, but one equal music; no fears nor hopes, but one equal possession; no ends nor beginnings, but one equal eternity; in the habitations of thy glory and dominion, world without end. Amen.

(Donne, n.d.)

Text and poetry therefore matter to us, all the more because of the pandemic. Art suspends disbelief and allows a web of imagination to hold our idiosyncrasies together. I know of few who do this better than Rilke:

This clumsy living that moves lumbering
as if in ropes through what is not done,
reminds us of the awkward way the swan walks.
And to die, which is the letting go
of the ground we stand on and cling to every day,
is like the swan, when he nervously lets himself down

into the water, which receives him gaily
and which flows joyfully under
and after him, wave after wave,
while the swan, unmoving and marvellously calm,
is pleased to be carried, each moment more fully grown,
more like a king, further and further on.

(Rilke, 1977)

What I have learned from the pandemic is that Australia needs help to deal with the pain of mass death. Artists can help us understand what loss is and provide an experience for those of us who no longer identify with a religious tradition. We might listen to Nick Cave singing about a non-interventionist god, *Tabula Rasa* by Avo Pärt, or any music as long as it means something to us. We also need music when we are faced with life and death.

Artists, pandemics and economics

We live in the economy that we chose. The 'gig economy', and the deregulation of labour that the term represents, is named after the lives of artists. I rang a number of jazz musicians in preparation for this chapter and asked what a jazz musician received per gig in 1980 compared to today. The answer was that a jazz musician received about A$150 per gig in 1980 and the fee has not changed since. This is a shocking disclosure. Imagine this happening in any other industry: well, we probably cannot, because it would never happen.

The Australia Council's longstanding project 'Making Art Work: An Economic Study of Professional Artists in Australia' has followed the working life of artists for over 30 years. The 2017 iteration describes the pre-pandemic situation thus:

> It is increasingly difficult for artists to make a living from their creative work, which is at odds with the increasing personal value Australians place on the arts, and the significant economic, social and cultural impact they have on our communities. Average total incomes for artists remain 21% below the Australian workforce average, and income from creative work has decreased by 19% over the last seven years.
>
> (Australia Council for the Arts, 2017)

The 2023 *Insight Report* details the Australian government's cultural expenditure from 2007–08 to 2020–21 and shows an increase in arts funding during the pandemic, demonstrating that arts funding can be directly linked to economic policy:

> Since the start of the pandemic, governments have directed $12.5 billion to cultural and creative industries in response to COVID-19, in the form of targeted COVID-19 support and wider economy COVID-19 support. This represents 46% of total government expenditure on cultural and creative industries (both COVID-19 and non-COVID-19 expenditure) in the last two financial years. $8.1 billion of this was in 2020–21.
>
> (A New Approach, 2023, p. 48)

The data are clear, our funding of the arts, relative to other territories, is poor:

> Government spending on recreation, culture and religion in Australia is below that of many of our international peers. In 2020, OECD countries on average spent 1.35% of total GDP for the purposes of recreation, culture and religion; Australia spent 0.98% of its GDP, placing us ahead of other English-speaking countries (the United States and United Kingdom) yet 23rd out of 31 OECD countries. Australia has remained below the OECD average from 2017 to 2020.
>
> (A New Approach, 2023, p. 48)

I find Australia's ranking of twenty-third out of 31 OECD countries to be revealing. The Anglosphere, like Australia, funds its arts poorly. Bill Browne's 2020 *Australia Institute Brief* states the case for greater funding by showing the inherent value of the arts:

- The arts and entertainment sector contributes $14.7 billion per year in value added (GDP).
- Arts and entertainment employs 193,600 Australians.
- For every million dollars in turnover, arts and entertainment produce 9 jobs while the construction industry only produces around 1 job.
- Arts and entertainment employs 51% women and 49% men.
- Arts and entertainment related industries (saw) the largest pandemic shutdowns.

> (Browne, 2020, p. 1)

The number of artists – 193,600 – is telling. Coal mining employs 49,600 Australians; engineering and construction, 107,700; and finance, 190,600. Only agriculture (281,600) and building construction (306,500) employ more Australians. Browne concludes that an expanded definition of the arts, which includes recreation services, information media and telecommunications, is possible. He quotes Cunningham and McCutcheon who calculate that 593,830 Australians were engaged in creative employment in 2016 (Browne, 2020).

The research also finds many artists are in precarious employment:

> There also have been some key shifts in the seven years since practising professional artists were last surveyed. Cost of living pressures experienced across the community are felt keenly by artists. Total income levels have gone backwards in real terms, driven by a decrease in income from creative work. Lack of income from creative work is now the biggest perceived immediate barrier to professional development, replacing lack of time. In this environment, artists are increasingly applying their creative skills outside the arts.
>
> (Australia Council for the Arts, 2017)

There are other studies that show the economic value of the arts but I think we get the message that 'we' would win any fair economic debate about arts funding, if there were to be such a debate. The reality is that there will not be a major debate about arts policy, despite the well-received changes in Labor government policy in 2022, because most of the country is pretty happy with the current level of funding for the arts.

I suggest that in having an economic argument we might lose the real debate. The debate I would like to have goes something like this: unless we value the arts for their indecipherable qualities, we will never fund them as we should, for there will always be a greater economic imperative than the arts. What government will drastically increase arts funding when homelessness, early childhood and aged care are in crisis?

My music school offers a case in point. ANU restructured its School of Music in 2012, ending its status as a conservatoire. Funding was reduced because of so-called economic realism: the school needed to change because its model of teaching musicians one-on-one was too expensive for the values of the university. The continuation of the school (and one-on-one teaching) was not achieved by a better economic plan; it was achieved by a community winning an argument about the inherent value of music to society and the loss that Canberra would suffer without a national standard music school.

What we might conclude is that we too often govern the arts with the presumption of a return on investment. In my opinion, this is fundamentally flawed, because, though economically justifiable, the arts are rarely successfully justified in this manner, despite the wealth of data:

> The arts and entertainment sector is labour intensive. For every million dollars of turnover in the *Creative and Performing Arts Activities* category, nine people are employed according to ABS estimates. Nine jobs per million dollars turnover is far higher than more capital-intensive industries. For example, the ABS's *Building Construction* category sees around 1 job per million in turnover, the whole *Mining* industry has 0.59, while the *Oil and Gas Extraction* category has just 0.25. In other words, $4 million in turnover is required on average for each job in oil and gas.
>
> (Browne, 2020, p. 4)

Technology as a disruptor

As the gig economy morphed into 'Work Choices', the technologies of art and music making revolutionised music, providing new hope for the independent artist and musician. This means that our data might be missing something significant – that there might be millions of Australian arts makers who are artists, without being part of the formal arts economy. Just as someone can be an aged carer without working in a nursing home, someone can be an artist without making art their employment.

I will concentrate on music as I know the discipline. Twenty-three years ago, my professional home recording studio cost over A$30,000. Ten years ago, I would have paid around A$10,000 for a comparable sound. Now that sound quality costs around A$400, meaning that a teenager can purchase equipment to make professional music in their home.

Earlier this year, I recorded a piece of music on equipment that cost less than A$200 and compared it to digital recordings I made in the year 2000. There is hardly any difference. It is, therefore, according to my calculator,

150 times cheaper to make a home recording than it was 20 years ago. The only other area I can think of that has had a similar growth in productivity in relation to price is computer chip processing.

The software has also been revolutionised. If you buy an Apple computer, entry-level audio and video software is supplied; the computer comes with thousands of audio loops in every conceivable style that can be dragged and dropped into a piece of music. A user does not have to play an instrument to make music; many computer programs automatically adjust music to the speed, time signature and key of a piece, meaning that a beginner can produce music immediately. Can't sing in tune? No problem in 2023.

Samples and synthesis are digital processes that allow sounds to be triggered by electronic or MIDI keyboards, meaning that acoustic instruments (and the years taken to master them) are no longer needed. Modern sampling started in earnest in the 1970s as part of the expansion of electroacoustic music practice. Fifty years later, samples are ubiquitous. When we turn on the television, the majority of the orchestras we hear are sampled. Every instrument, every articulation of an orchestra, has been recorded and processed, meaning that any bedroom musician can have access to a virtual orchestra, a suite of 'world' instruments, a concert grand piano and thousands of synthesised sounds.

To see how good sampling could be, I sampled some of my instruments with a company called Evolution Series. This was no small undertaking. The virtual oud (an 11-string fretless Arabic instrument) took two weeks to record and nearly two years to code. When completed, I could play my own instrument on a keyboard. The catch is that anyone else could play that instrument for US$139. This is how the marketeers described my virtual oud:

> This high-end instrument can best be described as having a lovely warm, full, yet precise tone. Engineered to the highest standards, Oud offers endless creativity. It was a true honour for us to create this inspiring instrument, and know you will enjoy playing it.
>
> (Ammar, 2023)

I have been working on a project called 'The War on the Critical Edition', my own personal music disruption process, for some years. It questions assumptions of art music and the privilege it inhabits within the canon. I started by recomposing from medieval scores primarily the music of the twelfth-century abbess, Hildegard of Bingen. I then cut up my own music into GarageBand loops and allowed others to make what they wanted out of my music.

In a series of papers, I then looked at the disruptions of technology. I incorporated this into my teaching. In my introductory musicology lecture at ANU School of Music, I play two versions of Debussy's *Claire de lune*. One is played on a Steinway and recorded onto analogue tape, the other on a A$100 MIDI keyboard, with its data used to trigger a synthetic piano. Fifty per cent of my listeners cannot hear the difference. It is not that technology is changing music, it is that music has already been changed. Music makers and schools are caught between two worlds: the responsibility to use and teach the important skills of previous generations; and the imperatives of music making in this century, which involve recording, data manipulation and artificial intelligence (AI). I quote a paper of mine from nearly 15 years ago:

> The computer has revolutionised music, and art music composers and institutions are only now coming to terms with the ramifications. The recording of music offers a potentially perfect copy of a performance that can then be transcribed or learnt orally, making it a meeting place between oral and written forms. It can be argued that notation, as we historically understand it, is now only one of a number of processes to preserve and record music. Innovations such as the Music Instrument Digital Interface (MIDI), the Digital Audio Workstation (DAW), and wave file composition (whereby the composition takes place after the recording of the individual parts), have replaced traditional scoring for many composers. In addition to this we now extend the term composition and composer well beyond the historical Western definitions.
>
> (Cunio, 2010, p. 15)

Let me offer a short example. One of my colleagues and PhD students, the jazz/rebetika saxophonist and composer Constantin Campbell, recorded an ensemble for his doctorate. The recording was constructed as jazz and traditional music: vintage microphones into a Neve console, no editing and almost no audio processing. The idea was to make a recording in the same manner that recordings were made in the mid-twentieth century. It sounded beautiful.

Normally such a recording would be taken to a mastering engineer, who would process the tracks with analogue equipment to impart what is commonly described as 'analogue warmth'. In this case, an AI mastering platform was used. The AI algorithm referenced seminal recordings and was able to create a realistic master through the tools of equalisation, compression, limiting and reverberance. It was, in essence, a self-driving car.

The wave of AI is breaking over music. Algorithmic composition, the notion of having computer systems that can respond to the music of a score or the music of an improviser, is not new, though it is moving out of the elite institutions that seeded it and becoming available to a wide range of musicians. It is already possible to program new music in the style of Bach and Mozart, and it seems conceivable that within 10 years we will have film and game scorebots (scoring robots) to generate and realise music without human involvement.

Technology goes further than AI. Not only can we sample instruments, but also voices. We can analyse a voice, select a virtual voice, type in some text and have a computer-generated replicant sing a vocal line. While this is not indistinguishable from a live singer, it will not be long until vocal samples are comparable to virtual instruments, meaning a whole pop album might be made in a bedroom without a note being played.

This is democratic capitalism in action. A lot of people are making music who would not otherwise have had a chance to do so. This could not be more different to the structures of a generation ago, in which music was owned by conglomerates who owned and charged the artist, recouping outlandish expenses from record sales, holding onto the rights of the music for decades after a record was made and had sold out. In other words, anyone can be an artist.

The artist and the pandemic

I would like to imagine a socially inclusive model of artistic participation as a possible response to the pandemic. Stenberg (2016) describes a project in Sweden in which visual artists are engaged to work and partner in organisations that deliver health and welfare, cultural policy and innovation for a period of eight months in a half-time position:

> To be able to understand the artists' working conditions in general, it is important to grasp how the present art field and cultural policy works. The use of the artist as a creative resource at workplaces is part of the current cultural policy in Sweden. This policy has changed over time. When the welfare state was at its peak in the 1960s and

1970s, the state policy was to support individual visual artists and artistic experiments with public funding. Since public resources later became limited, the cultural policy promoted artists to be oriented towards the market or to be involved in projects with different collaborators in society, as in the described projects. Politicians want art to become more popular among citizens in order to engage people in artistic activities and events, a policy called 'cultural democracy'.

(Stenberg, 2016)

Lauri Anderson's NASA residence is of interest to many artists because it lends credibility to the idea that an artist might make a meaningful contribution in areas such as the hard sciences. Anderson wrote for the *Smithsonian* magazine in 2008:

The opportunity came about completely out of the blue, as many things are in my life. Somebody called and said 'Do you want to be the first artist in residence at NASA?' and I said 'What does that mean in a space program?' and they said 'Well, we don't know what that means. What does it mean to you?' I was like 'Who are you people? What does it mean to me? What are you talking about?'

(Fletcher, 2008)

What we see is that an artist can be more than an entertainer or part of a creative industry. If there is a socially and economically justifiable role for artists that serves our society, which there clearly is, I suggest that we fund it. This moves us towards the idea of a universal basic income for artists, an idea that might have seemed ludicrous in pre-pandemic Australia.

In Finland, the idea of a basic income was trialled and reported on during the pandemic, as described in *The Guardian*:

The scheme also gave some participants 'the possibility to try and live their dreams', Blomberg-Kroll said. 'Freelancers and artists and entrepreneurs had more positive views on the effects of the basic income, which some felt had created opportunities for them to start businesses.' It also encouraged some participants to get more involved in society, by undertaking voluntary work, for example. 'Some found the guaranteed income increased the possibility for them to do things like providing informal care for their family or their neighbours,' said one of the researchers, Christian Kroll.

(Henley, 2020)

How might this look post pandemic? Artists would be able to drive innovation, development and multidisciplinarity – some of the skills that are most needed in our economy.

Responses

I would like to state my position. I described my artistic sensibilities for the *Music Trust* e-zine in 2021, remembering myself at 25, my first year of music school:

> Music was still burning but I had no desire to write the music I had been taught to write. I was a young man investigating Said's *Orientalism*, free improvisation and microtonality who loved mucking around with technology and I did not hear people like myself on the radio. I hankered for the scales of my childhood, and a melodic ease that might only be matched in a baroque cadenza. I wanted to hear it in new art music. In a moment of blind optimism that has informed the rest of my life, I realised that I might be able to live and work in these two worlds. I could be a musicologist composer, an activist composer.
>
> (Cunio, 2021)

With that disclosure in mind, I ask a question: how many people did you lose? It is a provocative question, one rarely heard outside of war. While there were not so many initial deaths in Australia, the worldwide numbers were staggering. I ask again: how many people did you lose? Knowing that you cannot ask me back I will share a little. I have lost five friends and a relative. Two of them were connected with this project. Not all of them died directly from the pandemic, but the pandemic changed the manner and timing of their deaths.

UK poet Hollie McNish wrote about her experiences in *The Guardian* in 2021, alongside the poem that follows this quotation:

> My maternal grandmother died during the coronavirus pandemic. She was my last surviving grandparent and one of the people I've felt closest to on this small, spinning planet. As with many other people grieving loved ones, I watched her funeral on a live stream.
>
> As the allotted time grew closer and a looped video of a calming waterfall assured me that my internet connection was working, I began panicking about what to wear, where in my house to sit, whether to have a glass of prosecco or a cup of tea, as if these decisions

were important. I was watching it on my own. I wondered what other people across the world were wearing and eating at funerals now that no one could see them disrespecting traditions.

(McNish et al., 2021)

chasing ceremony/convincing myself, by Hollie McNish [excerpt]
i'll not get to your funeral.
that's fine.
i know you'll not make Mine.
you hate the fussing anyway.
your favourite colour's yellow
not black.
on your street, when next door died
too soon before you did
neighbours clapped the passing hearse
as if the corpse were on a royal tour
you turned towards your daughters
here –
don't you dare do that for me
hair cradled into rollers
each night until the night you left
still lifting life with curls
the laws do not allow me
to stand and watch a lifetime
exit puppet-show-sized curtains
as tears try to console each other
two metres apart.

(McNish et al., 2021)

Covid Mantras

When COVID-19 struck I knew what I wanted to do. In the spirit of my studies into musical disruption I aimed for home studio perfection. I wanted to see how lifelike I could make new classical music, to break the ivory tower of the concert hall as the place where high art is made, so I made a 'song cycle' – it is posh for album! The project comprised two albums, one of songs (*Covid Mantras*) and one of poems (*Covid Sonnets*).

Covid Mantras was made at home during lockdown. I had built up my home studio some years ago, experimenting to find ways to make my home sound like a concert hall. This process started in 2006 during an ABC project, *The Sacred Fire* (music of Hildegard of Bingen). One of the pieces on the recording was subject to a technical issue and a stanza of the recorded text was lost. Before calling the ensemble back to the ABC, I analysed the reverberance of the Eugene Goosens Hall. I then used the same model microphone and pre-amplifier, recorded the passage in my lounge room and processed the recording with equalisation and reverberance. No-one could tell that I had inserted a 'fake' version of the Eugene Goosens Hall into a mainstream classical recording.

Back to the lockdown. I contacted a number of writers, who wrote and recorded poems of response onto portable audio recorders I posted to them. In the cases where we could (legally) meet, I recorded them. What did the writers do? They responded to loss, sometimes by looking at a major event in their own lives, sometimes by comparing social isolation to the climate crisis, and sometimes by processing their own grief and loss. This is *Covid Sonnets*. Listen to them on the following link: kimcunio.bandcamp.com/album/covid-sonnets.

After the poems were recorded, I spent some weeks conducting field recordings within the 5-kilometre radius I was allowed to cover on my daily walks. I combined them with the poems to complete the first stage of the project.

I then started *Covid Mantras*, a song cycle. I knew the cycle would be about loss, about people dying or withering away from the inside in social isolation. I wanted to make a requiem for those who lived and died alone, especially after one of the poets passed away during the project. Listen to *Covid Mantras* on the following link: kimcunio.bandcamp.com/album/covid-mantras-2.

The fact that the recording was undertaken in a bedroom is not new for popular music, though it is still a relatively novel process in art music. This was also the first piece of vocal music I composed entirely through improvisation. The piano parts were played in one take, with no pre-planning. Vocal parts were improvised over the piano, recorded onto my phone, then sent to the singer. There was no score.

The piano, a symbol of the dominance of the nineteenth and twentieth centuries is no longer the king of the heap. I played a nearly 50-year-old Kawai piano of limited sound quality. The music was recorded with as many microphones as I could fit around the piano. The voice was recorded after the piano, as with popular music.

Soprano Heather Lee, a long-time collaborator, recorded the song cycle on a tube microphone designed for popular music. This made the voice sound extremely close to the listener. Lee recorded mostly in one take, continuing the improvisatory aesthetic of the project. Both piano and voice were sent to an artificial reverb to give the impression of a concert hall, in this case, the splendid ANU music hall.

The work was recorded, edited and mixed entirely on headphones, something that is frowned upon by audio professionals, as certain frequencies are boosted unnaturally by them. There is also no crosstalk, the mixing of sound between two speakers, an effect that aids mixing. For brevity I will outline the songs as they are my primary response.

In the first song, I imagine Rumi as he might live in pandemic Australia. The piano plays a simple, almost folk-like minimalist in G Minor, with a sostenuto pedal, softening the tone.

> Come to me wherever you are,
> This is no time
> For loneliness.
>
> Walk with me wherever you want
> I do not mind where're we go,
> Wait for me wherever you are.
> This is no time
> For loneliness.
> There is already
> Too much despair.

A Prayer for the Time of Death is built around a 12-voice mantra, newly written, my response to the memorial prayers of Judaism, combined with bamboo flute and Vedic chanting from the nuns of the Vedanta order. The piano plays a long, slow progression in a minor scale, with everything built over its texture.

> May your passing not be in vain
> May someone for those whom have fallen
> Speak their name
> With love, and compassion.

This is followed by *Masks*, a song that looks to respond to daily life with masks. The piano plays sequential chord progressions that do not quite fit together.

What is it you are hiding?
As you don this mask
Will you fly like Harlequin?
Why do you fear this mask?

Too often we hide
My heart overflows with love,
What is it you are hiding?

We then have a piano solo. *Song to Jaie* was improvised to honour the death of a friend who passed away at this time. Next is *Loss*, a song that looks to respond to the daily struggle of living and working. It features vocal melisma and has the largest crescendo of the cycle.

This Groundhog Day
Is it every day from now?
I am waiting
For you to come to me.

You came to me in my dreams
You promised
Yes, I am going on
I am back at work now.
I wear my suffering on the inside
As I talk of things this Groundhog Day

I am waiting
You came to me in my dreams
You promised
Just close your eyes my friends
And see the well of suffering we own
And as we slow the wheel is
Ground down to the metal.
For all those whom we have loved
Are calling from too far away.

After *Loss*, we move to *Remembrance*, a song that works with a slow ostinato and simple melodic line. This is the first piece in a major key.

I miss you in the mornings
I miss you in those Summer breezes
I miss you how you'd make the tea
I miss you in the afternoon
I miss the way you would hear the birds sing
I miss the way that you would brush your hair

129

I miss the way that you would always care
About those that were alone
For you are in my memories

I miss you in the evenings
I miss the way you would call for second helpings
I miss your way of ending things
I miss you as you should be sleeping
I miss you as I should be feeling better
I miss you as I cannot believe
I am alone now
For you are in my memories.

The final song, *Night Mantras* combines the earlier mantra of *A Prayer for the Time of Death* with the *Om Asatoma* mantra of Vedanta Hinduism. It is played and sung in Rag Kalyan and the Lydian mode. It imagines the state of peace that I might aspire to at the time of my death.

Om Asatoma Sad Gamaya
Tamasoma Jyotir Gamaya,
Mrityoma Amritam Gamaya
Om Shanti Shanti Shanti.

Lead me from Unreal to real
Darkness to light,
Immortality, peace in this life
I am Peace, Peace, Peace.

I finish with two short invocations, the second a quote from an earlier paper.

May we remember the service that our artists gave us during the isolation of the pandemic. May we see the role of the arts as crucial to our wellbeing. May we be makers of art and supporters of the arts. May the arts inspire and delight us.

May each of us play a part in making a world of greater justice. May we meaningfully respond to the forced dispossession of our First Nations, for this land was never ceded. May we fix this planet before we burn it (Cunio, 2021).

References

Ammar, A. (2023). *Evolution series, world strings oud 2.0 world series.* www.evolution series.com/portfolio/world-strings-oud-2-0/.

A New Approach. (2023). *The big picture 3: Expenditure on artistic, cultural and creative activity by governments in Australia in 2007–08 to 2020–21.* newapproach. org.au/insight-reports/the-big-picture-3/.

Australia Council for the Arts. (2017). *Making art work: A summary and response by the Australia Council for the Arts.* creative.gov.au/workspace/uploads/files/making-art-work-companion-repo-5a05105696225.pdf.

Bender, A. P. (1894). Beliefs, rites, and customs of the Jews, connected with death, burial, and mourning. (As illustrated by the Bible and later Jewish literature) IV. *The Jewish Quarterly Review, 7*(1), 101–118. www.jstor.org/stable/1450333.

Browne, B. (2020). *Economic importance of the arts and entertainment sector* [Background brief]. The Australia Institute. australiainstitute.org.au/wp-content/uploads/2020/12/Background-Brief-Economic-importance-of-arts-and-entertainment-WEB.pdf.

Cunio, K. (2010). *The war on the critical edition volume 1* [Conference paper]. CreateWorld 2009: 'Mobile me – Creativity on the go', Brisbane, Australia. openresearch-repository.anu.edu.au/bitstream/1885/140962/1/63763_1.pdf.

Cunio, K. (2021, 4 October). Inside the musician. Kim Cunio: Cultural journeys and music making in a changing world. *Music Trust.* musictrust.com.au/loud mouth/inside-the-musician-kim-cunio-cultural-journeys-and-music-making-in-a-changing-world/.

Donne, J. (n.d.). *Bring us, O Lord God, sermon.* Republished as *A prayer by John Donne, contributed by Stuart Forster (2019).* scalar.fas.harvard.edu/resources-for-loss/a-prayer-by-john-donne-contributed-by-stuart-forster.

Fletcher, K. R. (2008, August). Laurie Anderson. *Smithsonian.* www.smithsonian mag.com/arts-culture/laurie-anderson-779875/.

Henley, J. (2020, 7 May). Finnish basic income pilot improved wellbeing, study finds. *The Guardian.* www.theguardian.com/society/2020/may/07/finnish-basic-income-pilot-improved-wellbeing-study-finds-coronavirus.

Mathews, R. H. (1909). Some burial customs of the Australian Aborigines. *Proceedings of the American Philosophical Society, 48*(192), 313–318. www.jstor. org/stable/984160.

McCaul, K. (2009). Review [of *Mortality, mourning and mortuary practices in Indigenous Australia*, by K. Glaskin, M. Tonkinson, Y. Musharbash & V. Burbank]. *Aboriginal History, 33*, 278–280. www.jstor.org/stable/24046846.

McNish, H., Armitage, S., McGough, R., Tempest, K., Bernard, J. & Antrobus, R. (2021, 8 May). Windows on the world: Pandemic poems by Simon Armitage, Hollie McNish, Kae Tempest and more. *The Guardian*. www.theguardian.com/books/2021/may/08/windows-on-the-world-pandemic-poems-by-simon-armitage-hollie-mcnish-kae-tempest-and-more.

Pearson, M. P. (2017). Dead and (un)buried: Reconstructing attitudes to death in long-term perspective. In J. Bradbury & C. Scarre (Eds), *Engaging with the dead: Exploring changing human beliefs about death, mortality and the human body* (pp. 129–137). Oxbow Books. doi.org/10.2307/j.ctt1vgw6s0.13.

Rilke, R. M. (1977). *The voices* (Robert Bly, Trans). Ally Press.

Stenberg, H. (2016). How is the artist role affected when artists are participating in projects in work life? *International Journal of Qualitative Studies on Health and Well-being, 11*(1). doi.org/10.3402/qhw.v11.30549.

White Lady Funerals. (2023). *About us*. www.whiteladyfunerals.com.au/about-us/.

8

'Ten footies, one small saltie': The Northern Territory experience and the shadow pandemic

Chay Brown

Introduction: Getting home

At the start of the pandemic, I was returning home from presenting my research on violence against women in the Northern Territory at an international conference in Edinburgh (Brown, 2020a). I was travelling with my mother – a visually impaired and deaf woman who is a survivor of domestic violence. We made it back to Australia a day before the borders closed but my mother had become sick on the plane. We landed at Sydney International Airport and immediately reported to health officials, who advised us to get on the next plane to our home, a remote town in the very centre of Australia called Alice Springs. There she could isolate in her home. Several Aboriginal community–controlled organisations[1] in Alice Springs had successfully lobbied the Northern Territory government to close the Northern Territory's borders. Once more, my mother and I had to race home.

---

1   Aboriginal community–controlled organisations are established by Aboriginal communities and led by Aboriginal and Torres Strait Islander people – the Indigenous people of Australia.

The Northern Territory is Australia's least populated state or territory. It is a vast geographical area roughly the size of Texas but with a population of less than 250,000 people. Approximately 130,000 of the Territory's population lives in the capital city of Darwin, while the remainder is dispersed across the vast country that extends from the red desert heart of Australia right through to the tropical north – this equates to around 0.16 people per square kilometre. My hometown, Mparntwe/Alice Springs,[2] has a population of approximately 25,000 and its nearest capital city is approximately 1,500 kilometres away.

Two days after the Territory's borders closed, I gave my final oral presentation for my doctoral thesis on what works to prevent violence against women in the Northern Territory (Brown, 2020b). The day after that, the lockdowns were announced. I remember my feelings of frustration and fear as government and public health officials made announcements and introduced public health measures, none of which recognised the increasing risk to women and children experiencing violence during this time.

It turned out that my mother did not have COVID-19, but I remember her saying to me: 'If this [lockdown] had been several years ago, it would have been the end of us.' She knew, just as I did, that violence would increase during this time. Our race home was illustrative of the uncertainty of the time and the fast pace with which decisions were made and measures introduced. Perhaps there was not the time to consider all eventualities, but the safety of women and children experiencing violence should have been centred.

No-one enjoyed the lockdowns; however, for many women and children around the world, they were unsurvivable.

I was born and raised in Mparntwe/Alice Springs and the surrounding communities. This is where I choose to undertake my research on violence against women, from the lens of lived experience and within my own home and connections. This is also where I lived throughout the COVID-19 pandemic. Much of what I refer to in this chapter is from my own lived experience, filtered from my research on violence against women and informed by all my relationships and connections with the service sector in the Northern Territory.

---

2   Mparntwe is the Arrernte name of the place now called Alice Springs. The Arrernte people are the traditional custodians and have lived and practised their lore and culture on Arrernte Country, including Mparntwe, for tens of thousands of years.

The chapter begins by providing some necessary context on violence against women in Australia, before giving an account of the Northern Territorian experience of the pandemic and public health measures. The chapter then theorises why violence against women increased during the pandemic, before concluding and offering some lessons that should have been learned but, perhaps, were not.

The Northern Territory

The Northern Territory is characterised by its extreme isolation and remoteness with respect to the rest of Australia. Most of the Northern Territory is neither urban nor regional, which means that access to basic goods, services and infrastructure is reduced. For example, for some remote communities, the nearest supermarket is an eight-hour drive away. In the Northern Territory, we often refer to these remote areas as 'out bush'. Many of these areas are inaccessible for large parts of the year when the wet season makes the rivers impassable; even during the dry season, there are few sealed roads. Communities are further isolated by the lack of phone network coverage and access to the internet.

Many Northern Territory communities also have inadequate access to housing. Homelessness in the Northern Territory is 12 times the national average, and many people live in overcrowded housing, often with more than 20 people living in a single dwelling (NT Shelter, n.d.). Some people live without electricity and running water, and many have only recently gained access to these basic services (Moyo, 2014; Wahlquist, 2017).

The Northern Territory is also set apart by its high Indigenous population (32 per cent compared to 3 per cent nationally) and its rich language and culture – more than 100 Indigenous languages can be heard spoken fluently on Territory streets every day (Australian Institute of Health and Welfare, 2022; Northern Territory Government, 2022).

The Northern Territory is also unique because, unlike other jurisdictions in Australia, it is not a state, meaning that its elected government does not have the same legislative or fiscal capabilities as the states. It is dependent on Australia's federal government for its funding and can be subject to federal intervention at any time, such as the Northern Territory Emergency Response 2007–22, which saw the federal government deploy the Australian military into the Northern Territory in response to allegations of child sexual assault within remote Aboriginal communities. Northern Territorians refer to this as 'the Intervention'. Many of the measures imposed during the Intervention are still in place today and have resulted in a culture of distrust of anyone from 'down south'. This term refers to anyone from urban south-eastern parts of Australia but, really, is used to refer to anyone from outside the Territory, especially those who position themselves as experts despite having little understanding of the Northern Territory context.

The Northern Territory's experience of the COVID-19 pandemic was, therefore, quite unusual, as the Northern Territory government became a leader in many ways. For instance, the Northern Territory was the first jurisdiction in Australia to close its borders (Allam, 2020). The experience of the pandemic was also different in the Northern Territory because of its high rates of violence.

What we know about violence against women

Violence against women, often referred to by its most common forms of domestic, family and sexual violence, is a problem that transcends geographic, social and cultural boundaries. In Australia, one in three women experience physical violence and one in five experience sexual violence from the age of 15 (Our Watch, 2021). Women most commonly experience violence at the hands of a current or former male partner, and, on average, one woman is killed each week (Our Watch, 2021). No matter the gender of the victim, violence is overwhelmingly perpetrated by men, and domestic, family and sexual violence is most commonly perpetrated by men against women and children (Flood et al., 2022).

The Northern Territory has the highest rates of domestic family and sexual violence in Australia. Sixty-three per cent of assaults in the Northern Territory are related to domestic and family violence, and women make up 63 per cent of the victims (Australian Bureau of Statistics, 2022). In 2021, domestic and family violence–related assaults were three times the national average, and five times that of most other jurisdictions (Australian Bureau of Statistics, 2022; Brown & Leung, 2023; Office of the Attorney-General and Justice, 2023). Domestic, family and sexual violence in the Northern Territory is also disproportionately severe, with weapons being used in two of every five assaults. In 2021, domestic violence–related homicides were approximately seven times the national average (Australian Bureau of Statistics, 2022; Brown & Leung, 2023).

However, these data only reflect incidents of violence that have been reported to formal services – most likely the most severe of cases. Globally, less than 40 per cent of violence against women is reported, and less than 10 per cent of that is reported to police (United Nations Economic and Social Affairs, 2015). Data on violence against women in Australia, and particularly in the Northern Territory, are flawed and overly reliant on administrative data from police and services that do not and cannot capture the full picture of violence against women.

National surveys that capture prevalence, although more reliable than administrative data, also have limitations because they do not collect data in institutional settings and in very remote locations. Excluding very remote locations means that national surveys, like the *Personal Safety Survey*, also give an incomplete picture of the scale and severity of domestic, family and sexual violence in the Northern Territory. Therefore, although official rates of domestic, family and sexual violence are high in the Northern Territory – in reality, they are far higher. The COVID-19 pandemic exacerbated these rates: for instance, the victimisation rate for assault in the Northern Territory in 2021 was the highest in the bureau's 27-year time series (Australian Bureau of Statistics, 2021).

Despite these limitations, the problem of violence against women is well known. Yet even the available data were not marshalled to inform policy and public health measures at the beginning of the pandemic. Rather, violence against women was an afterthought, eventually included in public health considerations as a result of direct advocacy from specialist services (Carrington et al., 2021). Prior to this, the message was 'stay safe, stay home' – and little to no space or messaging was given to those for whom home was not safe.

The Northern Territory's experience of the pandemic and public health measures

The Northern Territory closed its borders in March 2020 (Allam, 2020). The reason for this was the Northern Territory's uniquely vulnerable population: a high rate of chronic disease (Weeramanthri, 2003; Zhao, 2008) coupled with an under-resourced and over-stretched healthcare system (NT Health, Aboriginal Medical Services Alliance Northern Territory [AMSANT], Northern Territory Primary Health Network, 2020). With the closure of the borders also came lockdowns and biosecurity zones. Both measures remained in place for an initial 12 weeks, then were reinstated on and off according to need for the next two years (Department of Health and Aged Care, 2022).

Lockdowns in the Northern Territory manifested similarly to elsewhere: businesses were closed, all non-essential workers were asked to work from home, there were travel limits, limits on food items at supermarkets, and limits on the number of people allowed in homes and public venues. However, in the Northern Territory these measures had far greater impact. Whereas in urban areas of Australia, people can shop online and have groceries delivered to their homes, these services are extremely limited, especially in regional areas, and non-existent in remote areas. For example, in Alice Springs, where I live, wait times for online food orders were often two weeks or more. Many Aboriginal communities, including Town Camps (small Aboriginal communities on the social and geographical fringes of Alice Springs), do not have access to the internet, and many have no phone network coverage. This impedes people's access to basic communication and safety, let alone their ability to do their weekly food shop.

Further, in the Northern Territory, where overcrowding and homelessness are commonplace (I have received reports of up to 45 people in a three-bedroom house), imposed limits on the number of people in homes and isolating at home were near impossible (Brown, 2019). Communicating these public health measures to a population spread over a vast geographical space, living in extremely remote areas, many of which had English as a third, fourth or even eighth language, was also extremely challenging. New concepts had to be communicated, and many were done so creatively, such as AMSANT's guide to social distancing in the Northern Territory (see Figure 8.1). These communications show the leadership of Aboriginal community-controlled organisations, which, after successfully lobbying to shut the borders, took charge not only of educating the population, but also of coordinating the health response and vaccinations.

Figure 8.1: Social distancing in the Northern Territory, 2020.
Source: Aboriginal Medical Services Alliance Northen Territory.

Biosecurity zones were drawn up and enforced around Aboriginal communities in the Northern Territory, with the borders patrolled by police. In the lead up to this, there was a massive push to return people from regional towns, such as Alice Springs, back out bush, the idea being that it was safer for people to be in remote communities, protected by biosecurity zones, with all non-essential travel restricted. Only people with permits could enter and leave the biosecurity zones; even people who lived 20 kilometres outside

Alice Springs needed a permit to get through the police blocks. Hundreds of people were put on buses and sent back to communities. Services reported concerns about where people would be staying and living when they got back to the communities, especially people with special health needs, such as those on dialysis and on daily medications. A support service worker reported to me her concerns about placing an elderly woman on a bus to return 'out bush': she believed the woman would be sleeping on a mattress outside, with no close supports to ensure she had access to, let alone took, her daily medications.

Other concerns about the biosecurity zones included how people would access affordable food and materials. Food in remote communities in the Northern Territory is incredibly expensive, with prices up to 56 per cent higher than in urban areas (Beazley, 2022; NATSIWA, 2020). Normally, people living in remote communities travel to regional hubs to do their food shopping, as it is cheaper, as well as to buy other items not available in remote communities, such as clothing and car parts. I remember the day that the biosecurity zones were lifted: an endless line of cars waited at the border to travel into Alice Springs in single file, many of them to do their shopping.

After the initial lockdowns, the Northern Territory opened internally. Restrictions on capacity for venues and social distancing policies remained but, this aside, life carried on pretty much as normal. The borders remained closed. There was the occasional snap lockdown, but these were rare, and the Northern Territory was successful in keeping COVID-19 out, with the first cases of local transmission not occurring until late 2021. It was not until then, late 2021 to early 2022, that the Northern Territory introduced mask mandates and other measures commonplace in other jurisdictions.

Despite its success in managing the COVID-19 pandemic, the Northern Territory became the subject of intense scrutiny and notoriety from national and international voices, mostly in response to its strict vaccination policies (Allam, 2021). The Northern Territory implemented a mandatory vaccination policy for all government and essential workers. As misinformation about the vaccines spread like wildfire, some people chose to lose their jobs rather than receive lifesaving vaccinations. Misinformation had a huge impact on Aboriginal communities, many of whom were understandably fearful about the vaccines and health checks due to their living memory of government intervention (Australian Human Rights Commission, 2007). Once again, it was Aboriginal community-controlled organisations that spearheaded the vaccination communications and deliveries, and Aboriginal people in the Northern Territory were prioritised to receive the vaccines.

Even still, when the Northern Territory's borders were finally opened in late 2021, vaccination rates in some communities were below 50 per cent. When the first cases of COVID-19 swept through, many communities went into lockdown. During this time, many community organisations responded creatively, such as Katherine Women's Information & Legal Services (KWILS) that made 'women's business'[3] bags, which included supplies for women in remote communities and Town Camps in lockdown. KWILS knew that men would not go into bags labelled as 'women's business', so they could include safety planning and helpline numbers for women who may be experiencing violence.

In my hometown, specialist domestic, family and sexual violence services, themselves severely impacted by the pandemic and public health measures, pivoted and adapted to delivering services in extremely remote locations. The Tangentyere Council Men's Behaviour Change Program began delivering individual sessions with users of violence, including over the phone, to maintain engagement and monitor the risk men posed to their partners and children. The Ngaanyatjarra Pitjantjatjara Yankunytjatjara Women's Council delivered weaving materials to women in quarantine to continue engagement and support, and even chartered flights to evacuate women experiencing violence from remote locations. However, all of these creative and innovative responses were in spite of extremely limited resources, funding and support.

As COVID-19 spread throughout the Northern Territory, the perpetually stretched and under-resourced healthcare system buckled – but it did not break. Isolation, as predicted, proved to be a difficult and often comical thing to communicate. One support service reported to me that they were supplying their elderly Aboriginal clients in isolation with tobacco because otherwise they would not stay at home and were often found wandering around town looking for tobacco. 'What service would provide its clients with tobacco?', she laughed.

---

3   Women's business is a reference to women's lore and ceremony. This is strictly guarded and men typically respect and stay far away from anything associated with women's business.

However, other reasons people could not isolate included homelessness and overcrowding. How can you isolate when there are upwards of 15 people in your house? One service reported to me that two of their clients – both elderly Aboriginal men who had tested positive for COVID-19 – were sleeping in caves in the mountain ranges above Alice Springs because they had nowhere else to isolate, and so that people would not take their food, clothes and blankets. The service expressed special concern because both men had reduced mobility – they could not understand how they had gotten up there in the first place.

In spite of these challenges, the Northern Territory did not experience the waves of deaths it feared at the start of the pandemic. This was due to high vaccination rates and strong leadership from Aboriginal community-controlled organisations throughout the pandemic. Still, there had been 90 deaths attributable to COVID-19 in the Northern Territory at the time of writing (NT Health, 2023).

The shadow pandemic

> It's deeply disturbing that this pervasive violence by men against women not only persists unchanged, but is at its worst for young women aged 15–24 who may also be young mothers. And that was the situation before the pandemic stay-at-home orders. We know that the multiple impacts of COVID-19 have triggered a 'shadow pandemic' of increased reported violence of all kinds against women and girls ... Every government should be taking strong, proactive steps to address this, and involving women in doing so.
>
> (UN Women Executive Director Phumzile Mlambo-Ngcuka, WHO, 2021)

The problem of violence against women was severe prior to the pandemic, but public health measures designed to curb the spread of COVID-19 initially ignored the reality of domestic, family and sexual violence. Moreover, these measures may also have exacerbated the gendered drivers of violence and introduced risk factors, leading to an increase in violence against women throughout the world (Peterman et al., 2020). This global increase was labelled 'the shadow pandemic' (WHO, 2021).

Despite its limitations, the data show that violence against women increased, as predicted. In Brazil, there was an estimated 40–50 per cent increase in domestic violence; in Cyprus, calls to the domestic violence helpline rose by 30 per cent; and domestic violence reports in China tripled during the pandemic (UN Women, 2020, 2021). In other areas, such as Italy and Argentina, calls to helplines dropped sharply – but text messages, emails and WhatsApp messages increased (UN Women, 2020). In Australia, family violence reports in Victoria were the highest on record, up by 6.6 per cent in the first year of the pandemic (Crime Statistics Agency, 2020; Safe and Equal, 2021). In the Northern Territory, reported domestic, family and sexual violence increased by 25 per cent (Jonscher & Brash, 2020).

These increases were predicted by experts in the field, yet they were initially ignored. I myself wrote and spoke extensively at the beginning of the pandemic about the increased risk to women and children during this time (Brown, 2020b), but it was not until much later that 'escaping family violence' was included as one of the five reasons people could leave their home during lockdowns (Carrington et al., 2021). However, even this response was flawed, displaying a lack of understanding of family violence as a highly controlling pattern of abuse, power and domination. It is not always easy to 'just leave', especially when usual reasons and excuses – a trip to the shopping centre, dropping the kids off to school or to the hairdresser – are cut off.

So why did violence against women increase during the pandemic?

There are many reasons why violence against women increased during the pandemic, and in the Northern Territory particularly. The first reason is proximity. Women and children found themselves stuck in their homes with users of violence. Proximity plus increased stress and other factors meant that the risk of violence increased, while help-seeking behaviours were negatively impacted. For example, lockdowns and other public health measures prevented women and children from accessing safe places, such as schools and workplaces. At the same time, having the abuser in such close proximity made it very difficult for women and children to call for help, which could explain why women in many locations throughout the world began using alternative means, such as WhatsApp and other online chats, to seek help (Fitz-Gibbon et al., 2020; UN Women, 2020).

Not only did close proximity to users of violence make it difficult for women and children to leave, but it also isolated them from their social networks, which are key supports for women and children experiencing violence. It was difficult or impossible for some women and children to connect with friends, family and community groups due to public health measures. Rarely do women and children report directly to formal services; instead, they tend to use informal channels and social networks to access help and support. Measures like social distancing and lockdowns disrupted these social supports.

These restrictions and proximity factors were true for women all over the world, including Australia; however, they had a particular impact on women in remote areas. Women in remote areas already live in extreme isolation with respect to the rest of the country; this increased twofold during the pandemic, as there was no way in and no way out. It was not possible to leave communities during the lockdowns using formal channels, although there were reports of women using risky informal routes to travel to town to access services.

Violence against women also increased during the pandemic due to the introduction of increased risk factors (Usta et al., 2021). It is well known that violence against women and children increases in humanitarian and disaster settings (Care International, 2017; Peterman et al., 2020), such as the Black Saturday fires in Australia (Parkinson, 2014). Indeed, many women make their first report of violence in the aftermath of a disaster (Parkinson, 2014). It is theorised that this is because of the introduction of increased risk factors for violence in the household, such as trauma, alcohol and other drugs, relationship conflict and food insecurity. The pandemic increased the presence of these risk factors, placing extra stress on households and thereby increasing the likelihood of violence occurring.

Once more, this was exacerbated for women in remote communities. Aboriginal and Torres Strait Islander women in regional and remote areas were already disproportionately impacted by homelessness, overcrowding and food insecurity. In contexts where such risk factors already disproportionately existed due to the ongoing impacts of colonisation and successive government policies of assimilation, neglect and intervention (Australian Human Rights Commission, 2020), the pandemic and its measures added another layer of complexity, both increasing risk and reducing responses.

The pandemic also exacerbated gender inequality (Workplace Gender Equality Agency, 2020). Gender inequality is a key driver of violence against women, as gender-discriminatory or gender-insensitive structures, social norms, practices and relationships create an environment in which women are perceived as not being equal to men (Our Watch, 2018, 2021). These drivers also create and promote women's dependence on men, producing a power imbalance that can result in conditions in which violence against women not only occurs, but also is minimised, justified or condoned (Our Watch, 2021). When schools and workplaces closed during the pandemic, this increased women's unpaid care work in the home, as women took up increased roles of teaching and caring for children, while men's unpaid work largely did not increase (Workplace Gender Equality Agency, 2020). Women are more likely to be in low-paid and insecure employment, meaning that women were more likely to lose their jobs during the pandemic than men, increasing their financial dependence (Workplace Gender Equality Agency, 2020; UN Women, 2020). Moreover, 'feminised' industries, such as childcare and early learning sectors, were disproportionately impacted by the pandemic and less likely to be supported by government assistance (UN Women, 2021, 2022; Workplace Gender Equality Agency, 2020). These conditions exacerbated women's dependence on men and increased their isolation, therefore increasing the risk of violence.

Throughout the Northern Territory, where economic opportunities are already limited due to extreme remoteness, these effects were exacerbated. Many remote communities have limited, if any, access to schools, childcare and employment. It is theorised that Aboriginal and Torres Strait Islander women do more unpaid care work than non-Indigenous women (Australian Human Rights Commission, 2020). It is likely, therefore, that the pandemic compounded and exacerbated gender inequality in these settings, as opportunities for women's economic empowerment and participation became more scarce.

Not only did violence against women increase during the pandemic, but also it often intensified and became more complex (Carrington et al., 2021). For example, users of violence often made use of public health messaging to limit women and children's movements and control their healthcare decisions; some also used misinformation about COVID-19 or vaccinations to further control women and children (Gearin & Knight, 2020; Morley et al., 2021). Frontline services also reported that women and children presented with more complex needs: for example, some required assistance with food insecurity in addition to assistance with domestic, family and sexual violence.

Moreover, as violence against women increased around the world, the capacity of support services to respond to such needs was reduced (Carrington et al., 2021). This was because support services and their staff were also subject to public health measures and restrictions. In the Northern Territory, support services were already under-resourced and underfunded prior to the pandemic. The introduction of public health measures reduced such services even further. For example, caps on how many people could be in venues and rooms meant that fewer people could be accommodated. Moreover, much of the workforce was also working from home, and, with increased unpaid care work and the stress of the pandemic, many service providers had reduced capacity to respond. Further, critical work such as safety planning and working with users of violence is usually done in person for safety reasons. Transferring this work over the phone was not always safe, nor was it always possible. Many women in remote Australia have limited access to a phone; for those that do have a phone, there is no guarantee that they are in a safe enough location to undertake casework or conduct a welfare check (Brown et al., 2021).

Conclusions: What have we learned?

The WHO has declared the global public health emergency of COVID-19 over. Yet the shadow pandemic and the experience of gendered violence in the Northern Territory illustrate some important lessons about:

- *the strength and importance of Aboriginal community-controlled organisations and Elders who led advocacy, messaging and health responses throughout the pandemic*

  Responses to the public health emergency of violence against women would benefit from prioritising self-determination and community-driven initiatives and solutions.

- *the importance of data*

  Data inform policy and programmatic responses – what is declared important and what is not – yet the data are full of holes. Administrative data do not reflect prevalence, and national surveys and ways of collecting data were upended during COVID-19. National surveys exclude very remote locations in 'normal times' let alone during a pandemic. Data on domestic, family and sexual violence need to be strengthened and better mobilised to inform policy design.

- *the importance of a gender and domestic violence lens*

  All public health measures and public policy should be considered through these lenses so that unintended impacts can be mitigated and risks appropriately managed.

- *the importance of formulating policy according to remote experiences*

  Public policy is urban-centred and mainstream-focused and does not fit regional and remote communities, especially not Aboriginal and Torres Strait Islander ones. We cannot continue to have policy that speaks to an urban majority at the expense of remote communities.

- *the fact that violence against women continues to climb*

  In the Northern Territory, all forms of domestic, family and sexual violence increased during COVID-19 and have not returned to pre-COVID-19 levels. In fact, it continues to increase exponentially.

It is uncertain as to whether we have learned anything from the shadow pandemic.

References

Allam, L. (2020, 21 March). Northern Territory to close its borders from Tuesday. *The Guardian*. www.theguardian.com/world/2020/mar/21/ill-do-whatever-it-takes-northern-territory-still-considering-closing-its-borders.

Allam, L. (2021, 25 November). 'Tinfoil hat wearing tossers': NT chief minister and Aboriginal elders hit back at Covid 'false information'. *The Guardian*. www.theguardian.com/australia-news/2021/nov/25/tinfoil-hat-wearing-tossers-nt-chief-minister-and-aboriginal-elders-hit-back-at-covid-false-information.

Australian Bureau of Statistics. (2021). *Crime victimisation, Australia*. www.abs.gov.au/statistics/people/crime-and-justice/crime-victimisation-australia/2020-21.

Australian Bureau of Statistics. (2022). *Recorded crime – victims*. www.abs.gov.au/statistics/people/crime-and-justice/recorded-crime-victims/latest-release#northern-territory.

Australian Human Rights Commission. (2007). *Northern Territory 'emergency response' intervention*. humanrights.gov.au/our-work/aboriginal-and-torres-strait-islander-social-justice/projects/northern-territory-emergency.

Australian Human Rights Commission. (2020). *Wiyi Yani U Thangani Report (2020)*. humanrights.gov.au/our-work/aboriginal-and-torres-strait-islander-social-justice/publications/wiyi-yani-u-thangani.

Australian Institute of Health and Welfare. (2022, 7 July). *Profile of Indigenous Australians*. www.aihw.gov.au/reports/australias-health/profile-of-indigenous-australians.

Beazley, J. (2022, 21 May). 'Through the roof' food prices in remote NT are forcing Aboriginal families to make impossible choices. *The Guardian*. www.theguardian.com/australia-news/2022/may/21/through-the-roof-food-prices-in-remote-nt-are-forcing-aboriginal-families-to-make-impossible-choices.

Brown, C. (2019). *Where are the safe places? Safety mapping with Town Campers in Alice Springs* [Commissioned report]. Centre for Aboriginal Economic Policy Research, The Australian National University. doi.org/10.25911/5df8a0dfe3f6d.

Brown, C. (2020a). *From the roots up: Principles of good practice to prevent violence against women in the Northern Territory* [Unpublished doctoral dissertation]. The Australian National University.

Brown, C. (2020b). Isolated from COVID-19, endangered by domestic violence: The heighted risk of violence against women in the Northern Territory. In F. Markham, D. Smith & F. Morphy (Eds), *Indigenous Australians and the COVID-19 crisis: Perspectives on public policy. Topical Issue No. 1* (pp. 14–17). Centre for Aboriginal Economic Police Research, The Australian National University.

Brown, C. & Leung, L. (2023). *Evidence snapshot: What we know about domestic, family, and sexual violence in the Northern Territory – and what we don't*. The Equality Institute. www.equalityinstitute.org/media/pages/resources/evidence-snapshot-what-we-know-about-domestic-family-and-sexual-violence-in-the-northern-territory-and-what-we-don-t/6b0ee996d9-1686115013/nt_evidence_snapshot_eqi.pdf.

Brown, C., Yap, M., Thomassin, A., Murray, M. & Yu, E. (2021). *'Can I just share my story?' Experiences of technology-facilitated abuse among Aboriginal and Torres Strait Islander women from regional and remote areas*. The Office of the eSafety Commissioner.

Care International. (2017). *Suffering in silence: The 10 most under-reported humanitarian crises of 2016*. www.care.org.au/wp-content/uploads/2017/01/REPORT_Suffering_in_Silence__110117_PRINT.pdf.

Carrington, K., Morley, C., Warren, S., Ryan, V., Ball, M., Clarke, J. & Vitis, L. (2021). The impact of COVID-19 pandemic on Australian domestic and family violence services and their clients. *Australian Journal of Social Issues, 56*(4), 539–558. doi.org/10.1002/ajs4.183.

Crime Statistics Agency. (2020). *Victoria Police respond to record numbers of family violence incidents across the state* [Media release]. www.crimestatistics.vic.gov.au/media-centre/news/media-release-victoria-police-respond-to-record-numbers-of-family-violence.

Department of Health and Aged Care. (2022, 17 February). *Extension of biosecurity measures to protect remote communities in the NT* [Media release]. www.health.gov.au/ministers/the-hon-greg-hunt-mp/media/extension-of-biosecurity-measures-to-protect-remote-communities-in-the-nt.

Fitz-Gibbon, K., True, J. & Pfitzner, N. (2020, 18 August). More help required: The crisis in family violence during the coronavirus pandemic. *The Conversation.* theconversation.com/more-help-required-the-crisis-in-family-violence-during-the-coronavirus-pandemic-144126.

Flood, M., Brown, C., Dembele, L. & Mills, K. (2022). *Who uses domestic, family, and sexual violence, how, and why? The state of knowledge report on violence perpetration.* Queensland University of Technology.

Gearin, M. & Knight, B. (2020, 29 March). Family violence perpetrators using COVID-19 as 'a form of abuse we have not experienced before'. *ABC News.* www.abc.net.au/news/2020-03-29/coronavirus-family-violence-surge-in-victoria/12098546.

Jonscher, S. & Brash, S. (2020, 22 June). Significant increase in domestic violence recorded in NT during pandemic. *ABC News.* www.abc.net.au/news/2020-06-22/domestic-violence-increases-in-nt-during-pandemic/12379148.

Morley, C., Carrington, K., Ryan, V., Warren, S., Clarke, J., Ball, M. & Vitis, L. (2021). Locked down with the perpetrator: The hidden impacts of COVID-19 on domestic and family violence in Australia. *International Journal for Crime, Justice and Social Democracy, 10*(4), 204–222. doi.org/10.5204/ijcjsd.2069.

Moyo, M. (2014, 16 May). New look for Ilpeye Ilpeye Town Camp in Alice Springs. *Herald Sun.* www.heraldsun.com.au/news/new-look-for-ilpeye-ilpeye-town-camp-in-alice-springs/news-story/f74a0a55c610ffb93e48b65b8f3205bb.

National Aboriginal and Torres Strait Islander Women's Alliance (NATSIWA). (2020). *Submission to the House of Representatives Standing Committee on Indigenous Affairs: Inquiry into food pricing and food security in remote Indigenous communities.* natsiwa.org.au/docman/submissions/35-national-aboriginal-and-torres-strait-islander-womens-alliance/file.

Northern Territory Government. (2022, 20 May). *Aboriginal languages in NT.* nt.gov.au/community/interpreting-and-translating-services/aboriginal-interpreter-service/aboriginal-languages-in-nt.

NT Health. (2023, 3 March). *COVID-19 data.* health.nt.gov.au/covid-19/data [Site discontinued].

NT Health, AMSANT, Northern Territory Primary Health Network. (2020). *Strengthening our health system strategy (2020–2025).* health.nt.gov.au/__data/assets/pdf_file/0010/955495/Strengthening-our-Health-System-Strategy-2020-2025.pdf.

NT Shelter. (n.d.). *Educational resources.* ntshelter.org.au/educational-resources/.

Office of the Attorney-General and Justice. (2023). *Law reforms.* justice.nt.gov.au/law-reform-reviews.

Our Watch. (2018). *Changing the picture.* www.ourwatch.org.au/change-the-story/changing-the-picture.

Our Watch. (2021). *Change the story* (2nd ed.). media-cdn.ourwatch.org.au/wp-content/uploads/sites/2/2021/11/18101814/Change-the-story-Our-Watch-AA.pdf.

Parkinson, D. (2014). *Women's experience of violence in the aftermath of the Black Saturday bushfires* [Unpublished doctoral dissertation]. Monash University. doi.org/10.13140/RG.2.1.4265.9047.

Peterman, A., Potts, A., O'Donnell, M., Thompson, K., Shah, K., Oertelt-Prigione, S. & van Gelder, N. (2020). Pandemics and violence against women and children. *Working Paper, 528.* Centre for Global Development.

Safe and Equal. (2021). *Family violence statistics.* safeandequal.org.au/understanding-family-violence/statistics/.

United Nations Economic and Social Affairs. (2015). *The world's women 2015, trends and statistics.* United Nations.

UN Women. (2020). *COVID-19 and ending violence against women and girls.* www.unwomen.org/en/digital-library/publications/2020/04/issue-brief-covid-19-and-ending-violence-against-women-and-girls.

UN Women. (2021). *Measuring the shadow pandemic: Violence against women during COVID-19.* data.unwomen.org/publications/vaw-rga.

UN Women. (2022). *Gender-based violence: Women and girls at risk.* www.unwomen.org/en/hq-complex-page/covid-19-rebuilding-for-resilience/gender-based-violence.

Usta, J., Murr, H. & El-Jarrah, R. (2021). COVID-19 lockdown and the increased violence against women: Understanding domestic violence during a pandemic. *Violence and Gender*, *8*(3), 133–139. doi.org/10.1089/vio.2020.0069.

Wahlquist, C. (2017, 26 September). The native title campaigner whose people still have no power, water or sewerage. *The Guardian*. www.theguardian.com/australia-news/2017/sep/26/m-hayes-ampetyane-a-force-of-nature-for-her-people.

Weeramanthri, T., Hendy, S., Connors, C., Ashbridge, D., Rae, C., Dunn, M., Fittock, M., Cleary, J., O'Donohoe, L., Morton, S. & Swanson, N. (2003). The Northern Territory preventable chronic disease strategy – Promoting an integrated and life course approach to chronic disease in Australia. *Australian Health Review*, *26*(3), 31–42. doi.org/10.1071/ah030031.

Workplace Gender Equality Agency. (2020, 11 May). *Gendered impact of COVID-19*. www.wgea.gov.au/publications/gendered-impact-of-covid-19.

World Health Organization. (2021, 9 March). *Devastatingly pervasive: 1 in 3 women globally experience violence*. www.who.int/news/item/09-03-2021-devastatingly-pervasive-1-in-3-women-globally-experience-violence.

Zhao, Y., Connors, C., Wright, J., Guthridge, S. & Bailie, R. (2008, August). Estimating chronic disease prevalence among the remote Aboriginal population of the Northern Territory using multiple data sources. *Australian and New Zealand Journal of Public Health*, *32*(4), 307–313. doi.org/10.1111/j.1753-6405.2008.00245.x.

9

The impact of News Corporation scepticism on the COVID-19 pandemic: A case study from Victoria, June–August 2020

Tony Ward

> I know Victorians are with me when I say too many people are not taking this seriously. And too many people not taking this seriously means too many other people are having to plan funerals for those they love.
>
> (Andrews, 2020)

On 2 August 2020, Premier of Victoria Dan Andrews announced a state of disaster to tackle a second wave of COVID-19. Tough lockdown measures included nightly curfews, work and study from home directives, and one-hour limits on leaving homes each day. News Corporation media outlets were prominent among those 'not taking this seriously'. Typically, widely read columnist Andrew Bolt responded to the government restrictions by urging, on 4 August, 'Victoria, don't accept this!' (Milner, 2020).

This chapter analyses the impact of News Corporation scepticism through a case study of the Australian state of Victoria. Victoria suffered a 'second wave' of the virus from late June into July 2020, leading to the state of disaster announcement. The chapter estimates that News Corporation's scepticism materially worsened this second wave of the virus.

Influential News Corporation's coverage of COVID-19 in Victoria mirrored that in the United States, especially on Fox News. Many American studies have documented the noticeable impacts that COVID-19 scepticism from Fox News had on viewers' attitudes to the pandemic. This chapter uses those findings to illuminate a case study in Victoria. Victoria is a good example, as the News Corporation–owned *Herald Sun* is widely read in the state, and the paper both provided a platform for COVID-19 sceptics and was unrelenting in its criticism of state government actions.

The chapter presents a simple epidemiological model of the spread of the virus from late June to the peak of new infections in early August, when the government announced the state of disaster. Applying mid- to lower-end estimates of the impact of scepticism in the US, the modelling calculates that, without News Corporation's campaigns, the virus would have spread much more slowly, with perhaps half the number of new daily cases recorded in early August. Acknowledging uncertainties in response rates, the model uses sensitivity analysis to test the results. Even with an assumption of very low influence from the News Corporation media, there is still a significant impact.

The chapter has four sections: the first examines the literature on the impact of COVID-19 scepticism in the US, focusing on Fox News; the second provides an overview of the development of the pandemic in Victoria in mid-2020; the third looks at News Corporation's response to those events; and the fourth presents the results of the epidemiological model. The final section concludes the chapter.

US literature

From the start of the COVID-19 pandemic, there were significant differences between countries in the numbers of infections and the numbers of deaths. There were also differences within countries. Some of these differences reflected the incidence of the pandemic. Older and more disadvantaged populations were hit harder than younger and richer populations, and large urban areas had higher infection rates than remote rural areas (Helliwell et al., 2021b, p. 46). Another key factor in the differences was the responsiveness of communities to public health measures and entreaties: some communities were strongly affected by messages from political leaders and the media. This section shows that, in the US, Fox News' scepticism of COVID-19 had marked effects on compliance with public health measures.

Helliwell et al. (2021b) analysed the patterns of deaths from COVID-19 across the world in 2020. As well as noting other factors, they found significant impacts from political messages. Death rates were noticeably higher in countries such as Brazil and the US where political leaders were sceptical about the severity of the virus (Helliwell et al., 2021b, p. 48).

As well as political messages, the media also affected views on the severity of the virus and compliance with public health measures. This was especially marked in the US, particularly among conservatives. In Brazil, India and the UK, Altay et al. (2023) found that news and digital platform use had little impact on people's acceptance of COVID-19 misinformation. In the UK, there was little difference in political partisanship and vaccination rates (Klymak & Vlanda, 2022). That finding mirrored previous experience in the US: in 2014, Republicans were somewhat more likely than Democrats to be worried about the Ebola virus (Doherty et al., 2014, cited in Gollwitzer et al., 2020, p. 1195).

With COVID-19 in 2020–22, there were strong partisan responses in the US. The following literature overview demonstrates four things. First, Republicans were markedly less likely than Democrats to be concerned about COVID-19 and were also less likely to follow public health advice or be vaccinated. These patterns were encouraged and reinforced by political rhetoric, especially from President Trump. Second, as a consequence, infection rates and death rates were notably higher among Republicans. Third, Fox News had a marked impact, enhancing these typical patterns among its largely conservative audience. Last, the impact of Fox News was significant.

Partisan differences in responses to COVID-19

Numerous studies have found major partisan divides between Republicans and Democrats in terms of their responses to COVID-19. These have been apparent in initial attitudes, in adherence to social distancing and other public health measures, and, subsequently, in vaccination rates.

Gollwitzer et al. (2020) used the geotracking data of 15 million smartphones. They found that US counties that voted Republican in the 2016 presidential election exhibited 14 per cent less compliance with physical distancing between March and May 2020 than Democrat-voting counties. Partisanship had a larger impact than factors such as the number of cases, population density, median income, and racial and age demographics. Further, the observed partisan gap grew over time despite the pandemic worsening (Allcott et al., 2020).

The Kaiser Family Foundation has funded a regular COVID-19 vaccine monitor. This, and other surveys, have consistently shown a strong relationship between partisan identification and vaccination attitudes. Kirzinger et al. (2021), reporting in November 2021, found that the partisan divide on vaccinations had increased over time and that political partisanship is a stronger predictor of whether someone is vaccinated than demographic factors such as age, race, level of education or insurance status.

Partisan responses were amplified by messages from political leaders. In a survey of unvaccinated Republican voters, Pink et al. (2021) found receptiveness to messages from Republican leaders endorsing vaccination. However, those seeing a similar message from a Democrat leader were slightly less likely to vaccinate (see also Cowan et al., 2021).

Subsequent infection and mortality rates

Those partisan attitudes had impacts on subsequent infection and mortality rates. Gollwitzer et al. (2020, p. 1192) noted that rural counties typically had lower infection growth rates than urban counties. However, Republican-leaning counties suffered marginally higher COVID-19 infection and fatality growth rates than Democrat-voting counties.

Sehgal et al. (2022) tested the impact on mortality rates of partisan differences in attitudes towards COVID-19 and towards local policies requiring masks, social distancing and vaccines. They gathered data from a majority of US counties, comparing the number of COVID-19 deaths to the end of October 2021 with the Republican vote share in the 2020 presidential election. The analysis controlled for such factors as age, income and rural/urban populations. The findings suggested that the Republican vote share had a significant impact on mortality rates.

A now-standard measure of the mortality impact of COVID-19 is to compare actual death rates experienced in 2020–22 with previous death rates. The 'excess deaths' indicate the overall impact of the pandemic. Wallace et al. (2022) calculated excess deaths for Republican and Democrat voters in Ohio and Florida, comparing the figures in 2018–19 with those in 2020–21. They linked 577,659 deaths of individuals who died at age 25 or older with their 2017 voting records (both Ohio and Florida data sets allow such matching). Before vaccines became available, the excess death rate for registered Republicans was 22 per cent higher than that for registered Democrats. The disparity widened after vaccines were widely available – the Republican excess death rate was now 153 per cent of the Democrat excess death rate. The gap was particularly strong in more rural counties with low vaccination rates.

Influence of Fox News

Most viewers of Fox News tend to vote Republican, so that audience would be expected to share the above patterns. However, many studies have shown that Fox News viewers had even more hostile attitudes to social distancing, public health measures and vaccination than Republicans generally. Several have extended the analysis to show that there is a causal link.

In early March 2020, Jamieson and Albarracin (2020) conducted a phone survey of 1,008 respondents in the US. They gathered respondents' views on the seriousness of COVID-19 and checked their receptiveness to several conspiracy theories about the virus; they also checked these views against media consumption. The use of conservative media (such as Fox News and Rush Limbaugh) correlated with beliefs in the malign underlying motives of some at the Centre for Disease Control and Prevention and the Chinese origin of the virus. This reflected frequent claims on Fox News that the coronavirus was less dangerous than influenza and other media reports about it being a hoax (Gollwitzer et al., 2020, p. 1195). These results were robust after controlling for differences between Republican and Democrat voters.

Ash et al. (2020) studied the impact of Fox News in the early weeks of COVID-19 using data such as variations in mobile phone–based tracking of time spent away from home and distances travelled. In areas with higher Fox News viewership, people were less likely to adopt social distancing or purchase preparatory goods, such as cleaning products, hand sanitisers and masks. The researchers' finding that Fox News caused these behaviours was supported by two further patterns. First, the impact was apparent among Republican voters. Second, the strength of the results differed between different Fox presenters (see also Bursztyn et al., 2020).

By the end of 2020, Ash et al. (2020, p. 2) could conclude: 'Our analysis provides causal evidence of the effect of exposure to Fox News on viewers' adherence to social distancing measures and preparedness for the pandemic.'

Similarly, Gollwitzer et al. (2020, p. 1192), found that viewers of Fox News showed even less willingness to participate in social distancing than other Republican voters.

The Fox News influence extended from social distancing to vaccination. Choi et al. (2022) surveyed 789 adults in May 2021 to ascertain drivers of pro- or anti-vaccination attitudes. Pro-vaccine attitudes emerged among those who expressed worry about, and/or had greater knowledge of, COVID-19. Those who held stigmatising views of COVID-19, had experienced racial discrimination or had been watching Fox News were more likely to hold anti-vaccine attitudes. The impact of watching Fox News was much greater than any other variable. In terms of changing attitudes from the overall average, Fox News had up to twice the impact of other negative factors – and its ability to negatively impact attitudes towards vaccines was eight times greater than pro-vaccine factors (Choi et al., 2022, p. 9).

Pinna et al. (2022) found that Fox News had a strong impact on vaccine hesitancy and associated local vaccination rates across the US. From the start of the vaccine rollout in May 2021, higher local viewership of the Fox News Channel was associated with lower local vaccination rates. They verified that this was causal by controlling for other factors, such as local health policies, or local COVID-19 infections or death rates, and demonstrated that the impact was additional to partisan vote shares.

Estimating the size of Fox News' impact

Ash et al. (2020) calculated that an area with 10 per cent higher Fox News viewership than average would typically see increased time spent away from home (30 minutes per person per day) and decreased COVID-related expenditure ($43 per grocery store per day). From survey evidence, Ash et al. also found that Fox News viewers were 47 per cent more likely to believe that hydroxychloroquine was an effective anti-COVID-19 treatment, and 65 per cent more likely to prioritise economic activity over public health measures. Both were frequent talking points of Fox News presenters.

Bursztyn et al. (2020) compared the audiences for Fox News programs with different messages on COVID-19 in March 2020 and calculated significant differences in the COVID-19 transmission rate, peaking at 27 per cent. Simonov et al. (2020) also studied variations in regional compliance with social distancing recommendations. They specifically looked at stay-at-home behaviour, comparing data from April 2020 with January 2020 (i.e. before

COVID-19). They combined an impressive array of data: Nielsen's NLTV panel, measuring viewership of the two leading cable news channels – Fox News and CNN; Safegraph data tracking GPS locations from millions of US mobile phones; Homebase local business data, tracking daily hours worked for 695,782 employees and managers from 78,850 business locations, spanning 15,783 postcodes; and Facteus consumer spending data from some 10 million debit cards. They found that viewing Fox News had a significant and independent effect on people's willingness to ignore health recommendations. The average 'persuasion rate' was some 36 per cent among viewers of Fox News (Simonov et al., 2020, p. 25). Thus, one-third of those watching Fox News were likely to become less compliant with social distancing measures. Across the entire population, they concluded: 'We find a persuasion rate of Fox News on non-compliance with stay-at-home behaviour' of 28.4 per cent for homebound devices, 14.5 per cent for full-time work travel and 5.7 per cent for part-time work travel (Simonov et al., 2020, p. 26). This not only reflected the direct effect of those watching Fox News, but also indirectly, for if a significant part of the population was non-compliant, others were likely to think 'well, if they're not following the rules – why should we?'

Simonov et al. (2020) did not assess the impact of this on infection and mortality, reckoning it was too early at that time (mid-2020) to have good data. However, the above discussion clearly demonstrates the negative results of reduced adherence to health advice. The literature provides ample evidence to back Turnbull's (2020) dire warning that 'watching Fox News in the US may kill you' and Ingraham's (2020) statement that 'conservative media misinformation may have intensified the severity of the pandemic'.

COVID-19 in Victoria from March to August 2020

To provide background to the subsequent analysis of the impact of News Corporation's scepticism of COVID-19, this section summarises the path of the virus in the state of Victoria from March to August 2020.

Victoria's 'first wave' of COVID-19 infections started in mid-March 2020. On 16 March, Premier Daniel Andrews declared a state of emergency until 13 April: people were required to stay at home except for authorised activities; many food and recreation businesses were shut down; and other restrictions, referred to as Stage 3 restrictions, were put in place. This state of emergency was subsequently extended twice: on 12 April until 11 May, and then again on 11 May until 31 May, with slightly fewer restrictions.

Australia-wide, such restrictions had significant effects. Ian Marschner, professor of biostatistics at the National Health and Medical Research Council Clinical Trials Centre, University of Sydney, analysed the first wave of infections across Australia. He concluded that:

> the timing of government restrictions matched almost exactly with the flattening and downturn of infection numbers ... By clamping down early, we probably avoided tens of thousands of infections nationally.
>
> (Marschner, 2020)

Australia experienced a nationwide drop in the number of new cases in May, leading Victoria to further loosen restrictions from 1 June. However, the respite was short-lived, with cases climbing again from late June. On 20 June, the Victorian government announced some re-tightening of restrictions, especially on home gatherings.

On 30 June, the Victorian government reintroduced Stage 3 lockdowns across 10 Melbourne postcodes. On 4 July, an additional two postcodes were added, and very tight restrictions were imposed for a few days on nine public housing towers. On 7 July, after 191 new cases were reported, Stage 3 was again imposed on all of metropolitan Melbourne until at least 13 August. An additional restriction – the mandatory wearing of facemasks – came in from 23 July.

On 2 August 2020, the Victorian government announced a state of disaster until at least 13 September. It imposed Stage 3 restrictions across all of Victoria, and even tougher (Stage 4) restrictions for Melbourne. This included a curfew across Melbourne from 8 pm to 5 am, the shutting down of more businesses and the requirement that people stay within 5 kilometres of their homes at all times.

While the number of reported new infections kept climbing until the first week of August, the lockdown restrictions had remarkable effects. The effective reproduction number – a measure of how fast the virus was spreading – fell from 1.75 to 1.16. The Burnett Institute calculated that, while new infections in July numbered just over 8,000, without the restrictions that number could well have been 27,000 (Marschner, 2020; Scott & Kent, 2020).

It is important to note the range of factors that contributed to the second wave of the virus in Victoria. Prominent among these were failures in hotel quarantine, problems with contact tracing arrangements, poor preparation in aged care homes and the extent of community transmission. All played a part and better performance in any aspect would have significantly reduced the overall death toll.

With so many factors influencing the spread of the virus, those involved could readily shift blame, reinforcing the old adage that success has many parents while failure is an orphan. Of the 820 people who died of COVID-19 in Victoria, 655 (75 per cent of the total) lived in aged care homes. Despite aged care being a federal government responsibility, Minister for Senior Australians and Aged Care Services Richard Colbeck told a Senate Estimates Committee hearing that he did not 'feel responsible' for any of the deaths. Prime Minister Scott Morrison also ducked any responsibility. He argued instead that widespread community transmission in Victoria was the main reason so many people died (Russell, 2021). To get beyond such spin, it is worth noting the key features of each of the four factors.

Hotel quarantine

Failures in hotel quarantine of travellers returning from overseas sparked Victoria's second wave of the virus. Indeed, more than 90 per cent of infections in Victoria's second wave were traced back to one quarantine hotel, Rydges on Swanston. A board of inquiry, chaired by Justice Coate, investigated and delivered its final report on 21 December 2020 (ABC News, 2020). It found that a number of factors contributed to the failures in hotel quarantine. However, the key was a lack of preparation and planning. Both state and federal governments were aware from early 2020 of the possibility of a pandemic. However, mandatory mass quarantine was not a feature of any of their plans. This meant that the hotel quarantine program had to be conceived and implemented 'from scratch' in just 36 hours, which the inquiry found placed 'extraordinary strain' on the departments and people given the job of setting it up. According to Justice Coate, 'this lack of planning was a most unsatisfactory situation from which to develop such a complex and high-risk program' (ABC News, 2020).

The haste in setting up the program contributed to a series of other problems. First, there was uncertainty between two government departments about which was the lead agency. Such confusion caused 'considerable and significant problems with the way in which the program operated' and extended to finding out who made the decision to use private security in the quarantine hotels. It was ultimately not possible to pin the decision on anyone. The decision remained, Justice Coate wrote, 'an orphan, with no person or department claiming responsibility'.

The third major problem was poor training and supervision for the security guards. Justice Coate found that the process used to select security firms was 'not appropriate or sufficiently rigorous'. He said: 'It was made in haste and without any risk assessment, led by staff that did not have the requisite experience and knowledge, and without any public health oversight or input' (ABC News, 2020).

Contact tracing

Contact tracing arrangements were essential in tackling the virus once it had escaped from hotel quarantine and spread across the Victorian community. Stopping that spread was hampered by problems with the Department of Health's contact tracing arrangements. Several commentators noted that:

> A legacy of cuts left the Department of Health and Human Services under-resourced and highly centralised, meaning there was a smaller base upon which to build the surge contact tracing capacity.
>
> (Bennett, 2020)

Victoria's centralised approach was widely considered inferior to the system in NSW, which used decentralised local area health districts. Contract tracing there could draw on teams embedded in their local communities, with considerable local knowledge. These teams worked independently but in coordination with NSW Health.

Aged care

The problems with contract tracing in Victoria were slower to emerge than immediate failings in aged care. As noted above, 655 of the 820 COVID-19 deaths in Victoria were among aged care residents. Here, too, a major lack of planning occurred. Earlier in the year, a major site of the first wave of the virus from April to June was Newmarch House, an aged care facility in Sydney. That outbreak was much worse due to inadequate staffing and training. However, there was no effort to learn from the experience.

Far more residents of for-profit homes were infected with COVID-19 than residents of Victorian state government–owned homes. Some 98 residents died in just three Victorian for-profit homes alone.

In October 2020, the Royal Commission into Aged Care Quality and Safety confirmed that the federal government did not have a specific pandemic plan for the aged care sector and that there was 'a clear need for a defined, consolidated, national aged care COVID-19 plan' (Russell, 2021). Earlier in the year, a Senate inquiry report had stated that the government 'did not have adequate [public health] plans in place either before, or during the pandemic' and that it had 'failed to properly prepare the aged care and disability sectors for the pandemic'. The Senate inquiry also pointed out that the national health strategy was not clearly explained to the public until July 2020 (Russell, 2021).

Community transmission and restrictions

As noted above, Prime Minister Scott Morrison defended his government's record in aged care, arguing that widespread community transmission was the key factor underlying the spread of COVID-19 in Victoria. While Morrison's comments were patently self-serving, the extent and speed of community transmission was an important factor contributing to the overall dire result. The impact of community restrictions was evident in the data cited by Marschner (2020) above – namely, that the 'timing of government restrictions matched almost exactly with the flattening and downturn of infection numbers'.

It is clear that all four factors – failures in hotel quarantine, problems with contact tracing arrangements, poor preparation in aged care homes and the extent of community transmission – contributed to the second wave of the virus in Victoria. Better performance in any aspect would have significantly reduced the overall toll. As the two inquiries noted above showed, the failures were marked by poor initial planning and exacerbated by the haste with which people had to respond. In each case, a slower spread of the virus would have allowed more time for improved systems and training to take effect. The spread would also have been less had the community been less sceptical of initial measures to control the virus – and had the News Corporation media not encouraged that scepticism.

Responses by News Corporation media

As elsewhere, Victoria certainly had many people who were less receptive to restrictions. For example, on 20 August 2020, Victoria Police reported on fines they had levied the previous day for breaching the state's restrictions (*The Guardian*, 2020). These included a man and a woman not wearing facemasks while with their children at Lysterfield Lake Park in Melbourne's south-east. The family had travelled from Keysborough for a walk, breaching rules because the trip was more than 5 kilometres from their home. The police commented: 'When speaking to police, it was clear they were deliberately breaching the directions because they didn't think the virus was that serious' (*The Guardian*, 2020). Police also imposed a fine on a woman walking in Hobsons Bay during the 8 pm to 5 am curfew. She had visited a friend's house and did not think the virus was that serious.

Governments across Australia had long emphasised that success in battling the virus depended on community responses to its restriction measures. There were a range of reasons why some people were slow to accept such measures: some had insecure or casual work and could not afford to take time off; others, especially younger people, doubted they would be much affected by COVID-19 (Castillo & Petrie, 2020); still others were influenced by media sources, notably News Corporation. Bolt and other media commentators argued that people did not need to be particularly concerned, as the virus was not that serious and the government's measures were gross overreactions.

The *Herald Sun* and other News Corporation media outlets have a wide reach in Victoria; indeed, the *Herald Sun* alone claimed a daily newspaper audience of 567,000 readers in 2021, twice its rival, *The Age* (*Herald Sun*, 2021).

In late July and the first week of August 2020, several Australian writers took aim at News Corporation's coronavirus coverage. Muller (2020) warned: 'Whether a ratings chase or ideological war, News Corp's coronavirus coverage is dangerous'. Milner (2020) described 'News Corporation columnists [as] coronavirus superspreaders' and argued that the company 'should be closed under Melbourne's Stage 4 restrictions'. From the start of COVID-19, Bolt and other News Corporation columnists maintained a consistent line that government restrictions were going too far, even to the extent of arguing that the restrictions were worse than the virus.

According to the *Herald Sun*, Andrew Bolt is 'Australia's most read columnist'. From January 2020, Bolt, whose estimated annual salary is A$500,000, was sceptical about the threat of coronavirus, arguing: 'A real pandemic would look more deadly than the coronavirus' (Milner, 2020). On 20 July 2020, in response to masks becoming mandatory in Victoria – and ignoring extensive international research that showed that masks were effective against COVID-19 – Bolt wrote: 'I no longer trust what Premier Daniel Andrews says about the coronavirus. That includes his latest order to Victorians: wear face masks. On what medical basis is this necessary?' (Meade, 2020).

On 2 August, when Victoria announced a state of disaster and imposed tougher Stage 4 restrictions, Bolt declared: 'Victoria, don't accept this!' He followed by arguing that COVID-19 restrictions should be lifted because they are destroying the economy 'to save aged-care residents from dying a few months earlier' (Meade, 2020). Another *Herald Sun* and Sky News columnist, Rita Panahi, described the health measures as 'draconian' and people who backed Andrews as being 'in the thralls of Stockholm syndrome' (Meade, 2020). She referred to the Victorian premier as 'Ayatollah' (Milner, 2020). Alan Jones, also on Sky News, doubted the international medical evidence. He described mask wearing as 'alarmism', 'ineffectual' and not warranted by Australia's death rate. 'Only a mad person would believe a lockdown will wipe out the virus', he said (Meade, 2020).

There was a party-political aspect to the coverage. Denis Muller, from the Centre for Advancing Journalism at the University of Melbourne, compared News Corporation's treatment of government responses in NSW and Victoria (Muller, 2020), focusing on:

> the contrast between *The Daily Telegraph*'s coverage of the Ruby Princess debacle (Coalition government in New South Wales) and the *Herald Sun*'s coverage of the hotel quarantine debacle (Labor government in Victoria).

> My analysis of 464 articles in the *Telegraph* on the Ruby Princess showed the coverage was extensive, quoting many voices trenchantly critical of the way the government handled the case. However, the newspaper itself made no direct personal attack on Premier Gladys Berejiklian.

> A similar analysis I undertook of 411 articles in the *Herald Sun* about hotel quarantine and subsequent second wave likewise showed extensive coverage quoting many voices trenchantly critical of the government. But there was an additional dimension: direct personal attacks on Daniel Andrews.

A strong theme in News Corporation's coverage, as in Fox News', was warning about the economic damage that government shutdowns can produce. However, even in mid-2020, there was considerable analysis disputing that line, with Jericho (2020) arguing that 'analysis of the performance of OECD nations shows this thinking is completely wrong'. Much of the economic damage was being done by the virus itself and not the shutdowns. For example, Sweden, with limited restrictions, had a similar economic downturn to neighbouring Denmark, which had much tighter restrictions, but Sweden had much worse health results (Duckett & Mackey, 2020). Across all OECD countries, there was a clear relationship between the death rate from COVID-19 and the extent of the economic damage (see also Smithson, 2020). Muller (2020) concluded: 'Rupert Murdoch's News Corporation, in significant parts of its coverage of the coronavirus pandemic, has become a clear and present danger to the welfare of Australian society.'

Estimating the impact

News Corporation scepticism in Victoria followed similar patterns to that of Fox News in the US. Its impact on the spread of the virus in Victoria can be estimated using the US findings discussed above. To recap, Bursztyn et al. (2020) found that Fox News encouraged an increase in the rate of COVID-19 transmission up to 27 per cent, while Simonov et al. (2020) found that Fox News' 'persuasion rate' on noncompliance with stay-at-home measures was between 6 per cent and 28 per cent.

While it is important to acknowledge that the spread of the virus would have been affected by community responsiveness to any restrictions, News Corporation columnists consistently doubted the necessity of various health measures and lambasted the Victorian government for taking those measures, thereby encouraging noncompliance ('don't accept this') and reducing community responsiveness.

As Bursztyn et al. (2020, p. 27) commented for the US, 'estimating models of the COVID's spread is notoriously difficult'. Some COVID-19 modelling has been spectacularly wrong. A prime example was blazoned across the front page of *The Australian* on 6 August 2020 (Sheridan, 2020). The article reported 'secret' modelling forecasts of climbing new virus infections in Victoria throughout August, peaking well above 1,000 per day. In fact, the peak of new infections had already occurred when the article was published – peaking in the 700s on 29 July and 4 August. Not only were the figures wrong but also the source. The article claimed that the 'secret' modelling had been done by the state government. The government denied this and the author turned out to be a private individual.

Comprehensive modelling was commissioned by the Victorian government prior to it announcing a 'roadmap' out of COVID-19 restrictions on 6 September 2020. The model was:

> developed by researchers at the University of Melbourne and the University of New England. It simulates population movements in a simplified world, based on parameters that describe the spread of COVID and people's interactions with each other. In the real world, these patterns are highly random. So the researchers ran the model 1,000 times.

> (Bablani & Quakrim, 2020)

Even with such sophisticated Monte Carlo techniques, debate arose about the validity of the model's assumptions and consequent results. For example, some commentators asked about contact tracing – an area that had seen recent significant improvements.

COVID-19 modelling faced numerous challenges. First, once established, the virus spread could be exponential. Second, the virus spread in clusters, rather than in simple one-on-one transmission. Third, some people could be 'superspreaders'. For early strains of COVID-19, two major studies in mid-2020 in Hong Kong and India revealed as many as 70 per cent of infected people did not transmit the virus to anyone (Hyde, 2020). However, the remaining 30 per cent were indeed infectious, some capable of infecting large and accelerating numbers. About 10 per cent of infected people were responsible for about 80 per cent of secondary COVID-19 cases. There is, thus, an element of random chance in the precise spread pattern of the virus.

Nevertheless, modelling can produce useful information. The approach here follows the lead of Bursztyn et al. (2020, p. 27): 'we view our exercise as a back-of-the-envelope calculation to demonstrate that our observed treatment effects on deaths are consistent with reasonable changes in disease transmissibility'. The following epidemiological model is based on the growth factor for the virus – 'the one COVID number to watch', according to ABC journalists and Professor Catherine Bennett, chair of epidemiology at Deakin University (Elvery et al., 2020). In the simplest terms, that number is the change in the number of new cases each day, compared with the previous day's total. A growth number each day consistently above 1 quickly escalates to very large numbers of daily new infections.

The top line in Figure 9.1 shows the actual growth in total numbers of COVID-19 cases for Victoria from late June 2020, when the second wave started. The rapid climb in total numbers indicates a growth factor well above 1. Had the daily growth rate been consistently 0.9 or lower, the number of new cases would have diminished quickly, and there would indeed have been little need for public health measures or community response. So the model starts from a growth factor of 0.9. The gap between 0.9 and the actual growth rate measures the effectiveness of efforts to control the virus.

The lower line in Figure 9.1 estimates the path of total numbers *without* the influence of News Corporation scepticism. In the absence of News Corporation's opinions and criticisms, the noncompliance rate would have been somewhat lower – and the growth rate of new infections would have been less. The base case run of the model adopts a conservative approach: it assumes that News Corporation's impact on Victoria's noncompliance rate was 15 per cent. This is around the middle, or somewhat lower, than the range noted above for Fox News' impact in the US. Therefore, without News Corporation's impact, the model assumes 15 per cent greater compliance with the restrictions.

In calculating the model runs, it should be stressed that the 15 per cent figure is *not* applied to the entire growth number – it does not assume a reduction, for example, from a growth figure of 1.10 to 0.95. Rather, a much smaller adjustment is calculated. The model works from the above 0.9 baseline and applies the 15 per cent adjustment to any movement *above* that baseline. Thus, using the above figures, an actual growth figure of 1.10 is 20 percentage points above the baseline 0.9. Applying the 15 per cent reduction to the 20 percentage points reduces that difference to 17 percentage points. Rather than a growth figure of 1.10, the alternative scenario models a growth figure of 1.07.

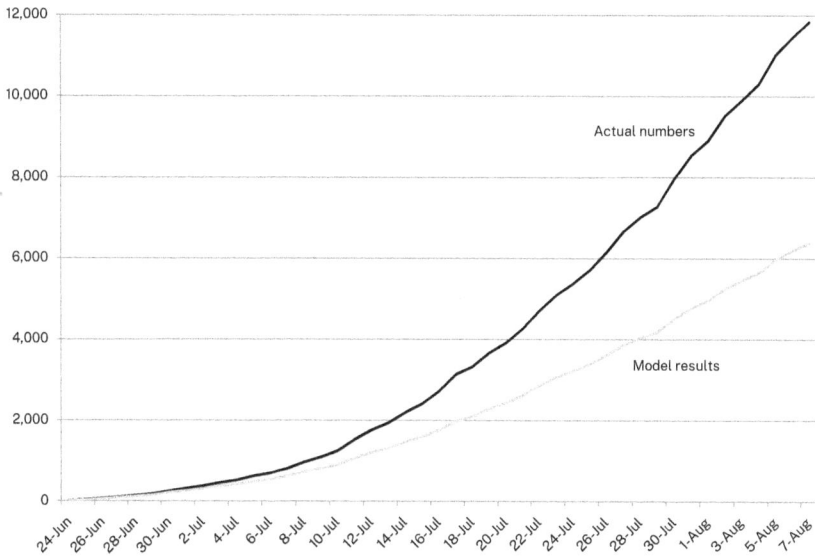

Figure 9.1: Victoria: Cumulative new cases of coronavirus from 24 June to 7 August 2020.

Source: Author's research.

Both the actual figures and the model estimates start from 24 June, when the state had 17 new infections. The difference between the two series is small at first but accumulates quickly. By 3 August, Victoria had recorded almost 10,000 new infections since 24 June, and there were around 500 daily new infections every day that week. The model, assuming greater compliance with COVID-19 restrictions, shows much lower figures. The accumulated total of infections since 24 June was 5,452 – 55 per cent of the actual total – and the average daily rate of new infections was 240, less than half the actual rate.

As infections grew at exponential rates, these results are sensitive to the assumptions used in the model. Based on the US studies, the analysis started from a conservative assumption, that News Corporation scepticism encouraged 15 per cent less compliance with COVID-19 restrictions. The model therefore estimated results for an alternative scenario, without News Corporation scepticism, and 15 per cent greater compliance with COVID-19 restrictions. This assumption can be varied in sensitivity analysis, showing the results in Table 9.1.

Table 9.1: Sensitivity testing

	New infections on 4 August	% of actual	Cumulative to 3 August	% of actual
Actual	398		9,909	
Model sensitivity				
10% greater compliance with restrictions	253	64	6,695	68
15% greater compliance with restrictions (base case)	198	50	5,452	55
20% greater compliance with restrictions	153	38	4,417	45

Source: Author's research.

Table 9.1 shows that the results are sensitive to the basic assumption of the influence of News Corporation columnists. However, even with a very low estimate of that influence – lower than the US data suggest – there is still a substantial effect, both on the daily numbers and on the cumulative total to 3 August.

Thus, even with very low assumptions about the influence of News Corporation columnists, the number of new infections would have grown much more slowly had they not voiced their opinions. Importantly, that would have given people more time to address the failures that were apparent in hotel quarantine, contact tracing and aged care. Such improvements would have engendered much more confidence in the ability of authorities to control the virus – and, in all likelihood, would have avoided the need for, and extent of, some of the 'draconian' measures taken in the Stage 4 lockdown.

Conclusion

Andrew Bolt's plea, 'Victoria, don't accept this!', responded to the government's announcement of the Stage 4 lockdown on 2 August. That lockdown was a direct response to the rapid growth in COVID-19 numbers in the previous five weeks. The model presented in this paper shows that an alternative scenario was possible, with much lower infection rates for the same period. In this alternative scenario, it is highly unlikely that such a strong response would have been required.

What is apparent from this chapter is that News Corporation's campaign in 2020 against coronavirus restrictions had numerous effects: it influenced people to pay less heed to government restrictions, which, in turn, considerably increased – perhaps doubled – the number of coronavirus cases in Victoria in July, resulting in the Stage 4 lockdowns. If News Corporation's columnists were indeed as concerned about the impacts of lockdowns as they claimed, they would have done considerably better by shutting up.

References

ABC News. (2020, 21 December). Victoria's COVID-19 Hotel Quarantine Inquiry has delivered its final report. Here are the key findings. *ABC News*. www.abc.net.au/news/2020-12-21/victoria-COVID-hotel-quarantine-inquiry-final-report/13002956.

Allcott, H., Boxell, L., Conway, J., Gentzkow, M., Thaler, M. & Yang, D. (2020). Polarization and public health: Partisan differences in social distancing during the coronavirus pandemic. *Journal of Public Economics, 191*. doi.org/10.1016/j.jpubeco.2020.104254.

Altay, S. Nielsen, R. K. & Fletcher, R. (2023) News can help! The impact of news media and digital platforms on awareness of and belief in misinformation. *International Journal of Press/Politics, 29*(2), 459–484. doi.org/10.1177/1940 1612221148981.

Andrews, D. (2020, 2 August). *Statement on changes to Melbourne's restrictions* [Media release]. www.premier.vic.gov.au/statement-changes-melbournes-restrictions.

Ash, E., Galletta, S., Hangartner, D., Margalit, Y. & Pinna, M. (2020, 27 June). The effect of Fox News on health behavior during COVID-19. *SocArXiv*. doi. org/10.31235/osf.io/abqe5.

Bablani, L. & Ouakrim, D. A. (2020, 6 September). 'Slow and steady' exit from lockdown as Victorian government sets sights on 'COVID-normal' Christmas. *The Conversation*. theconversation.com/slow-and-steady-exit-from-lockdown-as-victorian-government-sets-sights-on-COVID-normal-christmas-145558.

Bennett, C. (2020, 13 October). Where did Victoria go so wrong with contact tracing and have they fixed it? *The Conversation*. theconversation.com/where-did-victoria-go-so-wrong-with-contact-tracing-and-have-they-fixed-it-147993.

Bursztyn, L., Egorov, G. & Fiorin, S. (2020). From extreme to mainstream: The erosion of social norms. *American Economic Review, 110*(11), 3522–3548. doi.org/10.1257/aer.20171175.

Castillo, M. & Petrie, R. (2020, 20 August). Is there a clear pathway out of the pandemic? Australians disagree. *Melbourne Institute Research Insight, 22*(20). melbourneinstitute.unimelb.edu.au/publications/research-insights/search/result?paper=3468179.

Choi, J., Lieff, S. A., Meltzer, G. Y., Grivel, M. M., Chang, V. W., Yang, L. W. & Des Jarlais, D. C. (2022). Anti-vaccine attitudes among adults in the U.S. during the COVID-19 pandemic after vaccine rollout. *Vaccines, 10*(6), 933. doi.org/10.3390/vaccines10060933.

Cowan, S. K., Mark, N. & Reich, J. A. (2021). COVID-19 vaccine hesitancy is the new terrain for political division among Americans. *Socius, 7*. doi.org/10.1177/23780231211023657.

Doherty, C., Tyson, A. & Weisel, R. (2014, 21 October). *Ebola worries rise, but most are 'fairly' confident in government, hospitals to deal with disease.* Pew Research Center. www.pewresearch.org/politics/2014/10/21/ebola-worries-rise-but-most-are-fairly-confident-in-government-hospitals-to-deal-with-disease/.

Duckett, S. & Mackey, W. (2020, 29 July). No, Australia should not follow Sweden's approach to coronavirus. *The Conversation.* theconversation.com/no-australia-should-not-follow-swedens-approach-to-coronavirus-143540.

Elvery, S., Spraggon, B. & Martino, M. (2020, 10 April). The one COVID-19 number to watch. *ABC News*, www.abc.net.au/news/2020-04-10/coronavirus-data-australia-growth-factor-COVID/12132478?nw=0.

Gollwitzer, A., Martel, C., Brady, W. J., Pärnamets, P., Freedman, I. G., Knowles, E. D. & Van Bavel, J. J. (2020). Partisan differences in physical distancing are linked to health outcomes during the COVID-19 pandemic. *Nature Human Behaviour, 4*, 1186–1197. doi.org/10.1038/s41562-020-00977-7.

The Guardian. (2020, 20 August). Coronavirus blog: Update on Victoria's fines.

Helliwell, J. F., Huang, H., Wang, S. & Norton, M. (2021). World happiness, trust and deaths under COVID. In J. F. Helliwell, R. Layard, J. Sachs & J.-E. De Neve (Eds), *2021 World Happiness Report* (pp. 13–56). Sustainable Development Solutions Network.

Herald Sun. (2021, 22 November). Herald Sun readership surges latest Roy Morgan figures confirm.

Hyde, Z. (2020, 24 November). Children may transmit coronavirus at the same rate as adults: What we now know about schools and COVID-19. *The Conversation.* theconversation.com/children-may-transmit-coronavirus-at-the-same-rate-as-adults-what-we-now-know-about-schools-and-COVID-150523.

Ingraham, C. (2020, 25 June). New research explores how conservative media misinformation may have intensified the severity of the pandemic. *Washington Post*. www.washingtonpost.com/business/2020/06/25/fox-news-hannity-coronavirus-misinformation/.

Jamieson, K. H. & Albarracin, D. (2020, April). The relation between media consumption and misinformation at the outset of the SARS-CoV-2 pandemic in the US. *Special issue. Harvard Kennedy School Misinformation Review*.

Jericho, G. (2020, 13 September). Regardless of Covid restrictions, if people are dying in large numbers your economy is stuffed. *The Guardian*. www.theguardian.com/business/commentisfree/2020/sep/13/regardless-of-covid-restrictions-if-people-are-dying-in-large-numbers-your-economy-is-stuffed.

Kirzinger, A., Kearney, A., Hamel, L. & Brodie, M. (2021, 16 November). KFF COVID-19 vaccine monitor: The increasing importance of partisanship in predicting COVID-19 vaccination status [Technical report]. *Kaiser Family Foundation*. www.kff.org/coronavirus-covid-19/poll-finding/importance-of-partisanship-predicting-vaccination-status/.

Klymak, M. & Vlandas, T. (2022). Partisanship and COVID-19 vaccination in the UK. *Science Reports, 12*, 19785. doi.org/10.1038/s41598-022-23035-w.

Marschner, I. (2020, 13 August). Yes, it looks like Victoria has passed the peak of its second wave. It probably did earlier than we think. *The Conversation*. theconversation.com/yes-it-looks-like-victoria-has-passed-the-peak-of-its-second-wave-it-probably-did-earlier-than-we-think-144200.

Meade, A. (2020, 7 August). Andrew Bolt's views diagnosed as 'disgraceful' after coronavirus controversies. *The Guardian*. www.theguardian.com/media/2020/aug/07/andrew-bolts-views-diagnosed-as-disgraceful-after-coronavirus-controversies.

Milner, D. (2020, 5 August). Murdoch columnists are coronavirus superspreaders and should be closed under Melbourne's Stage 4 restrictions. *The Shot*. theshot.net.au/general-news/murdoch-columnists-are-coronavirus-superspreaders-and-should-be-closed-under-melbournes-stage-4-restrictions/.

Muller, D. (2020, 22 July). Whether a ratings chase or ideological war, News Corp's coronavirus coverage is dangerous. *The Conversation*. theconversation.com/whether-a-ratings-chase-or-ideological-war-news-corps-coronavirus-coverage-is-dangerous-143003.

Pink, S., Chu, J., Druckman, J. N., Rand, D. G. & Willer, R. (2021). Elite party cues increase vaccination intentions among Republicans. *Proceedings of the National Academy of Sciences, 118*(32), e2106559118. doi.org/10.1073/pnas.2106559118.

Pinna, M., Picard, L. & Goessmann, C. (2022). Cable news and COVID-19 vaccine uptake. *Nature Scientific Reports, 12.* doi.org/10.1038/s41598-022-20350-0.

Russell, S. (2021, 1 January). No plan PM: How government's lack of an aged care plan cost lives. *Michael West Media.* www.michaelwest.com.au/no-plan-pm-how-governments-lack-of-an-aged-care-plan-cost-lives/.

Scott, S. & Kent, L. (2020, 6 August). Melbourne's Stage 3 lockdown prevented thousands of coronavirus cases, research data shows. *ABC News.* www.abc.net.au/news/2020-08-04/melbournes-coronavirus-lockdown-worth-it-burnet-institute-data/12521434.

Sehgal, N. J., Yue, D., Pope, E., Wang, R. H. & Roby, D. H. (2022). The association between COVID-19 mortality and the county-level partisan divide in the United States. *Health Affairs, 41*(6), 853–863. doi.org/10.1377/hlthaff.2022.00085.

Sheridan, G. (2020, 6 August). Secret modelling reveals COVID cases peak still weeks away. *The Australian.*

Simonov, A., Sacher, S. K., Dubé, J.-P. H. & Biswas, S. (2020). The persuasive effect of Fox News: Non-compliance with social distancing during the COVID-19 pandemic. *NBER Working Paper, 27237.* doi.org/10.3386/w27237.

Smithson, M. (2020, 26 November). Data from 45 countries show containing COVID vs saving the economy is a false dichotomy. *The Conversation.* theconversation.com/data-from-45-countries-show-containing-COVID-vs-saving-the-economy-is-a-false-dichotomy-150533.

Turnbull, N. (2020, 27 July). Watching Fox News in the US may kill you. *Pearls and Irritations.* johnmenadue.com/noel-turnbull-watching-fox-news-in-the-us-may-kill-you/.

Wallace, J., Goldsmith-Pinkham, P. & Schwartz, J. L. (2022, 26 September). Excess death rates for Republicans and Democrats during the COVID-19 pandemic. *NBER Working Paper, 30512.* doi.org/10.3386/w30512.

10

Australia and forced displacement: A new research agenda?

Kate Ogg

Introduction

In the global and interdisciplinary field of forced displacement or forced migration studies, there is a significant focus on Australian laws and practices. There is a wealth of literature on Australia's treatment of those who come in search of international protection and how Australia's refugee policies have influenced legal developments in other parts of the world (such as the now abandoned refugee offshore processing agreement between the United Kingdom and Rwanda). In this body of scholarship, Australia is positioned as a refugee receiving state. Scholars of forced migration and forced displacement have traditionally not considered Australian laws and policies that cause or respond to the displacement of Australian residents. This is despite forced displacement being a central aspect of Australian life. The brutal history of post-invasion Australia is one of genocide and forced displacement of Aboriginal and Torres Strait Islander peoples.[1] Australia has a long history of bushfire, flood, drought and cyclone events that have resulted in people leaving their homes and communities temporarily or permanently.

---

1   In this chapter I use the terms 'Aboriginal and Torres Strait Islander', 'Indigenous', 'First Nations', 'First Nation Australians' and 'First Australians' interchangeably. There are mixed opinions among Indigenous Australians as to preferred terminology (Watson & Douglas, 2021). As a non-Indigenous Australian, it is not my place to weigh in on these debates and take a position. I intentionally use all commonly employed terms to reflect the diversity of opinions and practice among First Nation Australians.

However, the overlapping disasters associated with bushfires, floods and the COVID-19 pandemic from late 2019 have given rise to an emerging body of research on displacement within Australia and forced displacement of Australian citizens and permanent residents abroad. In this chapter, I provide personal reflections on this shift in research focus, chart the possibilities for a research agenda on Australia and forced displacement and indicate how this nationally focused research agenda can contribute to global knowledge and debates.

From the global to the local: An unexpected and uncomfortable transition

My COVID-19 experience was unexceptional. I was impacted by the pandemic and the overlapping disasters associated with bushfires and floods, but I did not directly suffer any tragedies or personal loss. In early 2020, I arrived in Australia after an overseas sabbatical but, for health reasons, could not return to my home in Canberra because it was blanketed in bushfire smoke. For weeks on end, Canberra had the worst air quality rating in the world (Remeikis, 2020). Medical research indicates that this may have long-lasting health consequences for those who had no choice but to live through it, especially pregnant women and newborn babies (ANU Reporter, 2020). Once the smoke cleared, there was about a one-week reprieve before COVID-19 started to spread in Australia, and isolation, lockdowns and travel restrictions became a part of everyday life. During the pandemic period, the town in which I grew up (Lismore, NSW) faced an unprecedented and disastrous double flooding event. Many people lost their lives and many more lost their homes and remain homeless. While Lismore floods every few years, the flood of 2022 was on such a scale that, for the first time, central institutions such as schools have chosen to relocate rather than rebuild.

When I returned to Australia, I was working on a monograph manuscript. The monograph was a global and comparative examination of the relationship between law and refugees' journeys within and across national borders. As a scholar of refugee and forced displacement law, my research mainly focuses on refugees, IDP, stateless people and victims of human trafficking. For the most part, and certainly before Russia's invasion of Ukraine, people in these situations have predominately come from non-Western lower- and middle-income countries (often referred to as the 'Global South' in forced migration scholarship) (United Nations High Commissioner for Refugees [UNHCR], 2022). I never imagined that my research agenda would broaden to include Australian citizens' and residents' experiences of displacement.

Early in 2020, when many countries temporarily shut their borders in response to the COVID-19 pandemic, I wrote a blog post for the Andrew & Renata Kaldor Centre for International Refugee Law on how border closures may affect people's international human right to seek asylum (Ogg, 2020). Soon after, I was contacted by a travel journalist who had read the blog and wanted an international human rights law perspective on Australia's COVID-19 border closures and travel restrictions. He was not interested in the impact of these laws and policies on refugees but, instead, wanted to know about the human rights implications for 'ordinary Australians'. I provided a brief opinion in between lockdown homeschooling and Zoom lecturing and did not think much more about it.

Those few quotes in a travel magazine I had never heard of triggered an avalanche of media requests. I received numerous requests from journalists each week asking for an 'international human rights law perspective' on Australia's COVID-19 domestic and international travel restrictions. These requests came from diverse sources. I spoke to many local and rural radio stations as well as one of Australia's main national radio programs. I was asked to give a live televised interview for a national news program. I was interviewed by the BBC about 'fortress Australia'. Even *Public Accountant Magazine* (the official journal of the Institute of Public Accountants) wanted an international human rights law account of Australia's domestic and international travel restrictions in relation to COVID-19.

I had mixed feelings about the media's sudden interest in international human rights law. Australia's relationship with human rights law is complex and a comprehensive discussion is beyond the scope of this chapter. Australia does not have a constitutionally entrenched bill of rights or a comprehensive national human rights framework. As a scholar who has published on refugee law, I have occasionally been approached by the media to discuss a refugee case before the courts or developments in migration law and policy. However, these requests are infrequent, and most journalists have been more interested in domestic legal frameworks as opposed to an international human rights law perspective. While I was pleased that international human rights law was becoming a part of the national conversation on the pandemic response, it made me question whether the media's fixation on human rights was self-interested. One of the main arguments against Australia adopting a national human rights framework is that Australia's legal system already works perfectly to protect rights. This argument is met with derision from many people who have experienced marginalisation and discrimination. For example, Behrendt (2003, p. 257) has written:

> When I hear people talk about how well our legal system works I can feel a great chasm between what their experience with our laws are and what those of my own family are.

Perhaps the increased media interest in human rights law was due to the fact that, for many Australians, the COVID-19 pandemic was the first time they had directly experienced what they felt to be an unacceptable encroachment on their personal freedoms. Could these experiences lead to a greater understanding of and solidarity with people who have endured much more grave human rights violations, such as refugees? These questions kept lingering.

As the pandemic continued, I became increasingly alarmed about the situation of 'stranded' Australians and both perplexed and aghast by the lack of sympathy and support they received from different sectors of society. With one exception (returns from India for two weeks in April and May 2021), Australian citizens and permanent residents were always legally allowed to return to Australia. However, the imposition of incoming passenger travel caps and hotel quarantine meant that tens of thousands of Australian nationals were essentially locked out of the country (Senate Select Committee on COVID-19, 2022). The cap on the number of people permitted to travel to Australia meant that it became very difficult to purchase airline tickets (Jefferies et al., 2021). For those who did manage to secure a ticket, flights were often cancelled and economy passengers were regularly bumped off flights (Jefferies et al., 2021). From some locations, it was only possible to travel to Australia by purchasing a first or business-class ticket or multiple tickets in case of cancellations (Evershed, 2021). For many Australian citizens and permanent residents, the exorbitant costs of airline tickets and hotel quarantine were prohibitive (Jefferies et al., 2021). At most times during these travel restrictions, between 30,000 and 40,000 Australian citizens and permanent residents were registered with the Department of Foreign Affairs and Trade as wanting to return to Australia (Senate Select Committee on COVID-19, 2022). Many faced situations of extreme vulnerability and hardship. Some had their visas expire, meaning they had no lawful right to remain in the country in which they were staying, some became homeless, some could not access essential medicine and healthcare, some lost all savings and income, and family members were separated meaning that essential care could not be provided (Ali et al., 2022; McDermid et al., 2022; Oster et al., 2022).

While the media reported on the plight of 'stranded' Australians and some politicians championed their return, there was a lack of outrage among the general public, a lack of leadership by human rights bodies and a lack of vocal dissent by public commentators (Simic & Ogg, 2023). There were no organised protests and many Australian residents expressed support for the border restrictions and blamed 'stranded' Australians for travelling overseas in online media commentary (Simic & Ogg, 2023). Human rights organisations provided clear and comprehensive information on many aspects of COVID-19 policy but advice on travel restrictions and border closures was brief and misleading (Ogg & Simic, 2022). I was surprised that there were few public commentators and few scholars who openly challenged and critiqued Australia's travel restrictions and border closures. Perhaps the one exception to this was when the federal government temporarily banned people who had been in India from returning to Australia. This prompted accusations of racism and racial discrimination from well-known media commentators, sports personalities and human rights lawyers (Simic & Ogg, 2023).

My reaction to the situation faced by Australians stranded overseas was informed by my background in refugee law. By putting in place policies that inhibited Australian citizens and permanent residents from returning, Australia was certainly in breach of international human rights law (in particular, a person's right to return to their country of nationality, which is discussed below). But, more fundamentally, by being unable to return to their homeland, many of these 'stranded' Australians were deprived of the sociopolitical frameworks that are essential to be able to live safely and with dignity. Refugee law's theoretical underpinnings recognise the need for a state-citizen-territory nexus. Harvey (2013) explains that the 1951 United Nations Convention Relating to the Status of Refugees ('Refugee Convention') provides a response to Arendt's polemic of refugees being beyond 'the pale of law'. Being beyond the pale of law does not mean that refugees are victims of the law's punitive effects but that no law exists for them. A refugee can be understood as a person who is outside of their homeland and no longer has the protection of that nation-state. The remedy they are entitled to in international law is surrogate state protection in another state (Hathaway, 1991). Far from presenting a challenge or alternative to the global nation-state system, refugee law's role is to insert the refugee back into the state-citizen-territory nexus (Harvey, 2013). In other words, international refugee law recognises that all people need access to the territory of a nation-state that will provide for essential needs and protect essential interests. The Refugee Convention does this by providing refugees with 'the ghostly substance of citizenship' (Harvey, 2013, p. 88). To be clear, I am not suggesting that Australians unable to return home during the COVID-19 pandemic were refugees within the meaning of international law. Instead, due to their inability to return to their country of nationality, the citizen-state-territory bond had been severed. This left many without vital legal protections, inhibited access to essential services such as healthcare and medicine, and fractured familial relationships.

As the pandemic continued into 2021, growing numbers of people became domestically stranded due to state border restrictions. For example, pursuant to Queensland's July 2021 border direction, most people who wished to enter Queensland (including Queensland residents returning from other parts of Australia) were required to apply for a Queensland Border Declaration Pass, enter the state at a designated airport and undertake hotel quarantine at their own cost. The Queensland border did not open until 13 December 2021. From July to December 2021, thousands of Queensland residents were unable to return home because they could not afford hotel quarantine and airline tickets (Ogg & Simic, 2022). Many of those with the means to pay for flights and hotel quarantine found themselves stranded due to delays in processing entry pass applications and lack of quarantine places (Ogg & Simic, 2022). A similar situation occurred in Victoria as a result of the Victorian government's decision to restrict travel across its border in July 2021 (Victorian Ombudsman, 2021). Again, there was a lack of compassion from many politicians and public sector actors and a lack of leadership from the human rights sector (Ogg & Simic, 2022).

My reaction to these situations of domestic displacement and the level to which they were accepted was also informed by forced displacement law and theory. Those who are displaced within their own country are not refugees. A person can only be a refugee, and thus entitled to surrogate state protection, once they are outside their country of origin or habitual residence. However, those who are displaced within their own country often are in similar situations to refugees. Due to being unable to return to their communities and ordinary place of residence, they often have difficulties accessing housing, work, education and healthcare and can be separated from family members. Tuitt (2004) argues that IDPs are, similar to refugees, beyond the pale of law in the Arendtian sense – they remain within their homeland but they often lack state protection. IDP law attempts to preserve or rebuild the state-citizen-territory relationship by preventing displacement, outlining special protections owed when a person is internally displaced and bringing an end to displacement (Kälin, 2008). Against this theoretical background, I understood that those who could not return to their homes, sometimes for months on end, were not merely inconvenienced, but had been cut off from vital safety nets and from everything that makes life worth living.

While I thought I understood the predicaments faced by those internationally and domestically displaced, reading a reflective piece by Associate Professor Olivera Simic about her experience of Australia's COVID-19 border policies revealed a layer of trauma the depths of which I have never experienced. Simic (2021) writes powerfully about the intersections between her experience of war and being a migrant in Australia and her inability to reconnect with family during the pandemic. As a legal scholar and transitional justice expert, Simic has traditionally focused on human rights violations in post-conflict countries rather than liberal democracies such as Australia. At first, we did not quite know where our research would lead us, but we were adamant that people's experiences of international and domestic border restrictions had to be documented and framed in a manner that underscored the gravity of the harm endured.

International perspectives on forced displacement in the Australian context: Emerging research

In light of the above discussion, it is perhaps unsurprising that scholars with expertise in refugee studies, statelessness, citizenship and displacement have led the scholarly analysis of the legal validity of Australia's international border restrictions. Jefferies et al. (2021, p. 224) describe Australia's COVID-19 international border restrictions as giving rise to 'arbitrary, functional exile' for 'tens of thousands of Australian Citizens and permanent residents'. They examine the right to return under domestic and international law and make a compelling argument that Australia's travel caps 'constituted an arbitrary restriction on Australians' right to come home' (Jefferies et al., 2021, p. 223). Simic and Rubenstein (2022) similarly examine Australia's international border restrictions from a domestic and international law perspective. They directly address the tension between states' public health obligations and rights to freedom of movement and conclude that the measures Australia put in place to protect public health eroded fundamental rights and freedoms.

McAdam's research on disaster evacuations directly brings an international forced displacement lens to Australian law and policy. McAdam (2022) focuses on the evacuations that occurred during the 2019–20 bushfires and 2022 floods in northern NSW and Queensland. She argues that the evacuees were IDPs with rights and entitlements under international law, even though evacuees in Australia and elsewhere are rarely considered IDPs and evacuation law and policy in Australia rarely references international human rights. McAdam (2022, p. 1332) argues that, by failing to recognise that people evacuated from natural disasters are IDPs:

> current domestic frameworks pay insufficient attention to protection needs that may arise – particularly for groups that may find themselves in vulnerable situations, such as children and people with a disability, and for people whose displacement becomes prolonged.

McAdam highlights that international law on internal displacement addresses these protection needs and offers an accountability framework. McAdam (2022, p. 1332) suggests that if 'law and policymakers were to consider the needs of evacuees through this lens, they could confront protection gaps head-on and thereby enhance the promotion of people's rights, wellbeing and recovery'.

In my research with Simic, we argue that those unable to return home due to state border closures were IDPs within the meaning of international law (Ogg & Simic, 2022). Bringing an international internal displacement law perspective to Australian pandemic law and policy exposes Australian legal and political actors' flawed and rudimentary approach to human rights proportionality analysis. Focusing on Queensland, we highlight that the Queensland government failed to consider the prospect of internal displacement when introducing laws enabling border closures. The government also took the position that public health objectives meant that freedom of movement rights could be forsaken whereas the approach provided by international internal displacement law is much more nuanced. International internal displacement law would not go as far as absolutely prohibiting any law or policy that caused displacement but would require that protections be put in place to reduce the incidence, arbitrariness and length of displacement, and that special protections and processes be put in place for children, indigenous persons and those with significant health care needs. Importantly, our research shows that international internal displacement law can inform existing laws and processes in Australia. Thus, some strengthening of human rights protection in relation to internal displacement can be achieved without the need to change existing laws.

In our analysis of public accounts written by 'stranded' Australians, Simic and I observed another connection between forced displacement scholarship and Australians' COVID-19 experiences (Simic & Ogg, p. 2023). Common themes that have emerged from these public accounts indicate an erosion of trust in government, a sense of betrayal by public authorities, a feeling of disconnection from fellow Australians and a sense of no longer having a 'home'. These tropes mirror findings on the consequences of displacement in transitional justice studies. While displacement within and across borders is a common aspect of conflict and mass atrocities, it remains an under-examined topic in the field of transitional justice. Nevertheless, there is a small body of literature that focuses on the relationship between transitional justice and displacement (see e.g. Bradley, 2013; Duthie, 2011; Harris Rimmer, 2010). This body of scholarship underlines the enduring role of the nation-state system for the protection of human rights, human security and a sense of identity, and emphasises that displacement results in a breakdown of the state–citizen social contract. Scholars of displacement and transitional justice highlight the need for processes that rebuild these sociopolitical connections (see e.g. Duthie, 2011). We highlight in our research that many displaced Australians report that the experience of displacement has fundamentally and, perhaps irrevocably, changed their relationship with their family, friends, communities and Australia more broadly (Simic & Ogg, 2023). Thus, displacement was not just a 'bad experience' from which people could eventually recover but, instead, was for many a life-changing experience. We suggest that understanding how sociopolitical connections can best be rebuilt is an important and pressing issue for Australia to address in the post-pandemic era. We outline the potential role of a 'people's inquiry' in addressing these objectives. Demonstrating the connections between pandemic and disaster displacement, the Citizen's Inquiry into the 2019/2020 Australian Bushfires (Australian Peoples' Tribunal, 2021) may provide a model for citizen-led transitional justice mechanisms to address the causes and consequences of displacement.

Another important research development prompted by Australia's COVID-19 border policies is a historical and legal project on Australia's medico-legal border practices during COVID-19 and previous pandemics. Jefferies et al. (2023) are examining Australia's laws and policies regulating human movement during COVID-19, the 1918–19 influenza pandemic and early twentieth-century smallpox outbreaks. In one of the first publications arising from this project, they observe that:

> human movement during pandemic times in Australia has been regulated in a manner that sees mobility as a risk to public health capable of mitigation through the strict enforcement of borders as a technology of both confinement and exclusion.
>
> (Jefferies et al., 2023)

There is some research on the human consequences of Australia's international travel restrictions. Existing research has a health, wellbeing and economic focus (Ali et al., 2022; McDermid et al., 2022; Oster et al., 2022). Simic and I are continuing our research on COVID-19 displacement through qualitative interviews with people affected by Australia's international and domestic travel restrictions. We are examining the sociopolitical consequences of displacement abroad and internally within Australia. This research is continuing. Below, in outlining a research agenda for Australia and forced displacement, I discuss some of our preliminary findings.

Internal and forced displacement in Australia: Unexplored issues and global contributions

As the above discussion indicates, the application of internationally developed legal and normative frameworks on forced displacement to the Australian context is a fledgling scholarly endeavour being led by scholars with a refugee studies background. This new direction in research has the potential to bring new perspectives to intractable injustices, provide crucial insights on current national law reform initiatives and make significant contributions to global scholarly debates and international policy priorities.

One salient question is the extent to which internationally developed legal and normative frameworks addressing forced displacement can and should be applied to historic and continuing injustices faced by First Nation Australians. These include the forced displacement of First Nation Australians from their lands, communities and families during the Frontier Wars (Reynolds, 1982) and the Stolen Generations (Australian Human Rights Commission, 1997), the contemporary closures of First Nation communities (Pugliese, 2015) and high levels of First Nations children in state care (Davis, 2019). Bringing an international forced displacement law lens to analyse these historic and contemporary injustices is an endeavour not without controversy. Scholarship by leading Australian First Nations legal scholars indicates an uneasy relationship with international law (see e.g. Watson, 2016). International law can be both a Western and colonial construct but also a space in which to resist continuing colonisation (Watson, 2016). Yet, there are important intersections between international law on internal displacement and international human rights of indigenous peoples. The United Nations Declaration on the Rights of Indigenous Peoples, in particular protections against forced removal from traditional lands and forcibly removing children, has developed international law relating to internal displacement (Kälin, 2008). The fields of migration studies and forced migration and displacement studies have developed without the inclusion of First Nation perspectives (Dauvergne, 2021a). A First Australians–led project of this nature would make important contributions to both national and international literatures on indigenous human rights and forced displacement.

One issue on which Australia could take a leading global role is legal and policy responses to internal displacement associated with events such as bushfires, droughts, floods and cyclones. McAdam (2020) highlights that the position of evacuees is underdeveloped in global forced displacement literature. Australia has a long history of these types of events and has the resources and infrastructure to continually improve preventative measures and disaster responses. The reforms McAdam (2022) outlines, if taken up, could inform other states' law and policy agendas as well as the development of international forced displacement legal and normative frameworks in the context of events that are traditionally referred to as 'natural' disasters, which will increase with climate change. Human rights bodies such as the Australian Human Rights Commission and state and territory human rights bodies can take the lead by advocating for these reforms and placing these issues within a human rights framework. In 2022, the office of the UNHCR along with others published a handbook for national human rights organisations that provides guidance on protecting IDPs (UNHCR et al., 2022). The handbook provides numerous examples of how national human rights bodies across the world are advocating for and protecting IDPs, but there is little discussion of initiatives with respect to disaster evacuees.

Another global research question on which an Australian study could provide valuable and unique perspectives is the extent to which lived experiences of displacement, especially with respect to citizens and residents of high-income countries, change attitudes towards refugees. An interesting pattern emerging from the interviews Simic and I are conducting with displaced Australians is shifting levels of engagement with, and compassion for, refugees in Australia and Australia's offshore processing centres. Some of our interviewees were already critical of, and politically active with respect to, Australia's treatment of refugees and their experience of displacement did not change their views. However, many of our interviewees reported that prior to becoming 'stranded' or separated from stranded family they were either unaware of or neutral towards Australia's refugee laws and policies. Their experience of displacement made them more aware of the challenges refugees face, aroused in them more compassion towards refugees, prompted them to change their political views on refugees and made them more open to becoming politically active with respect to resisting and critiquing Australia's treatment of refugees.

One of the pushbacks that researchers applying a forced or internal displacement lens to the Australian context may face is an assumption that such an endeavour is not worthwhile because there are greater displacement problems elsewhere. One of the reviewers for the article Simic and I wrote on internal displacement in Australia during the pandemic (Ogg & Simic, 2022) said:

> I'm not sure when put in the context of either other debatable human rights implications of Australian asylum/migration policy, or the global challenge of internal displacement, that this case study justified the lengths to which the article goes to construct a legal framework/analysis.

This is despite the article highlighting that some people died as a result of displacement, people were rendered homeless, cancer patients and pregnant women could not access vital medical treatment, and very young children were separated from their parents. There is no question that the scale of displacement is much greater in other countries and, in particular, in lower- and middle-income countries (see UNHCR, 2022). However, this does not render the challenges faced by Australian residents insignificant or unworthy of scholarly resources and attention. The development of the assumption that internal displacement is a 'Global South' problem is an issue ripe for critical analysis. In our article, we highlight that while the UNHCR's statistics indicate that there are no IDPs in higher-income nation-states, the Internal Displacement Monitoring Centre takes a different approach and counts bushfire victims in Australia and the United States as IDPs (Ogg & Simic, 2022).

Along similar lines, one interesting new research development is the application of internal displacement legal and normative frameworks to those who have fled family violence (see Bowstead, 2015). No country is free from family violence and yet there has been a tendency in refugee and human rights law to frame the issue as one predominately associated with non-Western cultures (Crawley, 2022). Further, refugee and forced displacement law has been slow to respond appropriately to gendered violence (Dauvergne, 2021b). Against this background, there are a number of important questions for research. Do existing internal displacement frameworks adequately address displacement associated with family violence? Were family violence victims considered in debates on the development of internal displacement law? If family violence victims can be considered IDPs, what does this mean for how we conceptualise internal displacement as a global phenomenon? What are the intersections between family violence displacement and other forms of displacement? An Australian perspective on the last question would be particularly valuable given Australia's history of disaster displacement and experience of displacement during the COVID-19 pandemic.

Studies of forced displacement of citizens or residents of higher-income countries such as Australia could also contribute to theoretical understandings of displacement. Two central themes in forced displacement research are 1) the fundamental importance of having a place in the world and 2) intersecting vulnerabilities in displacement contexts (Tuitt, 2004). The number of people displaced in Australia during the COVID-19 pandemic pales in comparison to the numbers of displaced people in other parts of the world. Also, the length of displacement (for some a few weeks or a few months and only in exceptional cases more than a year) is far shorter than the protracted displacement situations witnessed in other nation-states (see UNHCR, 2022). Australians who became displaced during the COVID-19 pandemic most probably had more safety nets than most other people experiencing displacement. For example, as residents of a higher-income nation, many were likely to have some financial savings or assets or may have been able to rely on friends and family. Nevertheless, accounts of Australians' experiences of COVID-19 displacement demonstrate how access to one's home and country is fundamental to rights enjoyment and how quickly a person or family can descend from relative comfort to destitution and despair when forcibly displaced (Ogg & Simic, 2022). A longitudinal study of those displaced in Australia during the COVID-19 pandemic and overlapping bushfires and floods would make salient contributions to understanding the longer-term consequences of displacement.

Finally, it is imperative that Australian experiences of displacement feed into the current debate on human rights protections in Australia. The Australian Human Rights Commission (2022) is pushing for the adoption of a federal human rights act and the attorney-general of Australia commissioned a review of Australia's human rights framework (Dreyfus, 2023). There are a few consistent perspectives arising in the interviews Simic and I are conducting with displaced Australians. One is that all of the interviewees have prefaced their story with some type of qualifying statement such as 'I know that I am luckier than others' or 'I understand that my situation is not as bad as other people's'. Second, all the interviewees understood and supported the need for some border restrictions to be put in place to prevent and reduce the spread of COVID-19. However, they objected to the rigid and arbitrary manner in which the restrictions operated and the length of time for which they continued. Third, they all spent extensive amounts of time and energy navigating complex public and private bureaucracies in order to return home or access essential services such as welfare and medicine. They felt that state, territory and federal governments provided inadequate assistance and were apathetic to their plight.

These three consistent themes raise important insights for the future development of human rights law in Australia. First, while it is important for any human rights framework to address issues such as torture and slavery, human rights have a role not just in preventing atrocities but also in enabling people to live safe and meaningful lives. A lot of our interviewees were uncomfortable using human rights language because they felt that they were more privileged than others in many ways. A reconceptualisation of human rights and their role in everyday life is much needed. Second, we need much more rigorous and nuanced understandings and applications of proportionality in human rights contexts. We need to find ways to more appropriately balance competing needs and interests as opposed to the utilitarian approach of sacrificing the lives and livelihoods of a minority to protect the majority. Third, Australia needs accessible and meaningful human rights remedies. One of the reasons why the federal, state and territory governments provided minimal assistance to displaced Australians was most probably that the prospect of a successful legal challenge to the border restrictions was unlikely. A reimagined national human rights framework should not only make human rights justiciable but also provide dispute resolution options for those who do not want to or cannot litigate.

Conclusion

Forced displacement is not a new phenomenon in the Australian context. However, the analysis of Australian law, policy and experiences through the lens of internationally developed forced displacement legal and normative frameworks is a novel research development that emerged during the overlapping disasters associated with the COVID-19 pandemic, bushfires and floods. In this chapter, I have identified key issues to be explored in forced displacement research focusing on Australia. Continuing this research agenda will not only address the lacuna of knowledge with respect to forced displacement in Australia, but also has the potential to contribute to global knowledge and debates and, on some issues, position Australia as a leader in law and policy reform addressing displacement.

References

Ali, K., Iasiello, M., van Agteren, J., Mavrangelos, T., Kyrios, M. & Fassnacht, D. B. (2022). A cross-sectional investigation of the mental health and wellbeing among individuals who have been negatively impacted by the COVID-19 international border closure in Australia. *Globalization and Health*, *18*, 12. doi.org/10.1186/s12992-022-00807-7.

ANU Reporter. (2020). *Bushfires and COVID take their toll on new mums and babies.* reporter.anu.edu.au/all-stories/bushfires-and-covid-take-their-toll-on-new-mums-and-babies.

Australian Human Rights Commission. (1997). *Bringing them home report: National inquiry into the separation of Aboriginal and Torres Strait Islander children from their families.* humanrights.gov.au/sites/default/files/content/pdf/social_justice/bringing_them_home_report.pdf.

Australian Human Rights Commission. (2022). *Position paper: A human rights act for Australia.* Free and Equal. humanrights.gov.au/sites/default/files/free_equal_hra_2022_-_main_report_rgb_0_0.pdf.

Australian Peoples' Tribunal. (2021). *Citizen's Inquiry into the 2019/2020 Australian bushfires: Did systemic failure by Australian governments, to care for Country, contribute to 'ecocide'?* tribunal.org.au/hearings/2021-tribunal/.

Behrendt, L. (2003). It's broke so fix it: Arguments for a Bill of Rights. *Australian Journal of Human Rights*, *9*(1), 257–262. doi.org/10.1080/1323238X.2003.11911100.

Bowstead, J. C. (2015). Forced migration in the United Kingdom: Women's journeys to escape domestic violence. *Transactions of the Institute of British Geographers*, *40*(3), 307–320. doi.org/10.1111/tran.12085.

Bradley, M. (2013). *Truth-telling and displacement: Patterns and prospects*. International Center for Transitional Justice/Brookings LSE. www.brookings.edu/wp-content/uploads/2016/06/TJ_TruthTelling.pdf.

Crawley, H. (2022). Saving Brown women from Brown men? 'Refugee women', gender and the racialised politics of protection. *Refugee Survey Quarterly*, *41*(3), 355–380. doi.org/10.1093/rsq/hdac021.

Dauvergne, C. (2021a). Introduction to the *Research handbook on the law and politics of migration*: Law, politics, and the spaces between. In C. Dauvergne (Ed.), *Research handbook on the law and politics of migration* (pp. 1–6). Edward Elgar. doi.org/10.4337/9781789902266.00008.

Dauvergne, C. (2021b). Women in refugee jurisprudence. In C. Costello, M. Foster & J. McAdam (Eds), *The Oxford handbook of international refugee law* (pp. 728–777). Oxford University Press. doi.org/10.1093/law/9780198848639.003.0041.

Davis, M. (2019). *Family is culture: Final report*. www.familyisculture.nsw.gov.au/?a=726329.

Dreyfus, M. (2023, 22 March). *Review into Australia's human rights framework* [Media release]. Attorney-General's Department. ministers.ag.gov.au/media-centre/review-australias-human-rights-framework-22-03-2023.

Duthie, R. (2011). Transitional justice and displacement. *The International Journal of Transitional Justice*, *5*(2), 241–261. doi.org/10.1093/ijtj/ijr009.

Evershed, N. (2021, 7 July). Data reveals Australia's new international arrivals cap is harshest yet. *The Guardian*. www.theguardian.com/news/datablog/2021/jul/07/australias-travel-restrictions-how-the-cap-on-international-arrivals-has-changed.

Harris Rimmer, S. (2010). Reconceiving refugees and internally displaced persons as transitional justice actors [Research paper]. *New Issues in Refugee Research*, 187. www.unhcr.org/sites/default/files/legacy-pdf/4bbb2a589.pdf.

Harvey, C. (2013). Is humanity enough? Refugees, asylum seekers and the rights regime. In S. Juss & C. Harvey (Eds), *Contemporary issues in refugee law* (pp. 68–88). Edward Elgar. doi.org/10.4337/9781782547662.00011.

Hathaway, J. C. (1991). Reconceiving refugee law as human rights protection. *Journal of Refugee Studies*, *4*(2), 113–131. doi.org/10.1093/jrs/4.2.113.

Jefferies, R., Barratt, T., Huang, C. & Bashford, A. (2023). Regulating movement in pandemic times. *Journal of Bioethical Inquiry*, *20*, 633–638. doi.org/10.1007/s11673-023-10292-1.

Jefferies, R., McAdam, J. & Pillai, S. (2021). Can we still call Australia home? The right to return and the legality of Australia's COVID-19 travel restrictions. *Australian Journal of Human Rights*, *27*(2), 211–231. doi.org/10.1080/1323238X.2021.1996529.

Kälin, W. (2008). *Guiding principles on internal displacement: annotations* (2nd ed.). Studies in Transnational Legal Policy, 38. www.brookings.edu/wp-content/uploads/2016/06/spring_guiding_principles.pdf.

McAdam, J. (2020). Displacing evacuations: A blind spot in disaster displacement research. *Refugee Survey Quarterly*, *39*(4), 583–590. doi.org/10.1093/rsq/hdaa017.

McAdam, J. (2022). Exploring the legal basis in Australia for evacuations from disasters: Avoiding arbitrary displacement. *UNSW Law Journal*, *45*(4), 1329–1366. doi.org/10.53637/OYFB2213.

McDermid, P., Sooppiyaragath, S., Craig, A., Sheel, M., Blazek, K., Talty, S. & Seale, H. (2022). Psychological and financial impacts of COVID-19 related travel measures: An international cross-sectional study. *PLoS ONE*, *17*(8). doi.org/10.1371/journal.pone.0271894.

Ogg, K. (2020, 16 April). *COVID-19 travel bans: The right to seek asylum when you cannot leave your homeland*. Kaldor Centre for International Refugee Law. www.unsw.edu.au/kaldor-centre/our-resources/legal-and-policy-resources/commentaries/covid-19-travel-bans.

Ogg, K. & Simić, O. (2022). Becoming an internally displaced person in Australia: State border closures during the COVID-19 pandemic and the role of international law on internal displacement. *Australian Journal of Human Rights*, *28*(1), 95–117. doi.org/10.1080/1323238X.2022.2094538.

Oster, C., Ali, K., Iasiello, M., Muir-Cochrane, E. & Fassnacht, D. B. (2022). The experience of individuals affected by Australia's international border closure during the COVID-19 pandemic. *Health & Place*, *78*. doi.org/10.1016/j.healthplace.2022.102928.

Pugliese, J. (2015). Geopolitics of Aboriginal sovereignty: Colonial law as 'a species of excess of its own authority', Aboriginal passport ceremonies and asylum seekers. *Law, Text, Culture*, *19*, 84–115.

Remeikis, A. (2020, 3 January). Canberra chokes on world's worst air quality as city all but shuts down. *The Guardian*. www.theguardian.com/australia-news/2020/jan/03/canberra-chokes-on-worlds-worst-air-quality-as-city-all-but-shut-down.

Reynolds, H. (1982). *The other side of the frontier: Aboriginal resistance to the European invasion of Australia*. Penguin Books.

Senate Select Committee on COVID-19. (2022, April). *Final report*. Parliament of Australia. www.aph.gov.au/Parliamentary_Business/Committees/Senate/COVID-19/COVID19/Report.

Simic, O. (2021). Locked in and locked out: A migrant woman's reflection on life in Australia during the COVID-19 pandemic. *Journal of International Women's Studies*, *22*(9), 400–426. vc.bridgew.edu/jiws/vol22/iss9/26/.

Simic, O. & Ogg, K. (2023). Australia's international and domestic borders as sites of dislocation, division and distrust: The socio-political impacts of COVID-19 travel bans. *Law in Context*.

Simic, O. & Rubenstein, K. (2022). The challenge of 'COVID-19 free' Australia: International travel restrictions and stranded citizens. *The International Journal of Human Rights*, *27*(5). doi.org/10.1080/13642987.2022.2058496.

Tuitt, P. (2004). Refugees, nations, laws and the territorialization of violence. In P. Fitzpatrick & P. Tuitt (Eds), *Critical beings: Law, nation and the global subject* (pp. 37–57). Ashgate.

UNHCR. (2022). *Global trends: Forced displacement in 2021*. www.unhcr.org/media/40152.

UNHCR et al. (2022). *Protecting internally displaced persons: A handbook for national human rights institutions*. www.unhcr.org/media/handbook-internal-displacement-national-human-rights-institutions.

Victorian Ombudsman. (2021). *Investigation into decision-making under the Victorian border crossing permit directions*. assets.ombudsman.vic.gov.au/assets/Investigation-into-decision-making-under-the-Victorian-Border-Crossing-Permit-Directions_Dec-2021.pdf.

Watson, I. (2016). *Aboriginal peoples, colonialism and international law: Raw law*. Routledge.

Watson, N. & Douglas, H. (2021). Introduction. In N. Watson & H. Douglas (Eds), *Indigenous legal judgments: Bringing Indigenous voices into judicial decision making* (pp. 1–22). Routledge.

Conclusions

11

Pandemic daze: From causal to casual

Mark Kenny

> It is time to move away from COVID exceptionalism, in my view, and we should be thinking about what we do to protect people from any respiratory disease. It does not mean we have somehow magically changed the infectiousness of this virus. It is still infectious.
>
> (Professor Paul Kelly, chief medical officer, 30 September 2022)

Australia and its management of the pandemic in overview

When the Australian of the Year was announced in January 2024, the two eminent melanoma specialists jointly awarded the country's top annual tribute snapped the public's patriotic reverie with a sobering corrective. Aware they were beaming into lounge rooms across the country, professors Georgina Long and Richard Scolyer, the latter afflicted with terminal brain cancer, used their pinnacle moment of good-vibes television to deliver an uncompromising reality check to a public wilfully defying a mortal risk: 'Tomorrow, [Australia Day][1] thousands of Aussies will be on the beaches, working on their tans, or as we see it, brewing their melanomas', Long said:

---

1   Australia's national day occurs on 26 January and is a public holiday around the country.

> A tan is skin cells in trauma in response to over-exposure to UV radiation from the sun. There is nothing healthy about a tan, nothing. Our bronzed Aussie culture is actually killing us.
>
> (Long, 2024)

They then called on advertisers and social media influencers to stop glamourising sun tanning in order to sell products. The parallel with a growing COVID-19 normalisation or what I will call here 'casualism' seemed obvious, even before noticing that the pair's live address came on 25 January, four years to the day since the first SARS-CoV-2 infection was confirmed in Australia (Margo, 2023). Like the causal relationship between sun exposure and skin cancer, Australians had managed to both know and yet unknow about COVID's ongoing prevalence. This 'unknowing' took the form of refusing to maintain observance of even relatively small behavioural changes to reduce personal exposure to an illness that had provoked profound fear and urgency upon its arrival.

Unlike the chronic skin cancer risk, the acute danger of COVID-19 in 2020 (and since) did not prompt a nationwide public health campaign, despite the crucial importance of individual preventative action and the clear need for community awareness (Crabb, 2023). Over 48 months, the nation has progressed through several phases of pandemic perception, beginning with acute fear and confusion and ending (to date) with an insouciance that, on the face of it, is at odds with a quantified risk. By year three, mask wearing had become rare in public places and what had been ubiquitous public venue signage designed to enforce social distancing and other 'safe' behaviours was either withdrawn or, in any event, widely ignored.

Moreover, an observable resistance arose towards any discussion about a return to onerous pandemic restrictions and that resistance quickly extended to nearly all COVID-19 talk undertaken by political representatives and medical authorities. It was as if the government-mandated deprivations of the early pandemic period were seared more deeply into many peoples' minds than either the trauma of the virus or the fear of contracting it. In social situations, Australians commonly now remark that they do not wish to even think about the pandemic anymore, let alone brook discussions about new infection prevention measures, should they be recommended in future outbreaks of COVID-19 infection or, indeed, in respect of an entirely new viral threat.

The swing in community opinion from outright fear to weary indifference was dramatic. In between these extremes had come a period of intense societal clamour for governments (state and federal) to act decisively to protect the population. Once instituted, however, those same public health measures – isolation, testing, compulsory reporting, rigorous contact tracing, travel restrictions and more – proved onerous and became increasingly unpopular. By the middle of 2021, broadly unpopular protests by so-called anti-vaxxers were becoming more common in capital cities and regional areas of the country (Noble, 2021). For those employees outside the information economy, working from home was either difficult or impossible. Thus, there were disproportionate effects of infection control policy, with lower-income workers tending to fare more poorly than those on higher incomes.

These measures eventually gave way to a second phase in which public scepticism about the quality of medical science and a general mistrust of the motives behind official decision-making was fuelled by a growing problem of mis- and disinformation. In the space of two years, Australians had travelled from a state of high COVID-19 alarm characterised by widespread social compliance with restrictive health rules to a delusional state of behaving as if the threat had passed, even though, statistically, it had not. This paradigm shift found its expression in both policy and politics. As Shirley Leitch and Sally Wheeler point out in the opening chapter of this volume, Australians had confronted the COVID-19 threat under a conservative Coalition government known for its reverence for market principles and a certain, albeit inconsistent, libertarian rhetoric. Its successful election narrative had valorised debt and deficit reduction, lower taxes and a return to a balanced budget. Faced with the pandemic, however, these objectives had to be jettisoned – a process of mental adjustment for the government that came in fits and starts.

This political branding was fortuitous because, while the unprecedented stimulus spending undertaken by the Coalition would have been undertaken by the Australian Labor Party (ALP) had it won the 2019 election, it seems likely that the Coalition, in Opposition, would have vehemently opposed the extent of new emergency spending. Such a political difference over policy would have denied the country the level of political bipartisanship that characterised emergency economic assistance in 2020. In fact, it was originally the Australian Council of Trade Unions that had recommended wage subsidisation by the government to avoid calamitous unemployment expected from lockdowns (O'Neil, 2020). This proposal was then supported by the ALP – a call notably rejected at first by the Morrison government on orthodox ideological grounds, before being agreed to, albeit in a modified form. The subsidies would go not to employees but to employers, and with minimal verification requirements to aid swift disbursement. In all, A\$88.9 billion was paid out in the program known as JobKeeper – equivalent to 4.5 per cent of GDP. This was the largest element of total pandemic support and was estimated at the time to have a final cost of A\$320 billion (Treasury, 2023). The JobKeeper scheme is analysed in some depth by Rohan Pitchford and Rabee Tourky in Chapter 4.

By the general election of 21 May 2022, however, the pandemic, and the Coalition government's handling of it, was regarded by both main parties to be unproductive terrain on which to campaign. COVID-19 minimisation measures, including debate over the delayed availability of vaccines, inadequate supply of PPE and access to affordable rapid antigen test kits (RATs), barely rated a mention against more pressing concerns around the economy, political integrity/corruption, women in politics and climate change. What had dominated the headlines only months before had come to be seen by the main parties as old news – a voter turn-off.

Even after the ALP succeeded in that election, its withering pre-election critique of its predecessor's policy failed to manifest in a serious change in governmental action, with no observable increase in public health messaging and little in the way of substantive new COVID-19 spending. As Chris Wallace (2023a) noted, within just eight months of its election, and despite the fact that only 30 per cent of voters thought the previous Coalition government had managed the crisis competently, the new ALP government led by Anthony Albanese appeared to opt for continuation rather than new interventions: 'The previous champion of muscular public policy slickly switched to a laissez-faire stance, with COVID-19 infection now declared a matter of "personal responsibility"' (Wallace, 2023a).

Noting that more Australians had died from COVID-19 during the Albanese government's first seven months in office than in the preceding 26 months of the Morrison Coalition government's handling of the pandemic, Wallace argues that medical experts had expected Labor to embark on a public health and awareness campaign aimed at educating Australians about the ongoing risks of infection and the ways that this risk could be minimised. Yet no such campaign materialised. It is likely that this substantial softening of Labor's promise to act on COVID-19 once in office stemmed from its political reading of the electorate. After two years of the pandemic, featuring movement restrictions and full lockdowns replete with stay-at-home orders and even night-time curfews in the southern state of Victoria, the new national government had evidently concluded that there was not only little appetite for a return to fetters on social and commercial activity, but also that there was a distaste for mentioning the pandemic at all.

Australians had gone from being seriously scared of the virus to being equally wary of returning to extreme COVID-19 containment measures (Booker & Najma, 2022). This rapid switch spawned the term 'lockdown amnesia' – the desire of many to 'close the chapter entirely, almost as if it had never happened' (Thorpe et al., 2024). Thorpe et al. argue that 'this desire to forget and move on … is understandable at one level. But it also risks missing the opportunity to learn from what happened'. They warn that individual memories of the pandemic period risk becoming increasingly inherently vague with time, and vulnerable to 'broader narratives (in the media or official responses)' that could overwrite personal recollections:

> Political calls to 'live with the virus' and media hesitancy to publish COVID-related stories due to perceived audience fatigue, can create a collective sense of needing to 'move on'. Looking back can be seen as questionable, or even attacked.
>
> (Thorpe et al., 2024).

The role of the media

Constant entreaties from conservative politicians and right-wing media contributed to a breakdown in community resolve to take measures to halt infection, even though it was widely reported that the virus posed a more deadly risk for some people than others. Feeding public cynicism, ironically, was the facility of direct access to the medical advice informing official policy in the early stages of the pandemic, which, of necessity, underwent some changes as the pathogen was more fully understood and its means of transmission – aerosol – became the focus (Lupton, 2024).

The bespoke elements of crisis communication in the internet and social media age were also, somewhat perversely, key contributors to a sense of confusion; while the instantaneous sharing of health information via internet-connected devices aided dissemination of health warnings, it also facilitated alternative information sources. Deborah Lupton (2024) contends that this is an important difference in the perception of risk across the community, because, in a pre-internet emergency, risk communication was a 'top-down practice' controlled by authorities – police, government leaders, health experts and the like. Whereas:

> The affordances of the internet and digital media allow for the public sharing of this information to take place rapidly and globally. This has meant that modes of communication are no longer solely in the purview of experts or authorities.
>
> (Lupton, 2024)

This top-down delivery of critical information during a crisis may have its weaknesses in that a single source of instruction increases the impact of wrong, delayed or just poorly communicated advice. But it at least does not have to compete with a vast array of putative authorities, including wild conspiracy theories and unscientific alternative treatments. The differential impacts of the pandemic as it unfurled – geographically but also economically, because lower-paid occupations tended to be less adaptable to a movement-restricted situation – combined with the dramatically altered media landscape of the hyper-connected digital age, fundamentally altered the way information flowed and the means adopted for its promulgation and receipt.

Prevention and mitigation strategies needed to take into account these new realities and the challenges of communicating with diverse publics with various media consumption modes, and perhaps much lower trust or confidence relationships with government, science and the validity of public health directions. The colossal, all-consuming nature of the pandemic threat meant that news media came to play the primary role. Transformed of necessity by accelerating advances in digital technology that made contemporaneous news coverage via the internet both technologically possible and commercially necessary, these companies (along with the two public outlets, ABC and SBS) quickly found themselves playing the role of COVID-first broadcasters (Kenny, 2023b). Daily press conferences called by state premiers and their respective chief health officers were broadcast live on rolling news channels – both free-to-air and subscription television. So normal did this become that the main ones, either in the bigger states or where outbreaks happened to be high at that time, were staggered in their scheduling so as to be able to be carried live across the nation.

As the crisis unfolded, journalists and, therefore, journalism itself became an instrument of public policy as media outlets carried official information to consumers, often uncritically, relating to infection numbers, hospitalisations and deaths, the need for social distancing and reporting symptoms, and measures for ensuring personal hygiene etc. In an environment in which the formal parliamentary Opposition had adopted a non-confrontational stance by actively eschewing 'politics' in order to enhance a sense of unified policy, the usual accountability role of journalists became both more necessary and yet medically, socially and politically untenable. As David Speers (2023) noted, drastic public policy measures based on nascent virology and emergent epidemiology required 'strong public trust and compliance for the measures to work'. Journalists and their employers were both chief conduit for that information and, potentially, the only protection for the public against capricious policy and state overreach:

> This dynamic presented a challenge for the media, particularly those with a role in scrutinising and analysing decisions of government. Were we to comply with the pressure to uncritically explain what the government was doing based on 'expert advice' in the interests of public safety? Or were we to test that advice against the opinions of other experts, expose contradictions and highlight consequences, all while avoiding any misinformation or exaggeration? The pressure on media wasn't just coming from federal and state governments. It was also coming, increasingly, from sections of the audience, understandably anxious about Covid and already shifting their viewing, reading, and listening habits.
>
> (Speers, 2023)

In the early months of the pandemic, the answer seemed clear enough. No vaccine existed nor was there any certainty that one would be developed. Moreover, the primary method of transmission (i.e. aerosol) was under-appreciated while other aspects were overstated (Kenny, 2023b). According to Lupton (2024), during this period, some people reported becoming confused, distressed and overwhelmed by the sheer volume of information coming at them, as authorities and medical specialists scrambled to understand the nature of the challenge and the public policy response. However, she found that these negatives were often assuaged by the act of seeking out information about what to do. This bilateral state of anxiety about the unknown scale of the danger and the access to information from chief health officers, infectious disease experts and epidemiologists characterised much of the first two years of the pandemic.

In the second two years of the pandemic, things shifted markedly. Trust in medical expertise, government policy and the necessity for ongoing COVID-19 deprivations began to decline. The possible role played by some commentators in the News Corporation media in this decline is discussed by Tony Ward in Chapter 9. Early support for strong pandemic measures undertaken and enforced during 2020–21 gave way to 'much lower support' in the second two-year period. Complacency replaced COVID-19 anxiety, which, according to Lupton (2024), was linked to the 'progressive withdrawal of strong public measures such as quarantine, mandatory isolation when infected, and testing and tracing regimens'. Both media and governments pulled back from daily discussion of the dangers of COVID-19, perceiving a widespread weariness in the broader public. According to some assessments, indifference about the real risk of infection rose against a concomitant fall in direct public entreaties on the need to wear masks and take other protective measures to avoid the virus (Lupton, 2024; Margo, 2023; Wallace, 2023a). It seems reasonable to conjecture that a withdrawal of what had been saturation media coverage about infection, hospitalisation and fatality numbers was received by the community as a sign that life was returning to normal. Thus, a reflexive loop may have emerged in which media – and political leaders – responded to a perceived public distaste for ongoing COVID-19 coverage, and the public increasingly read that as evidence that the worst was over.

It was into this changing dynamic that the pre-election positioning of both the Coalition and Labor began in the first half of 2022. Elected in May of that year, the new ALP government led by Prime Minister Anthony Albanese had been expected to make an observable step-change in public messaging about the dangers of COVID-19, and to prioritise the funding of measures to protect the vulnerable – particularly residents and staff in frontline aged care facilities and hospitals. Earlier, when criticised for the more energetic behaviour of other governments on behalf of their citizens, Prime Minister Scott Morrison had declared 'it's not a race', sparking widespread outrage in the community. Labor, while initially measured, had been critical of the Morrison government's perceived lack of urgency at important points in the crisis. 'It is a race. It's the most urgent job in the country right now', Albanese had said in May 2021, a year before the election:

> The cost of the Morrison Government's delays is being paid for by every worker who can't go to work, every business that has to shut, and every Australian who can't be with their loved ones.
>
> (Albanese, 2021)

Labor had previously condemned poor logistics and coordination in the acquisition and distribution of PPE for health workers, police and other essential services. Once it became clear that one or more vaccines were looking like gaining approval, the Morrison government had been seen to go slowly on securing enough supplies for the Australian population. Subsequently, as the emphasis on COVID-19 testing swung away from state-mandated (and provided) PCR testing towards self-testing, the government was criticised for failing to ensure adequate supplies of imported RATs.

Post-election positioning

Once finally in office, the ALP was expected to present a more front-footed approach to the ongoing pandemic threat. However, the material change was, according to some, hardly noticeable. Data obtained from the Victorian Health Department by the ABC in June 2023 revealed that at least 659 Victorians died from COVID-19–related illness while receiving treatment for other pathologies between 2020 and April 2023. The ABC stated that information released under freedom of information laws put the number of 'suspected' cases of hospital-acquired infections in state hospitals at 5,514 (Cook, 2023). The ABC report followed just weeks after the Monash Health Service in Victoria joined many other healthcare providers in softening its rules around COVID-19 protocols, reducing or removing front-entrance screening of members of the public and the mandatory wearing of N95 masks for frontline health workers, including nurses, orderlies and doctors.

The ABC story was just one of a plethora of reports on the apparent mismatch between the statistical realities of COVID-19 as an ongoing pandemic and the dramatically different levels of public and official consciousness about the disease and measures available to reduce its transmission. In July 2022, Minister for Health and Aged Care Mark Butler told a podcast on *The Conversation* site that the new federal government was not about to reintroduce strong pandemic management rules, such as movement restrictions, mask mandates or compulsory stay-at-home orders for those infected or exposed to those carrying the virus:

> What we don't want to end up with is a position where the community thinks government is being heavy handed or just continuing a situation which the community tolerated very well over … the first two years of the pandemic, but I think is starting to reach the end of their tether about.
>
> (Grattan, 2022)

The argument that 'the community ... is starting to reach the end of their tether' is telling in relation to a disease that is known to be both deadly and preventable, and which has been the subject of the greatest set of policy and budgetary provisions in relation to a public health matter in Australia's history. It is likely that this reflected a sociopolitical assessment by the Labor government as much as any health-based imperatives. The result was a framing of policy measures designed to address public impatience rather than an increase in public inpatients, despite the latter reflecting the reality of the ongoing community threat.

By February 2024, the ABC was describing the abandonment of specific infection minimisation measures in public hospitals as 'the Robodebt of medicine' – a reference to a notorious government debt recovery system that created bogus financial liabilities, hounded the poor and marginalised, and largely escaped major media attention until it had inflicted widespread social harm, including suicides. The ABC stated:

> Health departments insist the risk of catching COVID cannot be eliminated completely, and that hospitals maintain stringent measures to prevent infections and manage outbreaks. But senior healthcare workers in several states say vulnerable people – including transplant and oncology patients and others with compromised immune systems – are contracting COVID because even basic precautions are not being taken: a consequence, they say, of hospitals' failure to address airborne transmission, and the pervasive myth that COVID is 'just a cold'.

> (Gleeson, 2024)

Hospitals and aged care facilities that had been at the coalface of the pandemic emergency during 2020–21 had, somewhat jarringly, formed the vanguard of a new laissez-faire attitude to COVID-19 transmission, described by some as 'let it rip' (Wallace, 2023b). Simultaneously, these facilities emerged as nodes of many infections, causing some fatalities, and yet also as bellwethers of a new pragmatism in which it is accepted that the virus is practically unstoppable and, therefore, simply to be lived with. In a submission to the federal government's COVID-19 Response Inquiry, OzSAGE, which describes itself as a 'multi-disciplinary network of Australian experts from a broad range of sectors relevant to the well-being of the Australian population in the COVID-19 pandemic', characterised the rate of hospital-acquired COVID-19 infection as 'a national crisis': COVID-19 acquired in hospitals 'is causing a greater burden of disease than other nosocomial infections such as wound infections and antimicrobial resistance' (OzSAGE, 2023). OzSAGE cited data provided by Victorian health authorities that showed, in 2022, over 3,000 people acquired COVID-19 while in hospital in Victoria alone, and greater than 10 per cent of these died as a result (OzSAGE, 2023). Arguing that patients have an inalienable right to healthcare that does not put them at greater avoidable risk, and that prevention is a 'core responsibility' of infection prevention and control committees, OzSAGE reported that most states had 'removed the requirement for masking in healthcare' and that guidelines were not being followed regarding the wearing of masks when treating vulnerable patients (OzSAGE, 2023). The group joined a growing number of experts in medicine, public policy and related fields pushing for a re-tightening of anti-COVID-19 measures with particular emphasis on mask wearing in patient interface situations, improved ventilation in hospitals and public places, as well as greater community access to vaccines and to antiviral medications (Crabb, 2023; Lupton, 2024; Wallace, 2023a).

Some argue that once Labor achieved its goal of forming government, it lost the resolve it had shown on the Opposition benches to buttress public safety through high-profile public awareness campaigns and the reintroduction of restrictions on public contact when infections broke out. For Wallace (2023b), the new government's reluctance can be attributed to an 'asymmetry' in the public debate in which a small group of people with a sceptical attitude to the severity of the virus, the advisability of vaccines and the motives of governments has had an outsized influence. In some instances, this asymmetry may have intimidated politicians at a personal level via social media campaigns. Wallace says that these 'anti-vaxxer' voices have 'essentially hijacked the brains of the politicians who are responsible, state and federal, for public health in Australia'. She contends that social media 'massively inflamed' the issues around community protection:

> I think there's a great fatigue amongst politicians and policymakers about being subject to that kind of attack – I think as a result, there's been a very disappointing, indeed disturbing abandonment of public health fundamentals in this areas as something that governments state and federal should aspire to be high achievers in.
>
> (Wallace, 2023b)

In support of this view, Wallace (2023b) listed the tightly restricted availability of antiviral medication, the laissez-faire approach to vaccination in nursing homes, an unwillingness to actively recognise the reality that

COVID-19 is a 'respiratory infection' necessitating significant improvements in ventilation, and the paucity of proper metrics for monitoring COVID-19 morbidity and mortality.

A combination of community fatigue with inconvenient COVID-19 measures, right-wing and libertarian politicians disproportionately platformed by contrarian media, and government failure to provide leadership has licensed a growing mismatch between the reality of COVID-19 harm on the ground and the response at the official level. What had been a crisis of terrifying existential proportions in 2020, necessitating the biggest direct government interventions Australia has seen outside of wartime, has morphed into a more or less silent pandemic, as both governments and the public agree to pull back emergency measures even though the emergency itself continues.

The interplay of politics and policy

The words quoted at the beginning of this chapter capture the official mindset of policymakers perhaps more explicitly than any others articulated in the time since COVID-19 observance lost traction in the public square and the subject itself became an impolite dinner topic. Expressed by the chief medical officer at a joint press conference called by the prime minister, they reflect an uncommonly clear enunciation of a largely unheralded retreat from spectacular intervention towards a new policy stance for the long haul, widely described as 'living with COVID'.

However, infectious disease experts, epidemiologists and social policy observers hold strong reservations about the very precept. They cite the effects of COVID-19 exposure on the immune suppressed, the elderly, the poor and those with a range of health conditions, including lung disease and hypertension. The failure to maintain the salience of these concerns in the public mind at anything like the level they occupied at the height of the crisis explains something about the nature of Australian society and the human capacity for the accommodation of acute risk when it becomes chronic risk: that is, the normalisation of danger during sustained crises. Ironically, it may well be that because medico-scientific knowledge was being built and refined in full public view as the pandemic unfolded, those seeking to undermine the efficacy and motives of social separation, masks, isolation, quarantine rules and vaccines gathered so many adherents. Perhaps the biggest surprise though, given what that accumulated knowledge pointed to, is the failure of Australian governments, state and federal, to address the yawning gap in infection control: the inadequacy of up-to-date, properly resourced and enforceable indoor air quality (IAQ) standards. Doctors say that, while ventilation is not the same as viral elimination, it is arguably the most available proxy for that same outcome (OzSAGE, 2023). At present, Australia, like most countries, continues to fail on this most basic of requirements: the mandating of minimum IAQ. 'The shocking reality is that most countries, including Australia, do not have any IAQ standards or even plans to establish them', write Morawska et al. (2022, p. 578) in the *Medical Journal of Australia*.

The debate about the efficacy of emergency COVID-19 measures will continue, focusing, in particular, on the actions of the conservative Coalition government led by Scott Morrison when the pandemic started, and the Labor government from May 2022 when the political momentum seemed to ebb. For public health experts and economists alike, the dramatic actions of the Morrison government – closing the national border, banning social gatherings and ordering people to stay home – were pivotal. However, for a significant subset of the electorate, egged on by the populist press inspired by the US, the drama of COVID-19 was overblown and was used by a government already in trouble to be seen to be responding strongly. Said one prominent Liberal Party–aligned columnist:

> If you think it was political genius for a leader to shut the borders to an island nation, lock Australian citizens inside, prevent Australian citizens overseas from returning home, then Morrison is your man. There is another view. Morrison set the template for Australia's cruel, illiberal response. He didn't have the nous to sensibly balance risk. Instead, he chose a sledgehammer to try to eliminate risk.
>
> (Albrechtsen, 2024)

Arguably, both of the federal governments in power during the COVID-19 period responded partially to the health impetus and partially to the political/ electoral pressures as they understood them. The Morrison government was unpopular for its perceived neglect during the 'Black Summer' bushfire crisis of 2019–20, such that the embattled prime minister had glimpsed his own political mortality within less than a year of winning an unlikely election in 2019. Thus, the arrival of a dangerous new virus in January 2020 presented Morrison with both an obligation to demonstrate national leadership and an opportunity to show voters that he was capable of emergency leadership. Yet, by the time the election was due in May 2022, almost two years of working from home, interstate and overseas travel restrictions, and COVID-saturated news had worn thin with the public. Aided by the arrival of vaccines, Australia had gone from fear of the unknown to not wanting to know.

Politicians reflected this attitudinal vector as did media companies. When Labor took up governing after the 2022 election, its low-key response to the pandemic reflected this waning of public interest. An atmosphere of urgency invoked by the Opposition was replaced with a miasma of contingency and complacency. It took 16 months for the Albanese government to establish its long-promised inquiry into the handling of the pandemic, and, when it did so, the terms of reference were narrower than expected, excluding 'actions taken unilaterally by state and territory governments' (Australian Government, 2023, p. 2). This meant that the closure of state borders and the wisdom and efficacy of harsh lockdown restrictions – elements that had provoked strong community resistance – were beyond the inquiry's purview. Thus, federal Labor neatly sidestepped the examination of actions taken (or not taken) by second-tier Labor governments, some of which were due to face voters soon after the expected September 2024 completion date of the inquiry (Karp, 2023).

Politics dictated policy from the outset of the COVID-19 crisis, although, in the first year or so, this carried no cost to the Coalition government because of a clear alignment of the two major parties. A frightened nation looked to the government for protection, extending it an almost unchecked licence to enact whatever infection control measures it deemed necessary to defeat the virus. As time wore on, the two imperatives – robust public health policy and public hunger for life beyond COVID-19 – would begin to diverge. The Coalition tried to adjust, but, and perhaps to an even greater extent than other 'wartime' democracies dealing with the crisis, it carried public opprobrium for hardships caused by the emergency measures (Gauja et al., 2023). By the 2022 election, it would be to post-crisis political/ electoral pressures, rather than COVID-19, that the major parties would ultimately be most sensitive to.

References

Albanese, A. (2021, 30 May). *It is a race* [Status update]. Facebook. www.facebook. com/story.php/?story_fbid=334784481339728&id=100044245368721&pai pv=0&eav=AfZK5FMCrNTGIYwF7XEmzkuI60hCmWqPOVJPvFJ-HWL- CFhYPPZNOGQ2yE0LyLmAp2o&_rdr.

Albrechtsen, J. (2024, 13 February). From COVID to women, Morrison's legacy is an absolute shocker. *The Australian.* www.theaustralian.com.au/commentary/from- covid-to-women-morrisons-legacy-is-an-absolute-shocker/news-story/2e78c 6662a0f915c9ac363a4e7298cab.

Booker, C. & Sambul, N. (2022, 7 May). We're living with COVID but more of us are dying than ever. *Sydney Morning Herald.* www.smh.com.au/national/we-re- living-with-covid-but-more-of-us-are-dying-than-ever-20220429-p5ah7y.html.

Cook, H. (2023, 26 June). 'A death sentence': More than 600 people die after catching COVID in hospital. *The Age.* www.theage.com.au/national/victoria/a- death-sentence-more-than-600-people-die-after-catching-covid-in-hospital-2023 0621-p5di7x.html.

Crabb, B. (2023, 30 May). Does Australia need a new COVID-19 strategy [Audio podcast]. In *Democracy sausage with Mark Kenny.* podcasts.apple.com/au/podcast/ does-australia-need-a-new-covid-19-strategy/id1459965243?i=1000614960763.

Department of the Prime Minister and Cabinet. (2023, 21 September). *Commonwealth Government COVID-19 Response Inquiry terms of reference.* Australian Government. www.pmc.gov.au/resources/commonwealth-government-covid-19-response- inquiry-terms-reference.

Gauja, A., Sawer, M. & Sheppard, J. (Eds). (2023). *Watershed: The 2022 Australian federal election.* ANU Press. doi.org/10.22459/W.2023.

Gleeson, H. (2024, 11 February). Too many patients are catching COVID in Australian hospitals, doctors say. So why are hospitals rolling back precautions? *ABC News.* www.abc.net.au/news/2024-02-11/patients-catching-covid-hospitals- australia-infection-control/103442806.

Grattan, M. (2022, July 13). Politics with Michelle Grattan: Health Minister Mark Butler warns COVID wave will worsen. *The Conversation.* theconversation.com/ politics-with-michelle-grattan-health-minister-mark-butler-warns-covid-wave- will-worsen-186915.

Karp, P. (2023, 21 September). Covid-19 inquiry will exclude state and territory decisions, Anthony Albanese says. *The Guardian*. www.theguardian.com/australia-news/2023/sep/21/covid-19-inquiry-australia-government-response-state-territory-decisions-anthony-albanese.

Kenny, M. (2023a, 21 September). Anthony Albanese's COVID inquiry avoids key areas where lesson could be learned. *Canberra Times*. www.canberratimes.com.au/story/8359270/inconsistent-and-hypersensitive-a-covid-inquiry-to-match-nations-pandemic-response/.

Kenny, M. (2023b). Febrile nation. In T. Kirkland & G. Fang (Eds), *Pandemedia: How COVID changed journalism* (pp. 118–129). Monash University Publishing.

Long, G. (2024, 25 January). *2024 Australian of the Year recipients Professor Georgina Long and Professor Richard Scolyer*. YouTube. www.youtube.com/watch?v=5eO7yNBW3fg.

Lupton, D. (2024). COVID-19 and crisis communication. In B. Griffen-Foley & S. Turnbull (Eds), *The media and communications in Australia* (pp. 285–289). Abingdon. doi.org/10.4324/9781003280644.

Margo, J. (2023, 24 January). After three years of pandemic, welcome to the silent and deadly phase. *Australian Financial Review*. www.afr.com/policy/health-and-education/it-s-year-three-of-pandemic-so-where-are-we-20230123-p5ceu8.

Morawska, L., Marks, G. B. & Monty, J. (2022). Healthy indoor air is our fundamental need: The time to act is now. *Medical Journal of Australia, 217*(11), 578–581. doi.org/10.5694/mja2.51768.

Noble, F. (2021, 21 February). Anti-coronavirus vaccine protests held in Melbourne, Sydney, Brisbane, Adelaide, Perth. *9 News*. www.9news.com.au/national/coronavirus-protest-melbourne-brisbane-sydney-pete-evans/a328629b-4d7f-48b1-a13f-72fe42dd8c2b.

O'Neil, M. (2020, 21 March). *Australian workers need comprehensive wage support now* [Media release]. Australian Council of Trade Unions. www.actu.org.au/media-release/australian-workers-need-comprehensive-wage-support-now/.

OzSAGE. (2023, 15 December). Submission for COVID-19 Response Inquiry. ozsage.org/useful/uhzcus1h85qjs6myiqdnvr7yip2alb.

Speers, D. (2023). A question of balance. In T. Kirkland & G. Fang (Eds), *Pandemedia: How Covid changed journalism* (pp. 87–95). Monash University Publishing.

Thorpe, H., O'Leary, G., Nemani, M. J. & Ahmad, N. (2024, 10 January). Wanting to 'move on' is natural – but women's pandemic experiences can't be lost to 'lockdown amnesia'. *The Conversation*. theconversation.com/wanting-to-move-on-is-natural-but-womens-pandemic-experiences-cant-be-lost-to-lockdown-amnesia-218510.

Treasury. (2023, 16 June). *Independent evaluation of the JobKeeper payment* [Consultation paper]. Australian Government. treasury.gov.au/sites/default/files/2023-06/c2023-407908.pdf.

Wallace, C. (2023a, 5 January). Albanese has let Australian voters down on COVID-19. *Nikkei Asia*. asia.nikkei.com/Opinion/Albanese-has-let-Australian-voters-down-on-COVID-19.

Wallace, C. (2023b, 30 May). Does Australia need a new COVID-19 strategy [Audio podcast]. In *Democracy sausage with Mark Kenny*. podcasts.apple.com/au/podcast/does-australia-need-a-new-covid-19-strategy/id1459965243?i=1000614960763.

12

Proactive mitigation responses to COVID pandemics: Learning lessons needed to achieve a compassionate, resilient future

Robert L. Heath

Because they recur, events such as the COVID-19 pandemic remind us to learn from them, plan for the next iteration and be proactive. COVID-19 affected the entire globe in many ways, some places far more or less than others. Lots of people died; economies were harmed. By 2023 we could draw situationally relevant conclusions about the pandemic and seek to learn the lessons needed to prepare for the future. Risk management and communication protocols require learning lessons that come to grips with the resilience of coronaviruses and the problematics of humans' coping abilities. We need to understand the lasting, long-term impact of pandemics on medical science, public health, community norms and economies – the fodder of public policy. Strategic learning should mitigate the spread and damage of pandemics by fostering trust and building effective institutions; the opposite was often the case with COVID-19.

This project broadly asks: how will the COVID-19 pandemic change Australia? Conversely, how will Australia change the pandemic? A critical focus on strategies of pandemic mitigation suggests that one of Australia's wisest post-COVID-19 outcomes choices has been to apply an issues management, lessons-learned approach to public health management pandemic responses: to refine strategies and institutions regarding what to do and *what not to do* as this pandemic morphs or the next one occurs. National efficacy and government legitimacy require focused, science-based analysis coupled with compassionate policy that is implemented and communicated clearly, coherently and consistently. Experts must set subjective norms that can wisely be followed to achieve expert, personal and community efficacy. The challenge is to co-manage competing, conflicting and collaborating zones of meaning regarding response efficacy. A thoughtful focus on strategies for pandemic mitigation suggests that Australia's lessons learned should allow it to develop and apply modelled response data and protocols, compared to those of other countries, to know what to do and what not to do strategically during pandemics.

According to the WHO, as of May 2024, the global estimated total of COVID-19 cases was 775 million; deaths reached 7.1 million. Given how daunting this pandemic has been to define, monitor, account for and respond to, one can imagine these numbers could be off by a factor of at least three. Thousands of cases are routinely under-reported in the US. Under-reported cases were the norm from the beginning, for political and cultural reasons, and today the reporting of cases, unless severe, does not provide useful data. Many people have had COVID-19 and recovered, or died, without significant medical care or accurate diagnosis. Exposure to the virus, in the context of vaccination protocols, has become expected, accepted, even routine. Even in China, which employed strict lockdowns until late 2022, numbers are likely to be substantially under-reported. Crematoria activities in China may reveal more accurate numbers than other indicators.

As countries developed efficacious response protocols, including vaccines, citizens were looking for a 'new norm'. In the US, annual COVID-19 vaccinations are becoming on par with influenza vaccinations, yet sizeable populations are under-vaccinated. Mask mandates and social distancing are periodically re-implemented, especially in medical facilities.

A best-case future requires focused, science-based analysis, coupled with compassionate policy that is communicated clearly, coherently and consistently in ways that set subjective norms that motivate citizens to achieve expert, personal and community efficacy. Response efficacy can be increased by monitoring discourse regarding COVID-19 to understand whether misinformation, lies and false advice confound personal and communal efforts.

A risk communication, issues management approach to pandemic mitigation emphasises why public health communicators are more than 'channels' for 'transmitting' expert guidance. Science-based experts can often misunderstand or misjudge the subjective, cultural, political and economic implications of risk when it comes to public health communication. Politicians can distort the process, thereby fostering disorder rather than a concerted search for compassionate order. The overarching logic is that communities organise to communicate and communicate to organise. The challenge is to do both well.

Academic risk literature preaches the precept that risk management and communication are universally and recurringly challenged to define the quality of human societies. Compassionate resilience predicts the kind of future humans create. Communities are evaluated by the efficacy of their responses to disasters. The best public health paradigm is more matriarchal than patriarchal. Mothers and grandmothers know the virtue of compassionate prescription: put on your coat, don't get chilled, take your medicine.

The overarching theme of this COVID-19 discussion is that scientific information must be carefully developed and policy wisely tested: principled communication based on research and best practices can mitigate the impact of public health pandemics and protect economies by fostering resilient recovery. Risk management and communication research justify principled, multidiscipline, strategic development and implementation of public health policy through coherent, sustained, transparent, normative and compassionate strategic plans. (For emphasis on the risk communication process, see Heath, 2023.)

Lessons that forecast community efficacy and resilience

Countries develop protocols for identifying and responding to pandemics. Planning assesses past performance to refine protocols for future use. Consequently, in the US, the Obama administration left documented guidelines for the Trump administration to bring informed experience to bear the day a pandemic became evident. The key document is called *Playbook for Early Response to High-Consequence and Emerging Infectious Disease Threats and Biological Incidents* (Executive Office, 2016; see also Dale, 2020). Accumulated lessons learned recommended sound science, wise health management policy, trust-building communication and programs, and compassionate communication to blunt subsequent administrations' tendency to conclude: 'This is our first rodeo!'

Cavalier to the challenges of COVID-19 and narcissistically self-confident, Trump threw out Obama's *Playbook*, treated the pandemic as threatening his reputation as an effective president, politicised scientific discussions and called tested response protocols hoaxes. People died unnecessarily and economic damage resulted, as has been discussed elsewhere in this book, especially by Ward. That cautionary tale is a templated rubric for creating, implementing and evaluating national pandemic plans. Trump's administration struggled:

> The United States lagged in its response to the virus, from testing and tracking to implementing measures – such as mask mandates, social distancing, lockdowns, and later vaccines – to protect society ... pandemic-related issues ultimately became politicized.
>
> (Rothkopf, 2020, p. 164; see also Baker & Glasser, 2022)

President Trump's public presentations on pandemic control were performative; he claimed the virus to be a hoax. Politicians and other critics threatened medical experts such as Dr Anthony Fauci, then director of the National Institute of Allergy and Infectious Diseases, with violence and impeachment; they wanted him investigated, allegedly for aiding the Chinese government's strategic efforts to create the pandemic. Politicians argued that mask mandates were illegal, even in school and workplace safety and health contexts. Rather than merely ignoring scientists' public policy efforts, many opposed those voices' measured advice and protocols. *Lesson learned*: listen and improve, rather than dismiss and resist out of ill-advised motives.

Anti-vaxxers became 'freedom fighters'. Government leaders, namely Senator Ted Cruz (Republican, Texas), proposed in 2023 that senior military officers be prohibited from forcing personnel to be vaccinated, to be quarantined as necessary or to use face coverings to prevent the spread of the virus. His legislation would prevent officers from punishing military personnel, including forcing them out of the services, if they wilfully violated orders intended to mitigate the effect of the virus.

Risk assessment: Science, crisis consequence interpretations and response efficacy

Early in the US experience, COVID-19 became politicised. Two factors at play were citizens' worry about infection (threat perception, fear and dread) and the impact of the virus on the economy (threat perception, fear and dread). A factor in both perceptions was Trump's approval rating, which corresponded to political affiliation. A report was made on 11 June 2020, when deaths exceeded 115,000 and the stock market corrected after recent rises. In that report, 35.7 per cent of US respondents were somewhat worried about infection, and 28.5 per cent were very worried; in contrast, 21.3 per cent said they were not very concerned and 13.5 per cent said they were not worried at all about infection. On the matter of the economy, 50.8 per cent were very worried, 33.3 per cent were somewhat worried, 10.6 per cent were not very worried and 3.9 per cent were not worried at all. Trump's approval was politicised as 'public opinion'. Political affiliation affected poll results: Republican approval was 83.5 per cent, Independent 36.8 per cent and Democrats 10.8 per cent (Bycoffe et al., 2020). Many US citizens continued to believe that COVID-19 was a hoax created by the media ('enemies of the people') – Democrats and Chinese scientists who wanted to wound and defeat President Trump.

Early warning is essential, which means constant, systematic monitoring. As radar patiently scans for danger, so does an issue management approach to public health mitigation. A pandemic's scientific nature must be satisfactorily understood and integrated into evolving narrative conclusions and best operational practices.

Given that coronavirus is multidimensional and ever present, the point is not whether epidemics or pandemics will occur, but when and with what impact. Relevant to the social amplification of risk, Kasperson et al. (1988, p. 177) pondered the following question:

> One of the most perplexing problems in risk analysis is why some relatively minor risks or risk events, as assessed by technical experts, often elicit strong public concerns and result in substantial impacts upon society and economy. This article sets forth a conceptual framework that seeks to link systematically the technical assessment of risk with psychological, sociological, and cultural perspectives of risk perception and risk-related behavior. The main thesis is that

hazards interact with psychological, social, institutional, and cultural processes in ways that may amplify or attenuate public responses to the risk or risk event.

Proper assessment of these tipping points by type and magnitude, as well as by their idiosyncratic impact on specific populations at risk, is problematic. The first steps towards resilience include observing risk emergence, assessing it and using multi-channel protocols to share such assessment. Messages, appropriated by politicians, for instance, and reported in the media, can amplify or attenuate public responses. The first goal of science is to appropriately assess each risk while acknowledging the inevitable tug of war between amplification and attenuation.

Determining the probability of occurrence and magnitude of harm for each risk is necessarily polyvocal; ultimately, however, it requires scientific engagement – expert efficacy. How various voices speak about the probability and magnitude of risk is crucial to its mitigation. Mitigation begins with assessments of probability (high/low) and consequence (high/low). At the outset of COVID-19, the probability and consequence level of infection were contested, even politicised. Perceptions of citizens were guided by the planning, policy and political preferences and power expressions of individual voices through governments (national, state and local). The messaging of elites shaped and segmented public perceptions, thereby producing divergent, even conflicting, assessments.

As experts in the US worked to magnify the COVID-19 threat, President Trump downplayed its seriousness. Prescient of viruses' adaptability, the Obama administration used its experiences with Ebola and Zika to document a comprehensive response/mitigation game plan. This pandemic legacy, President Trump called, without critical justification, 'an obsolete, broken system' (Rupar, 2020, para. 2). Republican Senator Mitch McConnell alleged that the Obama administration had not provided the Trump administration with 'any kind of game plan' regarding a possible pandemic (Dale, 2020). These observations were political, unscientific.

In response to these charges, Ronald Klain, Obama's Ebola response coordinator, pointed to the *Playbook for Early Response to High-Consequence Emerging Infectious Disease Threats and Biological Incidents* (Knight, 2020). The last two paragraphs of that document read as follows:

In the event of a suspected or emerging biological incident (Phase 1c), the Federal Government may conduct enhanced public health surveillance and increase coordination among Federal partners and SLTT [state, local, territorial, or tribal] authorities. A Unified Coordination Group (UCG) may convene to facilitate information sharing and coordination. In this phase, DHS [Department of Homeland Security] and HHS [Health and Human Services] co-lead the UCG at the national level. If there is actionable intelligence of a deliberate incident, the FBI leads and coordinates law enforcement and investigative matters to counter the threat.

In conjunction with the national level, affected SLTT jurisdictions may engage with key stakeholders, including health departments, emergency management, law enforcement, environmental quality, and fusion centers in order to increase their information sharing and coordination. Early in a response, SLTT jurisdictions may also increase public health surveillance and sampling, develop public messaging strategies, and implement response plans. At the same time, affected SLTT jurisdictions maintain messaging strategies, and implement response plans. At the same time, affected SLTT jurisdictions maintain communications with Federal departments and agencies to provide situational awareness and to coordinate public messaging, as appropriate.

(Executive Office, 2016, p. 69)

The *Playbook* was developed to facilitate:

coordinating a complex US Government response to a high-consequence emerging disease threat anywhere in the world with the potential to cause an epidemic, pandemic, or other significant public health event, by providing a decision-making tool that identifies: (1) questions to ask; (2) agency counterparts to consult for answers to each; and (3) key decisions which may require deliberation through the Presidential Policy Directive (PPD)-1 process or its successor National Security Council Process.

(Executive Office, 2016, p. 4)

The Obama administration presumed that such documents would be updated as lessons were learned regarding the unique nature of any subsequent pandemic. Whether Trump was correct that the document was 'obsolete' might be contestable; however, McConnell's suggestion that there was no document was untrue.

By drawing on universal best practices, Australia can define, refine and reinforce its best practices so as to navigate current disaster responses and plan for its next pandemic.

Disaster mitigation: Setting the stage and gaining perspective

Disaster mitigation is inherently narrative, scripted and performative, but must also be strategic and situationally adjusted and compassionately enacted. The life cycle of viruses, as is true of all life, is understandable as a narrative. Critical measures of mitigation effectiveness entail individual, expert and community efficacy. Fear caused by the perception of disaster needs to be mitigated so that denial or misplaced blame do not facture trust and collective efficacy. Strategies should achieve a systematic reduction of chaos and uncertainty rather than amplify them. Response systems are fragile. Wise procedures, such as lockdowns or masking, should be presented and interpreted as compassionate efforts to achieve collective resilience.

The extended parallel process model (EPPM) differentiates fear-based and dread-based responses. When people encounter an event/situation that creates fear, EPPM predicts that their response may be dysfunctional. It can lead to denial, blame-placing and other responses that downplay or deflect fearful information. A constructive alternative is to react to information with a sense of dread (Maloney et al., 2011; Roberto et al., 2009; Witte, 1992; Witte & Allen, 2000). Expert efficacy begins by responding with dread before learning from science and best practices what policy development and implementation to effect to reduce potential harm. Dread offers a constructive approach to reducing the justification of 'fear'. Fearing the effect of knowledge can lead to denial, which prolongs the scourge, reduces response efficacy, and damages economies, public health and politics. Perceived expert, individual or community efficacy can shift analytical and response perspectives from fear to dread.

Disaster response principles and best practices can be modelled as DECMC: disaster and emergency crisis management communication. Such modelling presumes grounded expert efficacy: analysis, planning, implementation, monitoring and evaluation. However, much of pandemic disaster management and communication presupposes the desires and incentives of affected publics, variously at risk: the paradigm presumes that expertise can combat fear. The spear point of science and honed best practices drive strategic responses to satisfy at-risk publics' desire to know about a pandemic and preferred responses to it. Voids of expertise create vacuums that prompt information seeking and advice gathering, however inefficacious (Heath et al., 2021).

Mitigation campaigns can be modelled as protective action decision-making (PADM). Key factors are scientific investigation, organisation, strategic response (individual, expert and community), subjective norms, behavioural intention and narrative enactment. Response processes become more effective if experts monitor knowledge and manage the preparation, messaging and collective responses to see that sound knowledge and best practices are situationally adjusted (Lindell & Perry, 2012; see also Heath, Lee, Palenchar et al., 2009). Preferred behavioural norms must be clearly and compassionately communicated to satisfy interest group sensitivities.

A post-COVID-19 Australia can approach the next pandemic with deepened insights gained by refining its approach rather than developing uniquely new models. An overarching goal of risk mitigation is to prevent risks from manifesting issues and becoming crises that are fraught with uncertainty (Heath & Palenchar, 2009; Jaques, 2012). The overarching risk management logic is that pandemics are 'serial killers' rather than 'impulse murderers'. They keep going until stopped; they recur because the biological nature of viruses is to adapt by constantly changing to survive. An unscientific view of viruses sees them as not adaptable, resilient or capable of maximising their own 'relative' survivability. Viruses are resilient and adaptable; they can survive. Pandemic mitigation needs to be as resilient, enduring and adaptable.

Strategic responses to public health risks need science-based public health policy and risk communication that engages, creates and implements policy. This issues management approach to pandemics presumes that efficacious policy leads to containment and mitigation by looking forward to managing an uncertain future. Policy mechanisms monitor communication among all participants (expert, lay advice seeker, politician and lay response recalcitrant) to foster a coherent, shared sense of expert, individual and community efficacy.

Achieving predictable response efficacy

Mitigation presumes within-system, as well as between-system, institutional coordination and integrity. By mid-2020, the COVID-19 trajectory in the US seemed straightforward, but that changed as federal administration leadership became increasingly performative and transactional as Trump worried about his re-electability (Baker & Glasser, 2022). The virus persisted, mutated and aggressively demonstrated its novel adaptability.

Boiler-plated principles and response strategies necessarily had to become more complex. Principles such as 'one policy/one voice' had to be abandoned or modified as flaws amplified the reasons for cautious, systematic, adaptive approaches with layered responses and messages. To that point, if a mayor attempted to impose restrictions that seemed unpopular, the administration countered by reducing restrictions; the virus surged. Voices advocating restriction even met threats of lynching.

To counter viruses and mitigate their multidimensional presence in communities requires outcomes that depend on and emphasise resilient risk management interdependence between expert efficacy, individual (self-) efficacy and community efficacy. Mitigation increases as expertise (expert efficacy) is enacted individually (self-efficacy) and communally (community efficacy) through normative communication from similar/familiar sources whose messages are sensitive to the response-efficacy needs of individuals in communities (Heath, Lee & Ni, 2009).

Effective mitigation and resilient recovery require the development and implementation of layered, centralised communication plans based on flexible adaptation to scientific discovery regarding the unique and changing nature of each pandemic. Effective mitigation also requires agentic policy and clear, coherent and sustained polyvocal communication. Sources should be familiar to targeted audiences, and the content of messages should be sensitive to their interests and needs.

Pandemic communication is inherently discursive – a constructive mix of monologue and dialogue that produces coherent and not fractured or self-contradictory understanding and policies. Strategic communication planning works best when public health experts achieve expert efficacy by using sound science to achieve efficacious response policy. Pandemic communication requires constant issue monitoring to know the best science and what key spokespersons are saying. Messages should be coordinated to provide the most accurate information and the most agentic planning.

Public health planning and policy responses must be driven by sound medical science. Communication experts need to be embedded in the process in strategic ways to:

1. Monitor the quality of scientific, policy and normative information and create files that are available in public fora; one challenge is to monitor and track bad information and respond to it to ensure public access to the best available information.
2. Ensure that information acquisition is central to the enactable durability of the total mitigation plan, not merely a matter of periodic, even if frequent, public statements that debate opposing views authentically and transparently.
3. Specify, monitor and maintain the integrity of risk communication infrastructures and messaging in the public interest to set policy-based, subjective norms.

Mitigation communication presumes engagement, even if contentious, but should not privilege policy outcomes that are not scientifically grounded. Strategic management emphasises, as Jaques (2012) noted, the role of detection, including signalling systems, proactively addressing systemic flaws, knowing stakeholders and their views and interests, and learning and revising plans, systems, procedures and messages.

Public policy documents should assist government efforts to:

1. coordinate and communicate mitigating policy and information, such as Centers for Disease Control and Prevention (CDC) protocols and the pandemic *Playbook*
2. review risk communication, risk culture and public perception (interpretation and tolerance) of risk by using work by Ortwin Renn (2009), Katherine McComas (2006), Robert Heath, Tim Coombs (e.g. Olaniran et al., 2012), Roger Kasperson (e.g. Kasperson et al., 1988), Mary Douglas (1992), James Tansey and Steve Rayner (2009), Kim Witte (1992), Michael Lindell and Ronald Perry (2012), Matthew Seeger and Timothy Sellnow (2016), Robert Ulmer (e.g. Seeger et al., 2008) and others
3. avoid clumsy and irresponsible image-based, transactional responses.

High-quality risk management and communication infrastructure reduce risk through engagement integrity. Discursive infrastructure empowers pre-crisis preparation, crisis event response and post-crisis recovery through resilience and even renewal. Mitigation programs should shift crisis responses from reaction to pro-action. Response efficacy begins with the pre-crisis recognition that crises, especially public health events, are inevitable (Olaniran et al., 2012). Pandemic emergency management requires being as much ahead of the curve as possible to flatten the curve of infection and death.

Framing messages and best practices of pandemic emergency management

Agentic systems skilfully and compassionately learn lessons to improve public health protocols. Sophisticated countries with compassionate leaders devoted to science-based public health decision-making need not 'reinvent the wheel'. Precedence and institutional frameworks spark action once vigilant systems become aware that a public health crisis looms.

Arguably, the longer a public health crisis runs, the more divisive it is likely to become. Uncertainty motivates blame-placing, which confounds constructive engagement. Uncertainty challenges normative institutions. Institutional damage occurs and recovery becomes more difficult. COVID-19 challenged administrative credibility and authority at all levels (loss of perceived expert and community efficacy), the constitutive norms of management and self-governance, and the efficacy of medical and educational institutions.

In the US, President Trump's narcissistic paranoia and predilection for blame-placing motivated him to engage in image management, not issues management. He adopted a performative communication style. If he could keep the reported, versus actual, number of cases low, his administration would appear to be efficacious; he would be seen as an effective crisis leader. If he could convince key publics that no-one knew how to mitigate the damage or that it would go away on its own, he could be a cheerleader for ignoring the deadly virus. Could he blame China or Democrat governors and mayors or even Obama for public health failures? Could he wisely speculate about the efficacy of drinking bleach and installing lights into human bodies to kill the virus?

Mistake 1: Making political decisions that are not science-based and using communication strategically to undermine science and scientists. Making ostensibly scientific recommendations that are strategically politicised.

Early on, mythic interpretations contradicted mounting evidence. 'Happy talk' of hoaxes inspired some to believe that COVID-19 was ordinary flu. The virus spread. People died. Hospitals were overwhelmed. Testing was flawed or 'impolitic'. Trump created a response panel that was more show than substance.

Mistake 2: Sustaining divergent narratives: Scientific issue management/political image management.

These narrative divides were still vibrant when the White House targeted experts, especially Dr Anthony Fauci who had become a folk hero to many. A mid-June 2019 poll reported that 76 per cent of the public trusted Fauci and 26 per cent trusted Trump (Panetta, 2020). That the public liked Fauci more than Trump motivated the president to attack and marginalise rather than empower Fauci.

Cable news outlets and social media were flooded with COVID-19 messages that mixed political positioning and nixed science-based caution. States, cities, towns and regions battled over success/failure heuristics. Essential workers became puppets of the powerful. The economy became the story. Because schools had been closed (as had crowded commercial venues), Trump's focus on each became his spear point. 'Get back to work.' 'Get back to school.' 'Open up!' When data contravened happy talk, they were distorted or hidden. 'The pandemic will be over by Easter.'

Mistake 3: Believing that COVID-19 could be bullied or ignored. Science became inconvenient, as did risk caution.

Wearing a mask and social distancing were seen as capitulating to tyranny, loss of freedom and independence, or giving in to the Democratic Party. Politicised issue positions sparked resistance to public health caution and effective response norms. Governors who opted for caution and called for federal help were characterised as weak minded, weak willed and committed to violating citizens' freedom and independence. Public displays of opposition, encouraged by Trump, became fashionable, as did not wearing a mask or social distancing. A market emerged for fashionable masks. That trend was countered by defiantly not wearing masks. People spat on one another and on counters. Some screamed and brandished firearms. Store personnel were attacked for seeking to enforce corporate or community norms.

COVID-19 continued to win, at first harming the old, infirm and poor most and then becoming a death sentence to incautious younger people and people by political party. By this point, many countries were virtually at a new normal; meanwhile, the US was stumbling into the public health dark. The federal economy was taking a hit. Refrigerator trucks were deployed to augment morgues. Skip to September 2020, 2 million deaths, and the scenario was essentially unchanged, especially as the president flaunted his administration's guidelines.

The issues management approach presumes that successful organisations create and implement strategic policy, both private and public. Response efficacy requires an implementable policy by which multidisciplinary efforts align to produce mutual community benefit. Rather than use precedence, public health science and multidisciplinary guidance, the Trump administration opted for communicative efforts to minimise the risk perception of COVID-19. It shunned responsibility for leading the nation. It blame-placed rather than employing systemic, coordinated planning and implementation. Confusing and contradictory messages got the US response off to a troubled start, fostering unfocused peril.

The risk management and communication tradition in the US has produced hundreds of studies. Working groups have supplied theoretically sound research and developed and implemented (emergency) responses and mitigation protocols, such as those posted at the CDC.[1] US states have public health organisations of varying degrees of competence. One problem with the US response was leaving too much leadership to states; some states were incentivised to flaunt protocols and 'open early', creating a lack of uniformity.

---

1   For CDC's National Pandemic Strategy, see www.cdc.gov/pandemic-flu/php/national-strategy/ index.html.

The planning and implementation of pandemic responses can be grounded on the theory of reasoned action and framed as PADM (Lindell & Perry, 2004, 2012). PADM reasons that when people experience a threat, they want to learn what to do to reduce it. They monitor environmental cues (even direct and indirect experiences with the risk), social cues and information sources, and channel preferences that reflect receiver characteristics. They search for warning messages. Their pre-decision processes are shaped by information exposure, attention to specific information and comprehension.

Filtering leads to threat perceptions, protective action perceptions, and perceptions of subjective norms and preferences. These co-linear variables motivate idiosyncratic PADM. People engage in decision-making to know what actions others, especially experts as well as friends and family, recommend. Heath et al.'s (2008) study inquired whether social cues and norms predict behavioural intention to engage in PADM. If experts recommend social distancing and masks, that advice can produce subjective norms that predict behavioural intention. Conversely, if experts or politicians model different norms or modify science-based norms, then behavioural intentions change, vary and/or diminish. In setting norms and enacting them, the personal behaviour of leaders, including President Trump, influences public behaviour. As reporting on COVID-19 victims emphasised the aged, the poor and people of colour as being most likely to suffer, persons not in those groups assumed they were spared. Normative behaviour became predicated on false assumptions and misguided subjective norms. Young white people presumed they could live life as before.

With precedence, and research by virologists and epidemiologists, the Trump administration had ample advice to use to mitigate COVID-19. Its incentive was to use the pandemic as re-election leverage, especially as measured by the US stock market's performance. However, the chaos the administration created was contradicted by other leaders, the economy stumbled because response uncertainty damaged business continuity, and states were set against one another without effective national leadership and coherent coordination. As the lifting proved to be too heavy, Trump's administration opted for the single message: 'open up business to achieve speedy recovery' – or let the states take the lead as they wish in compliance with the subjective norm; business as usual.

The effects of this clumsy response became increasingly evident. By 17 June 2020, the US led the world in total COVID-19 cases (2,215,124) and deaths (119,269). By 16 September, total cases had become 6,610,000; deaths had reached 197,000. Monitors worried that by election day, 3 November 2020, deaths would exceed 200,000, even 225,000, and the economy would be on life support. Did citizens' willingness to engage in PADM predict the election's outcome? What can Australia learn from the US example as it imagines a post-pandemic future?

Monitoring sound science and resilient policy

Lesson learned: pandemic communication requires constant issue monitoring to know the best science, what influential spokespersons are saying, which messages provide the most accurate information, and which messages provide resilient planning and response efficacy. Mitigation presumes collective, normatively managed efficacy.

Contextually relevant policy must be based on best-case, issue-driven contests of fact, value, policy, identity, identification and place. Members of pandemic response teams play multiple, shared roles that overlap to generate, assemble and evaluate relevant information to develop policies that produce response efficacy. In the US, Trump enacted a strategically authoritarian, chaos-generating role. The most important link in the public health chain was the weakest.

Lesson learned: the gathering and use of scientific information must be closely monitored to ensure the formulation of coherent and coordinated responses. Kasperson et al. (1988) demonstrated that how and what the media communicates about risk necessarily affects the public's sense of risk (distorts, diminishes and amplifies). Trump fed false information and interpretations that were conveyed or combated by various news outlets. Instead of working for 'one message/one policy', Trump revelled in uncertainty and scorned the 'liberal media', which, he claimed, sustained the hoax about COVID-19 with the 'intent to bring him down'. His re-election was his motive, not keeping people safe and healthy.

A fully functioning narrative continuity approach to pandemics presumes that efficacy depends on people knowing and trusting appropriate response narratives, and being willing and able to enact them. Competing narratives amplified differently by media outlets result in chaos and failed coordination. People who do not know or are unable or unwilling to perform the best narrative pose grave consequences for efficacious risk response (Heath et al., 2008).

Baker and Glasser (2022) have provided a comprehensive analysis of the societal dysfunction Trump personally created for the US and, by extension, for other countries. Trump weakened public faith in the medical and scientific community as well as in science itself. He allowed and even voiced fantastical solutions to the virus. He demonstrated that one highly influential person, probably motivated by fear of losing an election compounded by clinical narcissism, can create a public health culture of nonsense and noncompliance. What should have been treated as wise medical advice to achieve individual and communal safety became politicised confusion and chaos. Institutions charged with public health responsibility were marginalised. Instead of calming consumers, his messaging, supported by sycophants, created a wary and distrustful workforce and hostile marketplace. Instead of strengthening institutions, they were purposefully weakened. What should not be politicised was.

Even slight differences in wording in public health messaging cause confusion that requires clarification. For instance, Maria Van Kerkhove, the WHO's technical lead on the COVID-19 pandemic, clarified an earlier statement on asymptomatic spread by stating that scientists did not actually know whether, when or how frequently asymptomatic cases of COVID-19 spread the virus. Previously she had claimed that such spread was 'rare' (Joseph, 2020). Issue monitoring needs to vigilantly guard against imprecision and ambiguity; it needs to watch for malicious communication.

In the US, internet chain letters supplied data, interpretations and advice that set subjective norms that confounded individual and community resilience. Such chains shared information that was wrong, even malicious. A case in point, the author of this paper received an email thread from a friend that contained forwarded messages: 'Somehow I do believe it but know nothing more. What do you know?' The subject was 'new info on treatment of Coronavirus' and claimed to be 'a MUST READ!!':

> Breaking Covid news!!
>
> Italy has allegedly discovered covid is not a virus, but a bacterium. It clots the blood and reduces the oxygen saturation from dispersing throughout the body. They went against the World Health Organization's [sic] that no bodies be autopsied.

When Italian Ministry of Health ordered many autopsies, they found the blood was clotted in all of the patients' veins. They immediately started using aspirin 100mg and anticoagulant medication. And have had immense success. 14,000 people were released from the hospital as healthy and covid free.

Italy is demanding Bill Gates and the World Health Organization be held accountable for crimes against humanity for misleading, misdirecting, and withholding life saving information from the world, which cost the lives of thousands. Ventilators and ICU [intensive care units] units were not necessary. A mandated vaccine is not necessary. Covid19 is a bacterium, easily treated with aspirin and anticoagulant.

Spread the word! Make this global. Hopefully our president will learn about this and do something about it before we lose all of our Constitutional freedoms.

After telling the reader that 'more follows', the following was added:

It is now clear that the whole world has been attacking the so-called Coronavirus Pandemic wrongly due to a serious pathophysiological diagnosis error. According to valuable information from Italian pathologists, ventilators and ICU were never needed.

Autopsies performed by the Italian pathologists has shown that it is not pneumonia but it is Disseminated Intravascular Coagulation (Thrombosis) which ought to be fought with antibiotics, antivirals, anti-inflammatories and anticoagulants.

If this is true for all cases, that means the whole world is about to resolve this novel pandemic earlier than expected. However, protocols are currently being changed in Italy who [sic] have been adversely affected by this pandemic.

The impressive case of a Mexican family in the United States who claimed they were cured with a home remedy was documented: three 500 mg aspirins dissolved in lemon juice boiled with honey, taken hot. The next day they woke up as if nothing had happened to them! Well, the scientific information that follows proves they are right!

Persons in the chain responded in supportive and contradictory ways.

The end of the pandemic

On 11 May 2023, President Biden announced the end of the COVID-19 Public Health Emergency response. No longer would the federal government mandate public health protocols. Even more recently, congressional Republicans moved to end federal funding for victims of the pandemic. People had pretty much sorted out what to do, both as advisories and personal responses. 'Masks optional' became public policy. Graduations at all academic levels celebrated the end of the shutdowns and other mandates. People attending such public events probably were more cautious about mass shootings than viral infection, at least that was the case during one college graduation.

Studies will be conducted by all disciplines and many countries to learn lessons about pandemics and about their lasting damage. Positive outcomes will undoubtedly be featured. One public/private cost for the US was 1.1 million deaths, although such numbers must be assumed to be skewed and lower than reality. Many deaths were unnecessary. Such deaths and the challenges of hospitalisation profoundly affected medical professionals, especially nurses.

Evaluative reflections began appearing, for example, in the *New Yorker* on 15 May 2023 (Khullar, 2023). This pointed out that, as the government response to COVID-19 was ending, costs associated with vaccination, masks, testing, medical treatment and medication would increasingly be borne by the least able to pay and most vulnerable. Assistance programs will end, resulting in food and housing insecurity. Perceptions of risk will lead to COVID-19 being ignored as a health problem and cause of death. Small businesses will not recover. The infusion of rescue money, coupled with the demand of large corporations to return to profitability and to restore executive compensation programs, will foster inflation, adding to housing costs, transportation costs and food insecurity. School districts have lost the ability to manage responses to public health because of culture wars. The contrast with the earlier pandemic response is stark: it was 'a time when many people had access to food, shelter, and medical care with a consistency they'd never had before' (Khullar, 2023, p. 16).

Overarching all matters is the hard challenge of what to call this public health event and its trajectory:

> Our understanding of COVID often suffers from a linguistic determinism. The words we use encourage a binary conception of viral threat: we are in an acute state of emergency – a pandemic – or we have entered a long-awaited, tractable endemic phase.
>
> (Khullar, 2023, p. 15)

By May 2023, 40,000 more people had died from COVID-19 in the US since 1 January. Many more have since died and will continue to die. Legislators are tired of funding programmatic responses. Political candidates are patting themselves on the back for never giving in to the virus. However divergent citizens and politicians are in their assessments, they are quick to say: 'See, I was right.'

'This changes everything!'

What will a post-COVID-19 Australia look like? How will the COVID-19 pandemic change Australia? These questions look to the future. Will the relevant parties learn the correct, most efficacious lessons? Will we be prepared, alert to harm and focused on how to minimise the chaos and harm from lack of preparation?

The major lesson learned is that good information must prevail against bad information – good information must drive bad information out of the marketplace of ideas. However, situationally, what constitutes 'good' and 'bad' information will become politicised. In the issues management tradition, responsible leadership must battle against politicised doubt, support wise responses and exhibit compassion. Public resilience depends on coordinated individual, expert and community agency.

References

Baker, P. & Glasser, S. (2022). *The divider: Trump in the White House, 2017–2021.* Doubleday.

Bycoffe, A., Goskopf, C. & Mehta, D. (2020, June 11). *How Americans view the coronavirus crisis and Trump's response.* FiveThirtyEight.

Dale, D. (2020, May 12). Fact check: Obama left Trump a pandemic response playbook. *The Mercury News.* www.mercurynews.com/2020/05/12/fact-check-obama-left-trump-a-pandemic-response-playbook/.

Douglas, M. (1992). *Risk and blame*. Routledge.

Executive Office of the President of the United States. (2016). *Playbook for early response to high-consequence emerging infectious disease threats and biological incidents*. Retrieved 9 June 2020, s3.documentcloud.org/documents/6819268/Pandemic-Playbook.pdf.

Heath, R. L. (2023). Mitigating crises: Analyzing, planning, organizing, mobilizing, and communicating to address natural disasters. In W. T. Coombs & S. J. Holladay (Eds), *The handbook of crisis communication* (pp. 285–300). Wiley Blackwell.

Heath, R. L., Horsley, S., Guest, G. & Glazier, C. (2021). Disaster and emergency crisis management communication. In Y. Jin, B. H. Reber & G. J. Nowak (Eds), *Advancing crisis communication effectiveness: Integrating public relations scholarship with practice* (pp. 92–109). Taylor & Francis.

Heath, R. L., Lee, J. & Ni, L. (2009). Crisis and risk approaches to emergency management planning and communication: The role of similarity and sensitivity. *Journal of Public Relations Research, 22*(2), 123–141.

Heath, R. L., Lee, J., Palenchar, M. J. & Lemon, L. (2009). Risk communication emergency response preparedness: Contextual assessment of the Protective Action Decision Model. *Risk Analysis, 38*(2), 333–344.

Heath, R. L., Li, F., Bowen, S. A. & Lee, J. (2008). Narratives of crisis planning and infectious disease: A case study of SARS. In M. W. Seeger, T. L. Sellnow & R. R. Ulmer (Eds), *Crisis communication and the public health* (pp. 131–155). Hampton Press.

Heath, R. L. & Palenchar, M. J. (2009). *Strategic issues management: Organizations and public policy challenges* (2nd ed.). Sage.

Jaques, T. (2012). Issue management as a strategic aspect of crisis prevention. In B. A. Olaniran, D. E. Williams & W. T. Coombs (Eds), *Pre-crisis planning communication and management: Preparing for the inevitable* (pp. 19–35). Peter Lang.

Joseph, A. (2020, 9 June). '*We don't actually have that answer yet': WHO clarifies comments on asymptomatic spread of Covid-19*. STAT News. www.statnews.com/2020/06/09/who-comments-asymptomatic-spread-covid-19/.

Kasperson, R. E., Renn, O., Slovic, P., Brown, E. J., Goble, R., Kasperson, J. X. & Ratick, S. (1988). The social amplification of risk: A conceptual framework. *Risk Analysis, 8*(2), 177–187.

Khullar, D. (2023, 15 May). Moving on. *The New Yorker*, [print edition] pp. 15–16. Online version: www.newyorker.com/magazine/2023/05/15/ending-the-covid-public-health-emergency-isnt-all-good-news.

Knight, V. (2020, 15 May). Evidence shows Obama team left a pandemic 'game plan' for Trump administration. *KFF Health News*. khn.org/news/evidence-shows-obama-team-left-a-pandemic-game-plan-for-trump-administration/.

Lindell, M. K. & Perry, R. W. (2004). *Communicating environmental risk in multiethnic communities*. Sage.

Lindell, M. K. & Perry, R. W. (2012). The protective action decision model: Theoretical modifications and additional evidence. *Risk Analysis, 32,* 616–632.

Maloney, E. K., Lapinski, M. K. & Witte, K. (2011). Fear appeals and persuasion: A review and update of the extended parallel process model. *Social and Personality Psychology Compass, 5,* 206–219.

McComas, K. A. (2006). Defining moments in risk communication research: 1996–2005. *Journal of Health Communication, 11,* 75–91.

Olaniran, B. A., Williams, D. E. & Coombs, W. T. (Eds) (2012). *Pre-crisis planning communication and management: Preparing for the inevitable*. Peter Lang.

Panetta, G. (2020, 13 July). Trump is reportedly rattled by Dr. Fauci's high approval ratings compared to his own poor polling on COVID-19. *Business Insider.* www.businessinsider.com/trump-is-spooked-by-faucis-high-approval-ratings-on-coronavirus-wapo-2020-7.

Renn, O. (2009). Risk communication: Insights and requirements for designing successful communication programs on health and environmental hazards. In R. L. Heath & H. D. O'Hair (Eds), *Handbook of risk and crisis communication* (pp. 80–98). Routledge.

Roberto, A. J., Goodall, C. E. & Witte, K. (2009). Raising the alarm and calming fears: Perceived threat and efficacy during risk and crisis. In R. L. Heath & H. D. O'Hair (Eds), *Handbook of risk and crisis communication* (pp. 285–301). Routledge.

Rothkopf, D. (2020). *American resistance: The inside story of how the deep state saved the nation*. Public Affairs.

Rupar, A. (2020, 20 April). Why Trump's efforts to blame Obama for the coronavirus make absolutely no sense. *Vox.* www.vox.com/2020/4/20/21227903/trump-blames-obama-coronavirus.

Seeger, M. W. & Sellnow, T. L. (2016). *Narratives of crisis: Telling stories of ruin and renewal*. Stanford University Press.

Seeger, M. W., Sellnow, T. L. & Ulmer, R. R. (Eds) (2008). *Crisis communication and the public health*. Hampton Press.

Tansey, J. & Rayner, S. (2009). Cultural theory and risk. In R. L. Heath & H. D. O'Hair (Eds), *Handbook of risk and crisis communication* (pp. 53–79). Routledge.

Witte, K. (1992). Putting the fear back into fear appeals: The extended parallel model. *Communication Monographs*, *59*, 329–349.

Witte, K. & Allen, M. (2000). A meta-analysis of fear appeals: Implications for effective health campaigns. *Health Education & Behavior*, *27*, 591–615.

13

Afterword

Shirley Leitch and Sally Wheeler

The challenge confronting researchers and policymakers alike is to resist strong pressures to simply 'move on'. This challenge must be especially tempting for those most deeply involved in the pandemic responses that have been soundly critiqued in this book and elsewhere. Many of the major mistakes of the pandemic – such as the colossal, flawed policy experiment that was JobKeeper – have already disappeared from political debate and, perhaps, from public consciousness. The intention of this book is that the lessons of such mistakes will not go unlearned or unremembered when we face our next crisis – as we inevitably will. COVID-19 is the fifth pandemic in the last 20 years or so and the ninth in the last 100 years. The Ebola outbreak of 2014 and the H1N1 virus spread of 2009 both offered lessons in what could occur, but the world moved on from those very quickly just as has happened this time. The concern at the time of writing is that the 'move on' camp prevails, with limited evidence of investment in proactive resilience strategies.

The defeat of the Morrison government in May 2022 might have been expected to open the pandemic response up to increased scrutiny and drive action. Replacing a government is certainly one way to effect change. The displeasure of the Australian electorate with the performance of the federal government had been evident when the ALP swept to power, aided by the success of Independents in formerly safe Liberal Party seats. Public dissatisfaction with pandemic management was a major contributor to the demise of the Morrison government according to the Australian Electoral Study (Cameron et al., 2022). That same study found that the prime minister himself had achieved the dubious distinction of scoring the lowest levels of popularity of any leader in the 35 years the team had been measuring such things.

This display of electoral displeasure was far from inevitable in a country that fared relatively well during the pandemic. For example, several of the state-level elections returned existing governments with increased majorities. In Western Australia, the Opposition was so decimated that cartoonists joked about the entire Liberal Party Opposition now fitting on a tandem bicycle. However, it may be that the Morrison government, as a third-term Liberal–National Party government, was facing an impossible task even before COVID-19 hit. Moreover, the incoming Labor government did not campaign on a platform of increasing Australian resilience or of 'opening the books' on the federal or government's policy responses. Given that Labor governments were the norm in the states, there was likely little appetite within the party for such scrutiny. And so, we 'move on'.

The incoming Albanese government inherited the massive public debt incurred by the pandemic response alongside economic indicators that were all headed in the wrong direction. Post-pandemic Australia faces the highest levels of inflation in decades, which has seen the Reserve Bank ratchet up the cash rate target 13 times, albeit from an historic low of just 0.1 per cent in 2020. The impact on mortgage holders has been immediate, especially for those who purchased during the housing boom that was driven by the pandemic and fuelled by those historically low interest rates.

Despite the controversy surrounding the Reserve Bank, this is textbook stuff, with similar institutional responses evident in many other nations, including the US, the UK and Canada. Concerns about the rising cost of living have moved to the top of voter concerns, leading to an increased focus on short-term economic management. At the same time, the Israeli–Palestinian conflict has muted the youth-led demands for climate action. These are not ideal conditions for driving a national debate on the policy changes and investment needed to build a more resilient and inclusive Australian society and economic base.

If the pandemic has taught us anything, we hope it is that paying attention to macro-level trends and indicators is important, but it is not enough. One of the central themes across the chapters within this book has been how COVID-19 policy responses played out across different groups both within Australia and elsewhere. At the micro-level, one size does not fit all. Our authors have identified multiple examples of policies that disproportionately and negatively affected the most disadvantaged, the most vulnerable and the least well equipped to deal with any new adversity.

It is worth recalling Martha Fineman's work on vulnerability within the human condition: it is a responsive state that provides a safety net for vulnerable subjects who find themselves under pressure to develop resilience in situations of neoliberalism (Fineman, 2017). The state, in the instances that the chapters in this book identify, failed to carry out the most basic of policy impact assessments; consequently, the already vulnerable found themselves exposed to new and additional risks as policy interventions and regulatory demands intersected with their current 'under pressure' lives. These groups needed special care and attention but did not receive differential support.

The most telling examples of such poorly designed policies may be found in Brown's chapter. Despite warnings from those working with women experiencing violence in the home, pandemic policies often worked to increase their risk of harm. Aboriginal women living in regional and remote communities were left especially vulnerable. Given the adverse health outcomes for Aboriginal people generally, a nuanced response to the pandemic should have provided additional protections rather than stripping away access to services and limiting their ability to escape from danger.

In 2024, a series of high-profile deaths saw violence against women once again grab the nation's headlines and the attention of politicians. However, the debate remains focused on statistics and the generic responses needed to better protect women and children. A more nuanced discussion would disaggregate the concept of 'women' to reveal that different approaches might be needed for women dealing with multiple and intersecting points of vulnerability.

It is no accident that family-based violence is on the rise in the context of a housing and cost of living crisis. Strengthening police protection for women at risk is vital but it is not the solution. A resilient and inclusive society is one that directly addresses the causes of risk rather than simply polices offenders or provides refuge to victims. The experts, such as Brown, are telling us these simple truths but decision-makers have yet to listen.

Another major lesson of the pandemic, which we seem to already be in the process of forgetting, is that many of the things that make life worth living cannot be reduced to economics, but they can be harmed by economic decisions. For reasons that have never been explained, the Australian government turned its back on the arts sector during the pandemic. Or, at least, as Cunio discussed in his chapter, they withheld support from artists while providing some funding for major arts venues. The buildings would stay open even as the artists struggled to survive. Artists were already numbered among the most disadvantaged occupational groups in our society and were left to fend for themselves. Yet, the pandemic was marked by multiple acts of generosity by artists who provided relief to the locked-down nation with music and comedy, for the most part without charge. The lesson is simple: a resilient and inclusive society needs a strong arts sector. Yet, for the most part, these major acts of philanthropy have yet to be recognised or rewarded.

The death and disruption engendered by the pandemic only partially explains our strong desire to move on and forward. History does not commemorate pandemics in the same way as it does other catastrophic events. Compare, for example, the focus in 2018 on the 100th anniversary of World War I and its 20 million dead, with the near silence around the 100th anniversary of the Spanish Flu, which killed 50 million. The official end of the pandemic in 2023 must not be allowed to mark the beginning of a similar 'great forgetting'.

Finally, as we type the last words for this book, the irony is not lost on us that one of us is recovering from a second bout of COVID-19 as cases rise across Australia. The other of us has already had COVID-19 on five occasions in three countries. The pandemic may be over, but the virus is very much with us.

References

Cameron, S., McAllister, I., Jackman, S. & Sheppard, J. (2022). *The 2022 Australian federal election: Results from the Australian election study*. The Australian National University. australianelectionstudy.org/wp-content/uploads/The-2022-Australian-Federal-Election-Results-from-the-Australian-Election-Study.pdf.

Fineman, M. A. (2017). Vulnerability and inevitable inequality. *Oslo Law Review*, 4(3), 133–149. ssrn.com/abstract=3087441.

www.ingramcontent.com/pod-product-compliance
Lightning Source LLC
Chambersburg PA
CBHW050647270326
41927CB00012B/2910